Date Due

FEB 21 '95			
MAR 1 '95			
MAR 1 '95	DISCARDED		
OCT 04 1995			
OCT 30 1995			
MAR 06 '96			
MAY 8 '97			
9·18·99			
MAY 10 2002			
OCT 21 2004			
FEB 16 2006 MAY 11 2008			

Car Suspension and Handling

Car Suspension and Handling

Third Edition

Donald Bastow,
BSc(Eng), CEng, FIMechE, FSAE, MSIA (France)

Third edition revised by

Geoffrey P. Howard
BSc(Eng), ACGI, MSAE

PENTECH PRESS
London

SOCIETY OF AUTOMOTIVE ENGINEERS, INC.
Warrendale, USA

First published 1993
by Pentech Press Limited
Graham Lodge, Graham Road
London, NW4 3DG
and
Society of Automobile Engineers, Inc.,
400 Commonwealth Drive, Warrendale, PA 15096-0001, USA

© D. Bastow, 1993
1st edition 1980
2nd edition 1987

BRITISH LIBRARY CATALOGUING IN PUBLICATION DATA

British Library Cataloguing in Publication Data

Bastow, Donald
  Car Suspension and Handling. – 3Rev.ed
I. Title II. Howard, Geoffrey
629.243

ISBN 0-7273-0318-x

Library of Congress Cataloging-in-Publication Data

Bastow, Donald
  Car suspension and handling / Donald Bastow. — 3rd ed. / rev. by
Geoffrey P. Howard
    p.   cm.
  Includes bibliographical references and index.
  ISBN 1-56091-404-1 : $69.00
    1. Automobiles—Springs and suspension—Design and construction.
  2. Automobiles—Steering-gear—Design and construction. I. Howard,
Geoffrey. II. Title.
  TL257.B37   1993
  629.24′3—dc20   93-8678
                                                                CIP

Printed in Great Britain by Bookcraft (Bath) Ltd.

Preface to 3rd edition

The challenges facing the motor industry in the remainder of this decade have never been greater in the whole of its history. A revolution is taking place throughout all the design, development and manufacturing processes involved in vehicle production, from first concept to marketing and sales. In the field of car suspension and handling the pace of change has accelerated steadily since this book was first published, making the task of updating the content from the 2nd to the 3rd editions a formidable assignment.

Since the 2nd edition of 1987 the original author has died, after a long and distinguished career in the automotive industry that began several years before I was born and never really ended. Donald Bastow's early work for, among others, the legendary W. O. Bentley, gave him an insight into vehicle engineering that formed the basis of his deep understanding of principles and concepts. In preparing the 3rd edition I have tried therefore to keep as much of his original theory as possible intact, but only where it can still be applied to modern vehicles with their more developed and complex systems. To this I have added several new sections including chapters on drive layout arrangements and computers in suspension design. The remainder has been rearranged and restructured to provide both a primer and a text book that is intended to lead the reader through the complexities of the subject in a logical and progressive way. I have also added more background information where it is appropriate and updated many of the figures and tables.

As Donald Bastow pointed out in his preface to the 1st edition, 'a car suspension reconciles the sensitivity of the human animal to disturbances with what the road surface would like to inflict.' He added that 'a suspension is a compromise between conflicting requirements and almost certainly also inflicts individual idiosyncrasies' – a fact that is only too familiar to anyone who has ever been involved in subjective vehicle appraisals or the analysis of motoring press comments.

By way of dedication I would like to pay tribute to the various groups of suspension and handling engineers all over the world whose day-to-day job is to make cars more comfortable to ride in and safer to drive. In the course of the past 30 years I have probably met about 1,000 of them in Europe, the USA, Australia and Japan, and have never failed to be impressed by their dedication and expertise. It is to them in general and a couple of dozen in particular that I am indebted for much of the information I have been able to add to this book.

Anyone who takes the trouble to compare the standards of road behaviour of today's cars with those of only a few years ago will find ample proof of the progress that has taken place in vehicle design, both across the board in general and in terms of suspension behaviour in particular. By the time the reader reaches the end of this book he will probably understand how and why the differences are so great.

February 1993   Geoffrey Howard

Preface to 1st edition

A car suspension reconciles the sensitivity of the human animal to disturbances with what the road surface would inflict on it if no suspension were present. As in engineering generally, a suspension is a compromise between conflicting requirements and almost certainly also reflects individual idiosyncracies. I have tried in this book to provide the basic theory, to list the conflicting requirements and to give, where they can be helpful, examples to illustrate the application of that theory, using values which fall within the fairly wide range of car sizes which continue to be made. The compromise is always made easier by being able to put values on the conflicting requirements and I hope that this book may be able to help in this.

The later chapters provide examples of past and present practice in the application of the theory. For illustrations of the applications and assorted information I am greatly indebted to vehicle and component manufacturers. The illustrations are individually acknowledged; it would be more difficult to tag all the items of information with their sources and in some cases it might also be embarrassing. I would like therefore to record here my indebtedness to all those who have helped me in this way: I am very grateful to them. I should like also to record my thanks to Mr. M. S. Crosthwaite for verifying the examples and various other calculations.

Donald Bastow

Contents

ix

Notation

A = acceleration; initial displacement

D = dynamic magnifier; dimension across flats of nut; deflection; diameter

E = Young's modulus

F = force

G = shear modulus

H = height of centre of gravity, above ground or above roll axis; height

I = moment of inertia

K = discomfort factor

L = wheelbase

M = moment; torque

P = pressure (inflation of tyres); force

R = radius, effective radius, of link, steering tube, spring leaf, steering lever wheel, etc.

S = spring rate

T = track

W = weight or mass

X = value of $k^2/ab > 1$

Y = distance of oscillation point behind centre of gravity, greater than b

a = acceleration; distance of centre of gravity from front wheels

b = distance of centre of gravity from rear wheels

c = horizontal distance of instantaneous centre from contact point; distance; ratio coil diameter/wire diameter of springs

d = distance, diameter

e = exponential function; offset; error

f = frequency; stress; distance, in suspension

g = acceleration due to gravity; distance in suspension

h = height, of centre, etc.

k = radius of gyration

n = factor or ratio as defined

p = proportion of total braking on front wheels

r = radius

t = time, thickness

v = velocity

x = deflection, vertical; distance of weight from centre of gravity; proportion of spring rate; value of roll inertia to $T^2/4$; value of $k^2/ab < 1$

y = distance of oscillation point behind centre of gravity less than b; deflection of wheel; deflection; length of contact patch

α = angle of movement of contact point to vertical, side view; angle of steering lever to perpendicular to steering tube

δ = damping as proportion of critical = F_d/F_{dc}

θ = angle; drift angle; angle of movement of tyre–road contact point or wheel centre to vertical in side elevation; roll angle of car on suspension

φ = pitch angle of car; angle of friction (tan $\varphi = \mu$); angle of link to horizontal; angle of steering lever to fore and aft or datum; roll angle of car on tyres; camber angle of wheel

ω = angular velocity

μ = coefficient of friction

Suffixes

a = front

ap = anti-pitch

b = rear

bp = ball pin

c = combined, cornering, critical, at resonances, between centres

ci = combined including partial tyre rate

d = damping

dc = critical damping

e = effective

f = front

g = gyroscopic; centre of gravity

i = inner, ideal

k = kingpin

l = longitudinal; link

o = outer

p = polar; pitch

r = rear

rc = roll centre

s = spring; sprung; screwthread

sl = steering lever

sp = spring; sprung

st = steering tube

t = tyre; total; nut face; transverse

tr = track rod

tf = transfer

us = unsprung

usa = average unsprung

v = vertical

w = wheelbase

x = part of rate of tyre as spring

1
Introduction

1.1 THE FUNCTION OF THE SUSPENSION SYSTEM

A vehicle exists to carry someone or something from one place to another. Implicit in that statement is that in doing so there shall be as little disturbance as possible of who or what is being carried. If the load is inanimate, the less the disturbance the less in the way of special packing will be necessary. If animate, then the better the condition after the journey, the longer the journey can be without fatigue. In the case of the driver of the vehicle, the less the fatigue, the greater the levels of concentration that can be maintained and safer the driver's performance, especially towards the end of the journey.

The basic need for a suspension system in a vehicle[1] is not entirely caused by human susceptibility to the discomforts of vibration, although isolation from road-induced disturbances is certainly a highly desirable design aim. Maintaining contact between the wheels and the road surface is far more fundamental, as the control and stability of the vehicle relies upon it totally. To add isolation and insulation in the simplest way they could devise, early coachmakers developed the simple leaf spring, preformed to the shape of a semi-ellipse and rolled at the ends to provide easy and flexible attachments.

The attraction of the leaf spring in the early days of suspension design was its ability to be handled and manufactured in the primitive smithy. Easily malleable mild steel could be formed to the required shape using only an open coke furnace, anvil and hammer, then tempered by quenching in water, before being hung from the chassis on flexible pivots and shackles and clamped to the axle with U-bolts and plates. It used everyday blacksmith technology that was easily performed and well understood.

In the very early days of car development, the absorption

1

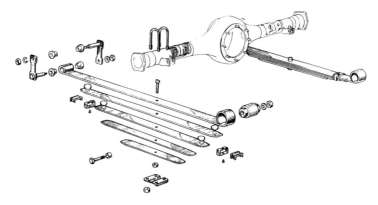

Fig. 1·1   The typical leaf spring comprises several separate leaves and is mounted on a bushed pivot at one end with a swinging shackle at the other. The axle tube is clamped to the central portion by U-bolts

properties required by the rigid tyres of the cartwheels made the double semi-elliptic leaf spring the most commonly used type of springing medium. Cars like the original 1886 Daimler used a pair at each corner[2], with the axle clamped below the lower set and the chassis clamped above the uppers. For several decades until well into the 1960s, multi leaf-spring live-axle rear suspensions of the type shown in Fig.1.1 were well established as the standard design for mass produced cars and are still the most common form of suspension to be found on commercial vehicles right through from medium vans to heavy trucks. Other pioneering designers mounted the springs transversely so that a single pivot steering system could be used for the front axle. Sixty years later transverse leaf springs were still in use on cars like the Chevrolet Corvette and A.C. Ace, separated by the depth of the hub to act as independent transverse links. Their current use is mainly confined to small rugged off-road vehicles of the type inspired by the war-time Jeep.

In its structural role the leaf spring is simply a flexible beam, as shown in Fig. 1.2, supported at each end with a point load W at its centre. In this typical offset design, the front end reaction is $W_a = WL_d/L$ and the rear end reaction $W_b = WL_b/L$. The relatively wide but thin cross-section of a leaf-shaped spring allows a high stiffness in the horizontal plane, for positive axle location, to be combined with flexibility in the vertical plane, for good isolation. But the internal stresses of a single-plane leaf (or a beam) supported in this way are far from uniform and much higher at the centre. To distribute them more evenly, the vertical section depth must taper in

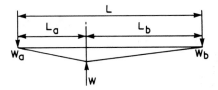

Fig. 1·2 Offsetting a semi-eliiptic spring produces unequal forces at the two ends and resists driving and braking torque more effectively

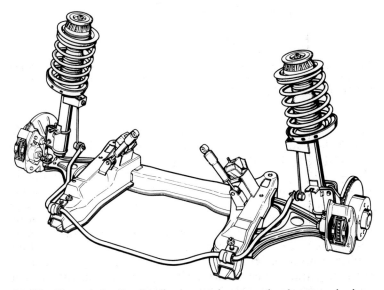

Fig. 1·3 The typical coil spring front suspension uses splayed struts and a lower locating arm, usually A-shaped on two inboard pivots. In the MacPherson type the anti-roll bar acts as a locating member for the lower strut ends

proportion to the distance from the input point. If this section were produced in solid material it would be uniformly stressed but also very rigid. But if secondary leaves are added instead as a series of laminates following the same tapering section, flexibility and the ability to store energy are greatly improved. As each leaf then deflects towards its elastic limit it transfers additional loads to the next leaf in the stack, with a small degree of relative sliding motion at each interface.

The birth of the coil spring as shown in Fig. 1.3 as the primary suspension medium did not appear until the more general trend towards independent front suspension after World War II, and even then it was usually used in conjunction with leaf springs at the rear. The advantage of the coil spring lay in its almost total lack of internal friction (derived from the interleaf sliding action on a leaf spring design), which allowed the damping function to be confined to a more precisely controlled shock absorber unit, and its greater package efficiency.

Leaf springs were easy to arrange in the flat ladder-type structures of the separate chassis unit: They required widely-spaced attachments in the same horizontal plane as each other. Coil springs, although much more efficient in their ability to store energy and deflect through large displacements, need to react against members vertically above their input pads. The concept of the coil spring is inseparable from the integral body or the three-dimensional space-frame chassis.

Suspension design today has polarised towards coil springs in a variety of forms, typically used concentrically with telescopic dampers struts as shown in Fig. 1.3. The flexibility of their design criteria and their ability to be manufactured relatively cheaply in large quantities with consistent characteristics has brought coil springs to the forefront of modern suspension design. In the modern, highly optimised bodyshell they also feed road loads into well-spaced and stiff areas of the engineering structure.

In the history of suspension development there has probably been more progress in the understanding of the effects of wheel geometry and kinematic changes than in any other related field. Only in the 1980s have the ideas of self-aligning wheels that can compensate for any imbalance in the braking system or tyre drag, of negative roll in corners or the fine-tuning of handling through rear wheel steering started to become feasible and viable for popular cars. In the 1990s, the availability of affordable electronic systems is having an even more dramatic effect on eliminating the traditional compromises between ride and handling qualities.

By definition, a suspension system[3] is used to support a load from above, which is exactly how the early engineers and mechanics saw the role of the springing medium (as their primitive carriages hung from their supports) and why the apparent misnomer came into general usage. In reality, the mechanisms that isolate the occupants of a modern car from road disturbances are compression systems, but it is inconceivable to make such a basic change to the convention at this stage in history.

Springs, of course, are the flexible elements in the suspension system which are able to store the energy applied to them in the form of loads and displacements. The basic concept of a sprung

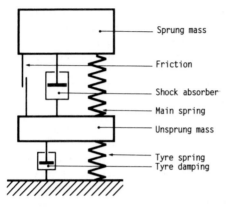

Fig. 1·4 Vehicle suspension systems contain several elements, with a main spring supporting the sprung mass and the shock absorber (or damper) dissipating the energy stored in the spring during movement. The tyre acts as a secondary spring system, acting on both the unsprung masses of the suspension and the sprung mass of the loaded vehicle

vehicle suspension unit is shown in Fig. 1.4. Different types of springs have different abilities in this respect (see Chapter 3). Spring flexibility in most countries is measured as the rate at which loads cause spring deflection. Newtons per metre are typical SI spring rate units (France is one of the exceptions where *flexibilité* in metre/ Newton is sometimes used).

Spring energy is converted to heat and dissipated partly by the friction of the system and mostly by the dampers, more often and erroneously called shock absorbers. Usually in the form of pistons working in cylinder filled with hydraulic fluid, dampers exert a force which is proportional to the square of the piston velocity (see Chapter 4). The damper's function is to restrain undesirable bounce characteristics of the sprung vehicle mass and to also restrain the wheel assembly from losing its contact with the ground by being excited at its natural vibration frequency.

The mechanical elements in a suspension system other than the main springs and dampers are provided to locate the wheel assemblies and control the geometry of their movement under dynamic laden conditions. Some of these elements are simple links, others may be compound multi-role members like the relatively thin transverse torsion bars used to stabilise the vehicle in corners by restricting roll (the often quoted 'stabiliser bar' or 'anti-roll bar', sometimes shortened to 'roll bar').

Mechanics in engineering terms describes the science dealing with the action of forces on objects or structures. It forms the basis for all mechanical design - the analysis of loads, functions and motion which is at the root of everyday life in the modern, industrialised and mechanically-oriented society enjoyed by the civilised world.

Under the influence of forces, all objects may be either in motion or at rest, relative to some other defined system or reference point. The part of mechanics which deals with motion is called dynamics (statics are concerned with forces in equilibrium and kinematics refer to the theory of motion without reference to the forces involved).

Quantities which combine speed with direction are known as vectors, the most commonly used vector in vehicle terminology being velocity (which is therefore clearly differentiated from speed). The rate of change of velocity for an object is its acceleration, and its velocity times its mass is its momentum. The actions of forces and momentum are governed by several laws of motion which explain the behaviour of everything we see moving around us every day.

1.2   VEHICLE DYNAMICS

As already mentioned, the primary function of a vehicle's suspension system is to isolate the structure (and the occupants) from shocks and vibrations generated by the road surface. It must do this while maintaining stability, steering control and the overall handling precision of the vehicle in its dynamic behaviour. Each wheel is therefore connected to the integral body of a modern car by a system of links, to control the kinematics of the suspension movement, and a system of springs and dampers, to provide flexible but restrained wheel movement. The diameter of the tyre, the flexibility of its sidewall (which acts as a secondary spring system), the size of the contact patch between the tyre and the road, the (unsprung) weight of the wheel, tyre and axle assembly all affect the magnitude of the shock transmitted to the suspension unit. The spring rate or stiffness, the damping effects of the shock absorber and the ratio of sprung to unsprung masses affect the amplitude of the wheel motion and the load transmitted to the body structure through the spring seats and suspension attachment points.

Apart from the forward longitudinal velocity of the vehicle u and any cornering forces generated by steering action to provide a side velocity v, the total vehicle system is therefore subjected to many different degrees of free movement, acceleration and vibration, simplified in most analyses to act about three perpendicular axes, X,

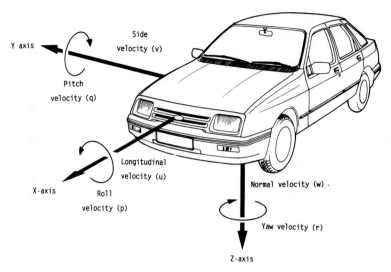

Fig. 1·5 A moving vehicle has up to 17 different degrees of freedom that must be considered about the three main axes

Y and Z as shown in Fig. 1.5. In addition to moving vertically on its springs with a normal velocity w, it is free to yaw about the vertical Z axis with a yaw velocity r, to pitch with a pitch velocity q about the lateral horizontal Y axis and to roll with a roll velocity p about the longitudinal X axis passing through the front and rear roll centres (provided all wheels remain in contact with the road surface).

The interaction of these movements, each with its own velocity, acceleration and frequency makes a sprung vehicle one of the most complex systems in the field of dynamics. With at least 17 different degrees of freedom, analysis of what takes place during a complex road manoeuvre (which often involves coincidental roll, pitch and yaw) cannot be undertaken adequately without computer aids, especially when there are additional variables to be considered like body flexibility, suspension link deflections, compliance in the attachment bushes and geometry changes caused by torque inputs to the wheels and by suspension movement.

Modern cars mostly use independent coil spring suspension front and rear, highly developed to provide dynamic characteristics that combine good ride qualities with outstanding handling and driver control. Earlier car designs, many of today's vans and most trucks use rigid axles, for sound engineering reasons. Over the years a number of other suspension designs has been tried, usually without success in the long term, although the way ahead seems to lie with a combination of variable-rate air spring and hydraulic control under the influences of an on-board micro computer which senses many different inputs and responds at high speed (see Chapter 9).

The primary function of a suspension system has changed little, however, even if the understanding of its behaviour and the quality of its ride comfort have both made quantum leaps ahead. A suspension spring is still required to absorb the shock loadings produced by bumps in the road surface, which it does by being initially compressed and subsequently expanded against the total mass of the car. The rate at which energy is stored depends on the spring rate[4], or stiffness, and the rate at which it releases this stored energy is controlled by the natural frequency of the sprung system, typically in the 1 to 1.5 Hertz (or cycles per second) bracket.

Effective damping is essential to control wheel and body movements. The subtlety of suspension design in ride terms depends to a large extent on the balance between spring stiffness and damping effect, interacting with the amount of wheel travel available and the means of restricting it. Progressive springing can be achieved either by inherent spring characteristics (such as coils wound from tapered-section wire) or by introducing flexible bump stops, or snubbers, to the system.

Major constraints to this aspect of suspension design concern the ability of the total vehicle to carry loads without reaching the wheel travel limits under normal running conditions. In this respect there is much to be gained from load-levelling control systems, although their complication adds considerably to the basic component costs.

If each wheel could be considered as a separate system, suspension design would be a much simpler process. But all the springs are linked together by the structure of the body and all the wheels by the reaction of the ground, which makes their interactions extremely complex and their characteristics very interdependent. A car is free to bounce equally at both ends together, to pitch about the front or rear axles, to roll about a longitudinal axis and to combine any or all of these effects together. How the static masses are distributed, how the wheels are connected and how the spring rates are balanced make a fundamental contribution to the behaviour of the vehicle under dynamic conditions.

1.3 SUSPENSION GEOMETRY

Kinematic variations in wheel angle and movement are generally

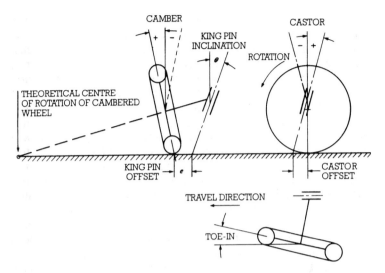

Fig. 1·6 Front suspension geometry is calibrated by a number of variables. In the horizontal plane, the alignment of the wheels is identified as toe-setting. In the transverse vertical plane, wheel inclination is measured as the camber angle, while the king pin inclination θ and the king pin offset e are also critical. In the longitudinal vertical plane, king pin inclination is known as the castor angle

described by their geometry and the science of wheel control has become as complex as ride quality development. To understand the various systems in detail it is first necessary for the variables to be defined, as illustrated in Figs. 1.6 to 1.11.

Toe setting: This is the very small angle, Fig. 1.6, between each wheel and the longitudinal axis of the car. It is usually measured under static conditions by the difference in the distance between the front and rear edges of left and right wheel rims at centreline level. Under dynamic conditions toe settings often change due to longitudinal and lateral compliance of the suspension and body components.

Castor angle and mechanical trail: Usually a steered wheel is arranged to trail by a small angle, so that forward movement gives a stabilising effect. That angle of trail, Fig. 1.6, is known as the degree of castor. Most modern cars use the self-aligning torque of the front tyres and the front weight bias to provide self-centring of the steering system and true running, so castor angles are modest and typically around 1 or 2 degrees.

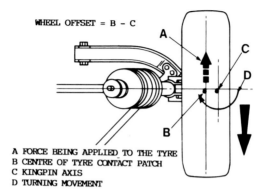

WHEEL OFFSET = B – C

A FORCE BEING APPLIED TO THE TYRE
B CENTRE OF TYRE CONTACT PATCH
C KINGPIN AXIS
D TURNING MOVEMENT

Fig. 1·7   Wheel offset is significant in determining the self-stablising characteristics of front wheel kinematics. Negative offset between points B and C causes uneven braking torque to be cancelled out

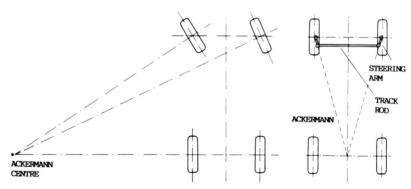

STEERING ARM

TRACK ROD

ACKERMANN

ACKERMANN CENTRE

Fig. 1·8   To enable all four wheels to run around a common centre in bends, the steering arms for the front wheels must be angled inwards so their projected operating angles meet at the rear axle. This characteristic is known as the Ackermann effect

Camber angle: This is the angle between the plane of a wheel and the vertical, as shown in Fig. 1.6. It is described as positive when the top of the wheel leans out and negative when the top leans in. Camber angles usually change slightly under the geometry influences of wheel travel. As camber angle also affects the pressure distribution of the tyre footprint on the road, it plays an important part in the balance of cornering power and handling characteristics.

The more positive the camber angle, the greater the slip angle for a given cornering force and the slower the onset of complete

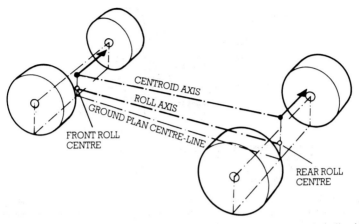

Fig. 1·9   The axis between the front and rear roll centres is known as the roll axis. Its inclination plays an important part in determining the handling characteristics

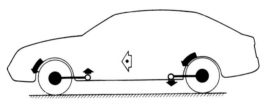

Fig. 1·10   Front-end dive effects under braking can be counteracted by using a leading arm geometry that generates an upward reaction in response to retarding wheel torque

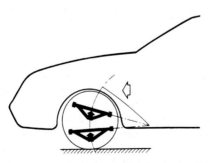

*Fig.*1·11   In double wishbone or strut suspension layouts, anti-dive characteristics can be introduced by arranging for the inner upper and lower pivots to operate with opposed inclinations

breakaway. The more negative the camber angle, the higher the ultimate cornering force but the more sudden and rapid the total breakaway becomes. For maximum traction as well as cornering power, high performance cars with wide tyres need to run with low camber angles on their driving wheels and as little change as the suspension installation allows.

Wheel offset (or scrub radius): The lateral distance between the point where the swivel axis of a steered wheel meets the ground and centre of the tyre footprint is known as the offset, as shown in Fig. 1.7. If the axis passes inside the footprint centre, the offset is positive and if it passes outside it is negative. If it coincides, the system is termed centrepoint. Negative offset provides stability advantages in the event of uneven braking torque or a tyre deflation, but is often claimed to reduce steering 'feel'. Positive offset is also claimed to generate more self-centring but increased steering effort, although opinions on these factors often differ.

Ackermann effect: This is the degree by which the inner wheel in a turn is arranged to cover a tighter radius than the outer wheel, as shown in Fig. 1.8. Full Ackermann effect is provided by angling the steering arms slightly inwards so their projected lines meet at the rear axle and all four wheels run around a common centre in bends. The importance of full Ackermann geometry has declined with advancing tyre technology, although Ford investigations into the optimum balance between offset and Ackermann effects have produced a system, first introduced on Sierra, which combines low steering effort with excellent feel.

Roll centres and roll axis: Under lateral cornering forces, the body will roll on its springs about centres at both ends of the car, as shown in Fig. 1.9. The line joining these centres is the roll axis and its inclination to the horizontal plane plays an important part in the handling characteristics. Determining the roll centres for a MacPherson strut suspension or an independent trailing arm system involves some geometrical plotting (it is usually just above ground level), but both types allow it to be adjusted through the design geometry of the various links involved. On a MacPherson strut system this roll centre moves vertically with jounce and rebound and from side to side with body roll. To restrict roll, left and right suspension arms are often linked by a slim torsion bar spring, often called a stabiliser.

Anti-dive and anti-squat: To resist front-end dip under heavy braking, or rear-end squat under acceleration, suspension pivots are usually angled to provide upward reactions automatically in response to high wheel torque inputs[5]. Some movement is preferred by most drivers to improve the braking feel, but it is well controlled in most modern cars.

Torque-steer: With powerful front-drive cars, there can be an interaction of the drive system on the suspension geometry which causes directional influences on the steering, known as torque-steer effects. They are detected as an easily-countered pull on the wheel when accelerating hard, usually associated with a tendency for the car to steer the opposite way when the engine power is suddenly reduced.

Torque steer is one of the most difficult design challenges with front drive, and the difficulty multiplies with increased power levels. Common causes of torque steer include unequal drive shaft stiffness, unequal drive shaft length, compliance steer effects and unequal changes in drive shaft angles between opposite sides of the car, or a conflict between drive shaft, suspension or steering geometry[6]. The basic forces involved are shown in Fig. 1.12 and the subject is discussed in further detail in Section 8.9. In this case where the driveshaft angles α and β are different, the net torque steer couple C_t is given by the equation:

$$C_t = C_r - C_l = T\left(\tan\frac{\alpha}{2} - \tan\frac{\beta}{2}\right) \qquad (1.1)$$

Roll steer: There are several ways in which the effects of roll can cause either front or rear wheels to steer the car slightly, and this characteristic may be used for fine tuning of a car's handling. In some cases, the toe setting may change as the outer wheel becomes

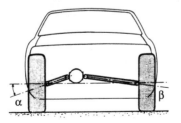

Torque steer   Torque steer
couple to right C_r couple to left C_l

Fig. 1·12 Front wheel drive cars with unequal length drive shafts and a nose-up attitude when accelerating will pull to the right if the left-hand drive shaft is shorter than the left

more loaded in a turn, or the outer wheel may creep forward slightly (as the inner wheel creeps backwards), to create a steering effect. Rear roll steer is often used to counter front understeer, either through the primary geometry of the system or by secondary loading of the compliance bushes. Too much roll steer, however, can lead to excessive tyre wear and disturbing bump steer effects on long-wave single wheel movements like those experienced on motorways.

REFERENCES

1. Ford Motor Co., 'Vehicle Dynamics' Booklet (1981)
2. Howard, G., 'Chassis & Suspension Engineering', *Osprey Publishing Ltd.* (1987)
3. Newton, K., Steeds, W. and Garrett, K., 'The Motor Vehicle', Butterworths, (1989)
4. Campbell, C, 'Automobile Suspensions', *Chapman & Hall*, (1981)
5. Murakami, T., Uno, T., Iwasaki, H. and Noguchi, H., 'Development of a New Multi-Link Front Suspension', *SAE Technical Paper No. 890179* (1989)
6. Bulmer, C., 'Argumentative Torque', *Car Design & Technology* (November 1991).

2

Disturbances and sensitivity

2.1 ROAD IRREGULARITIES

Before making any analysis of vehicle suspension it is desirable to know at least the probable height of the road irregularities against which the system is intended to insulate. Measurements first made as long ago as 1936[1] using a 16-wheeled apparatus as the averaging-out base are just as valid today in most territories of the world[2]. The results of this exercise were expressed in terms of integrated inches per mile of the irregularities, with the index for the best roads tested being 75 to 85 in/mile (1.18 to 1.34 m/km), while values obtained on main roads ranged from 100 to 250 in/mile (1.58 to 3.95 m/km). The view was expressed that surface undulations having amplitudes of 0.75 in. to 1 in. (0.019 to 0.025 m) were likely to cause discomfort at normal speeds. Amplitudes of less than 0.013 m meant medium quality roads, while amplitudes under 0.005 m meant a very good surface.

If we relate the amplitude of 0.005 m and the index of 1.18 m/km, both representative of good roads, we obtain a figure of 236 or more bumps per kilometre or a pitch of about 4 m. With some of the irregularities lying below the figure of 0.005 m the average pitch will be less than 4 m. The average distance traversed per wheel revolution is less than 2 m.

Although the figures date from a long time ago there is still very little evidence to suggest that they differ much from the range occurring in roads in general use today, though the proportions of the different levels of integrated irregularities has undoubtedly changed.

2.2 SPECIFIC SURFACES

Performance and durability of suspension components is one of the most critical factors in vehicle design and dynamic control on the road. Throughout the motor industry advanced suspension testing facilities have been developed to ensure that every part of the suspension system meets stringent performance criteria over a long and dependable life in service.

Designing mechanical components for the suspension system, like the other parts in the vehicle, starts from a realistic initial assumption of the stresses likely to be experienced in the most severe conditions of service. The performance of prototype parts is then validated and the design developed under controlled test conditions to reach maximum levels of efficiency, cost effectiveness and manufacturing feasibility.

Although the suspension system appears simple in concept, compared to a power unit or transmission, its function and its effect on vehicle behaviour are complex. Performance criteria of suspension components are based on a combination of engineering experience and input data from instrumented vehicles operating over real road conditions and scientific simulations. Many of the most severe surface features to be found anywhere in the world are now faithfully reproduced on special road systems at the various industry proving grounds as a common standard for developing suspension systems for ride comfort and suspension components and sub-assemblies for durability, to save valuable engineering time.

The first of these is known as 'Belgian Pavé', the original of which was the product of neglect, at least during World War 2, on the typical stone block surfaces found in parts of Belgium, France, the Netherlands and Germany. The test track surfaces are actual reproductions of a typical surface measured in Belgium, with the stone blocks set in concrete to maintain consistency of the disturbances produced over long periods of severe use. Early postwar cars in use on the continent of Europe found these pavé surfaces produced not only rapid deterioration in hydraulic shock absorber performance but also structural breakages of various forms. It is now generally considered that if a prototype or development car survives 1600 km of the pavé testing it is unlikely to develop structural faults during a normal lifetime. The Belgian pavé of this type at the British Motor Industry Research Association's (MIRA) proving grounds[3], which is a typical example of the industry standard, has been installed using stone blocks of random length between 0.15 and 0.23 m long. There is a random height variation of ± 0.025 m and a pattern repeat every 4.5 to 6 m.

The second special surface commonly used has a washboard or ripple texture representative of surfaces found further afield in undeveloped countries, such as East Africa where road maintenance

is minimal and seasonal deterioration extreme. Any car manufacturer wanting to develop or maintain a market for his products in
these territories must design and develop suspension components
capable of withstanding sustained use in these conditions. The
washboard surface at MIRA has a spacing between its corrugations
is 0.75 m ± 0.05 m. To allow for any variation of relative timing on
the two sides of the car, a part of the surface has the ripples at right
angles to the direction of travel and they are then angled back. The
ripples have a height of 0.025 m.

The third surface which is interesting for the suspension designer
is the long wave pitching track. This has sinusoidal waves 12 m long
and of 0.1 m amplitude. This tends to excite the sprung mass at
speeds from 55 to 65 km/hr, which implies 1.3 to 1.5 Hz. These
surfaces are provided for two reasons: they are permanent reproductions of actual surfaces; they allow a manufacturer to ensure that his
vehicle can travel at a reasonable speed over such surfaces; they also
allow endurance tests to be carried out on actual vehicles using large
amplitudes of suspension travel.

Other surfaces increasing being reproduced for vehicle appraisals
under the controlled and secure environment of the proving ground
include specific sections of badly maintained roadways, meticulously
reconstructed to high precision levels. Ford of Europe has a whole
network of these appraisal roads at its Lommel Proving Grounds in
Belgium, two of which are shown in Fig. 2.1. The Inner Paris Road
has been particularly useful in developing suspension systems that
are acceptable to discerning French car buyers.

2.3   TEST AND APPRAISAL METHODS

Multi-channel tape recordings made of road input data both at the
proving grounds and during test sessions conducted at all the
extreme geographical locations are later transformed into digital
computer codes. This process allows many hours of testing to be
condensed on to a single tape so that laboratory test sequences on
typical components and complete suspension assemblies can be
generated. Fig. 2.2 shows a typical application of these techniques to
a vehicle on a 'four-poster' hydra-pulse machine installed in an
environmental test chamber at Ford. Relationships between test
cycles and component life are determined by stress level analysis,
now performed by computer-aided techniques for rapid and reliable
production of test rig control tapes, level count distributions and
frequency analysis of noise and vibration recordings.

Fig. 2·1 Blocks of Belgian pavé set in concrete and reproductions of specifically bad road sections like these three examples at Ford's European Proving Grounds are now part of the special test surfaces used in suspension development all over the world

Fig. 2·2   Road load data from pre-recorded tapes is fed into four hydraulic actuators positioned under the road wheels to assess the noise, vibration and harshness levels inside a test vehicle under controlled laboratory conditions

2.4 DAMPER PERFORMANCE STANDARDS

Although the springs, links, bushes and insulators of a modern suspension system all require meticulous design and development for high standards of vehicle behaviour to be achieved, the role of the damper within the system has changed completely. From a simple set of friction discs to a hydraulic damping piston, it has evolved to play an integrated part in the primary ride characteristics, putting new demands upon it and requiring new ways of developing and testing its vital performance standards.

The often conflicting demands of vehicle ride and handling, and the increased performance of the modern car with its large section low-profile tyres, result in very high peak forces and velocities in the suspension system. Some systems using lightweight undriven rear axles have recorded vertical wheel velocities approaching 5 m/sec on rough roads, which is several times the peak values traditionally assumed for suspension design. At the same time on smooth roads, damper seal friction forces need to be as low as possible to ensure the ride is not compromised in any way by stickiness in the stroke of the piston rod. Damper performance is a fundamental part of both the handling control of the vehicle and in the comfort levels felt by the occupants. The damper settings must meet tight performance and durability targets, even though these components are usually bought in from outside suppliers. Most of the large manufacturers build a very wide product range of cars (Ford models, for example, span a range from a small hatchback like the Ford Fiesta to a large luxury saloon like the Ford Scorpio in size and from modest diesel power to turbocharged high-performance petrol engines) incorporating several different designs of suspension system for both front and rear wheel drive. Damping equipment specified also covers the full field of designs including gas dampers, single-tube, gas pressurised dampers, twin-tube, emulsion tube and self-levelling types supplied by a total of up to a dozen different major European damper manufacturers.

To ensure that these units meet each company's performance standards, the car makers each develop their own acceptable criteria on prototype vehicles which are translated into damper performance curves, commonly called damper carding specifications (because traces were originally recorded on small hardbacked graphs). Durability of the units in association with the total vehicle is determined by running accelerated and general durability routes at various proving grounds, where there are many different special road surfaces including broken concrete, washboard, long-pitch waves, cobblestones, canted slabs, road blocks, chuckholes, railway crossings, square-edged holes and staggered bumps. Test schedules are available with a predetermined severity index that condenses several years' average customer usage into only a few weeks testing.

With the range and complexity of suppliers and types, it becomes too expensive and time consuming to cover all durability aspects on road test. Efforts have therefore been made, as with all other components, to transfer as much testing as possible to the laboratory. Laboratory tests can be accelerated more readily, can be controlled to give more repeatability and accuracy and performance can be continuously monitored.

Damper tests today are usually conducted on the latest computer-controlled machines used in development and in the setting of the quality control standards that the suppliers must meet. Some of this equipment can complete more than 3.5 million test cycles in less

Fig. 2·3 Four dampers are tested simmultaneously in special machines for performance and durability over a wide range of stroke velocities and temperatures

than four days, equivalent to about 10,000 customer kilometres per day.

One of these new machines installed at the Ford component laboratories in Essex is shown in Fig. 2.3. It took five years to develop and is used to investigate seal and valve durability over a wider spectrum of velocities and temperatures than was possible in the past. It is supported by all the previous performance and durability tests which are still carried out as well, including those for strength, corrosion, fatigue and noise level.

Four dampers are mounted together in the machine for simultaneous performance and endurance testing, as they would be on a car. Servo hydraulics under computer control provide vertical motion, while pneumatic actuators apply side loads at the same time, accurately reproducing ride and handling effects from data collected on instrumented cars. Water jackets control the operating temperatures automatically, while computerised recording and shutdown facilities allow unattended operation 24 hours per day.

A servo-hydraulic actuator, mounted in the base of the machine frame, provides vertical and axial motion to the four shock absorbers. Adjacent to this actuator and mounted on the sides of the machine frame are four pneumatic actuators which are coupled via a cable and pulley arrangement to apply a side load to each unit according to a fully programmable input from the controlling computer. The shock absorbers can reproduce any vehicle installation angle between 0 and 30 degrees to the vertical and there is on-line compensation for any non-linearity in the bounce or rebound input, for accurate reproduction of wave forms.

The control computer, which is shared between two other test machines, has 112 kilobytes of operating system memory and stores all data on two 5 megabyte hard discs. An automatic plotter can present data in the form of force against displacement, force against velocity for a cycle or a summary of force against peak velocity for a complete performance test over a range of inputs.

With this highly developed aid, all of a vehicle's dampers can now be tested more effectively and the performance and durability standards controlled more accurately. It is just one example of the investment and methodology that has recently been applied to improve suspension systems and their behaviour in production vehicles.

2.5   INFLUENCE OF WHEEL SIZE

The road surface cannot be considered on its own as its effect on the car depends on several other key factors. Primarily, the size of the wheel and tyre assembly that traverses the road (and the associated tyre rate at a primary spring) have a significant influence on how road shocks are transmitted. Small wheels drop into pot-holes more easily, for example, and large wheels climb up sharp square edges with less effort. Secondly, the size of the wheel and tyre assembly affects the unsprung mass that must be moved for the suspension to absorb movements resulting from road irregularities.

The effect of wheel radius assuming a sharp-edged step and a rigid wheel is easily calculated. Fig. 2.4 shows that for a step of 0.025 m, a drop in wheel radius from 0.37 m to 0.25 m gives an increase in wheel vertical velocity over the first 20% of the lift of about 15%. What this amounts to in practice is more difficult to predict. The larger wheel will be heavier; but it is hard to say if it will yield more or less readily to the intrusion of the square corner. The issue is also clouded by the initial deflection of the tyre, the length of the contact patch implied by this and the resulting earlier contact with the step, in both cases, than the rigid wheel would imply. Even with the sharp-edged step a lot more tyre information is needed to attempt the calculations about movements of two different radii wheels. The effect of wheel radius when the tyre drops into a hollow

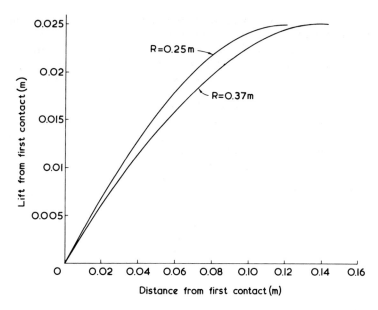

Fig. 2·4   Rigid circular wheels of different radii, 0.37 m and 0.25 m, behave differently when they meet an obstruction in the form of a step 0.025 m high. At zero lift the velocity ratio is 1:56; at 0.005 m lift it has slightly diminished to 1:36

in the ground is just as difficult to predict. A rigid wheel cannot follow a ground contour that has an effective radius smaller than the wheel. At a stage depending on the relative radii, two-point contact will occur. With a tyred instead of a rigid wheel the length of contact patch and the rigidity of the tread affect the way the wheel starts to drop into a hollow and complicate calculations. What we can be reasonably sure about in both cases is that a larger radius wheel should show less abrupt departures from a given path than a smaller radius wheel, but the final effect on the car's own suspension system will depend also on the difference in the unsprung weight of the different sizes of wheel. The real effect of the wheel radius change may be less therefore than indicated by the curves in Fig. 2.4.

2.6   DISCOMFORT LEVELS FELT IN THE CAR

Levels of comfort (or discomfort) in a car, van or truck and the amount of fatigue experienced during travel are essentially subjective elements of ride quality assessment. Disturbances, vibrations, noise levels and harshness can all be measured in various ways, but the correlation of these readings to what is felt by the occupants has never been straight-forward or universally realistic. So suspension engineers have recently been taking new initiatives to develop objective techniques for quantifying ride levels, with some very promising results.

Ride quality assessments are usually measured by what is described as a subjective system rating, using a team or panel of test personnel drawn from all areas of company management. The procedure involves a process of detailed and precise comparison between vehicles and suspension settings driven over a wide variety of surfaces with everything rated on a scale of 1 to 10. Below the half-way mark is where the average customer starts to notice bad characteristics and it takes skilled and developed senses to make a half rating distinction on some of the finer subjective qualities such as secondary ride or steering wheel fight.

From complete compilations of the results, long lists of average ratings are then drawn up to cover all major aspects of the total behaviour, from single bump absorption and pot-hole shocks to the less obvious, but often more intrusive qualities like noise, vibration and harshness (NVH). Production vehicles, competitive designs and future proposals are fully appraised, dynamically over all types of road surface both under controlled conditions in the proving grounds and over public roads in a 'real world' environment. Each development team has its own special location where the characteristics of the surfaces are well known and the resultant suspension behaviour well understood.

Component and vehicle engineers working in the field of ride quality have previously had little quantitative means of measuring their own achievements. Whilst noise and vibration analyses in anechoic chambers provide valuable development methods for improving refinement levels, the suspension engineer has traditionally been restricted in his approach and forced to rely far more on subjective judgements and undefined comments from highly experienced experts.

2.7 HUMAN SUSCEPTIBILITY TO DISTURBANCES

For inanimate cargoes experiments can be made to find out if damage occurs on a journey. It should then be possible to form some opinion of why and how and to decide if it is simpler to modify the vehicle or the packing of the cargo. One might at first imagine that it would be easier to deal with human beings as drivers or passengers, because they can be asked questions and can give answers. However, just as the possession of absolute pitch is rare, so is the ability to maintain in the mind an unchanging standard of reference in regard to comfort, unaffected by surroundings in the car, fatigue or freshness, random or continuous noise, the external scenery and other distractions. A variety of experimenters have tried to eliminate these human variables, principally by carrying out their experiments on as many subjects as possible with widely diverse characteristics and background.

The medical effects of vibration on the human body have been studied for many years now, with all manner of conclusions reached, although most of these are more concerned with health under work conditions than simple comfort levels from exposure to road disturbances inside a vehicle. F. W. Lanchester[4] suggested as long ago as 1907 that a suspension frequency less than 1.5 Hz was desirable if attainable. H. S. Rowell[5] went rather further in the 1920s and suggested that the suspension frequency should be between 1.5 Hz and 2.3 Hz, basing this conclusion on enquiries and experiments. His argument was that as walking with a pace of 30 in (0.76 m) at speeds between 2.5 and 4 mph (1.12 and 1.79 m/s) was comfortable for most people, frequencies between 1.5 and 2.3 Hz must be acceptable to the human body.

Generally speaking, it seems that those vertical frequencies which seem to be the most uncomfortable fall either in the relatively high range from 20 to 200 Hz (although there is also evidence that fatigue occurs most rapidly when subjected to vibrations in the 4 to 8 Hz range) or in the very low band below 0.75 Hz, where dizziness and motion sickness can result. Lateral or fore-and-aft frequencies in the same ranges are also uncomfortable because they disturb the balance mechanism of the inner ear. Natural frequencies of suspension systems are therefore normally designed to fall within the acceptable mid range, although the total analysis of vehicle vibrations usually contains higher frequency – but lower amplitude – elements derived from tyre resonances (50–100 Hz) and bushing compliance (15–50 Hz).

In addition to vibration frequency, measurements of human susceptibility have also demonstrated that the duration of the exposure and its strength (as measured by the Root Mean Square of the acceleration amplitudes†) are also critical factors in fatigue levels recorded. Recommendations by the International Standards Orga-

---

† Root Mean Square (RMS) values are derived by taking instantaneous measurements of acceleration over a complete frequency cycle, squaring them and then taking the square root of their average.

nisation specify vibration levels likely to cause 'fatigue-decreased proficiency' as a series of contours based on these terms.

Earlier work on vehicle ride quality has demonstrated that the Root Mean Square of the vertical acceleration at the seat cushion in a vehicle correlates well with subjective ratings determined by appraisal teams. The first generation of 'ride meters' therefore measured this quantity over a specified time with the ability to use different frequency filters if desired.

More recent developments in this field have extended the scope of this basic approach to the much more complex system shown in Fig. 2.5, where human susceptibility to accelerations is measured about each of 12 separate axes. Three linear accelerations (in the X, Y and Z planes) are recorded at chest, buttock and foot levels, together with yaw, pitch and roll accelerations at the seat cushion, for subsequent analysis against amplitude and frequency weightings.

From a weighted combination of these 12 RMS measurements, an overall ride value can be computed which has so far correlated very closely with the subjective ride ratings on ride quality. It provides an extremely useful development tool for making rapid comparisons between vehicles or suspension settings. For an immediate read-out of overall ride values, a simplified six-channel meter has also been developed to supplement the full analysis of 12-channel recordings on a laboratory computer system.

To avoid exciting frequencies which the human body does not like is obviously important. From a variety of sources the following information has been derived:

(1) If the vestibular apparatus of the inner ear is subjected continuously to linear and/or angular accelerations between about 0.5 and 0.75 Hz dizziness and seasickness will be produced. Sensitivity in some individuals or circumstances may extend towards 1 Hz. The frequency for highest sensitivity depends upon the individual; so also does the time before the symptoms manifest themselves.

(2) The visceral region objects to frequencies between 5 and 7 Hz. The frequency depends upon the individual and the amplitude; greater amplitude increases the frequency to which any given individual is sensitive. Another indication of the effect of visceral region sensitivity is that a given tolerance level may permit a 6 Hz only 0.7 of the acceleration at 15 Hz giving the same discomfort. Even so the amplitude of sinusoidal vibrations implied by this acceleration relationship is, at 6 Hz, 4.36 times that at 15 Hz.

(3)   The head and neck are sensitive to frequencies between about 18 and 20 Hz.

(4)   Another early researcher discovered sensitivity to vertical accelerations at 11 Hz. Purdue University tests[6] in the 1930s showed higher than average sensitivity to frequencies of 4.25, 8.25 and 12 Hz.

(5)   Later researches indicated sensitivity to longitudinal and transverse vibrations at 1.5 Hz and did not differentiate between the two directions in sensitivity.

There is relatively immediate objection on the part of the subject to the frequency range of items (2) to (5) above.

Attempts to obtain correlation between subjective impressions can be influenced by vehicle size, appearance, noise level, interior furnishings and possibly also by the external environment; there are even suggestions that vehicle colour may have an influence.

Work by Ford reserarchers[7] also led to the development of specialised ride assessement dummies of the type shown in Fig. 2.5.

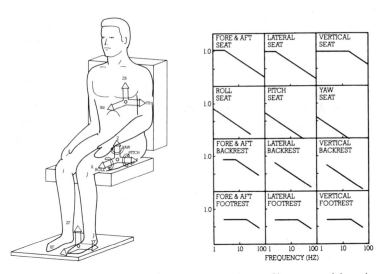

Fig. 2·5   Evaluation techniques used today involve the use of instrumented dummies with tri-axis accelerometers positioned at chest, buttock and foot levels. The human susceptibility to accelerations about 12 separate axes are shown alongside

2.8 SELF-LEVELLING AND ITS EFFECT

Ride comfort is often handicapped by the need to maintain adequate suspension travel in the fully laden static condition, which can demand spring rates stiffer than the optimum for driver-only or two-occupant operation. One solution is to use some kind of progressive springing that increases its stiffness with load, and another is to add a self-levelling system that restores ride height automatically whenever static wheel travel is detected.

Progressive rate springs may be wound from tapered wire or provided by second-stage assistance from the latest type of bump stops or snubbers, made from new-generation plastic materials and designed to operate very early in wheel travel sequence. Various different types of self-levelling suspension usually applied to the rear struts (see Chapter 7) are able to maintain ground clearance and keep wheel geometry closer to its optimum for more consistent handling.

REFERENCES

1. 'Surface Irregularity of Roads', DSIR Road Research Board Report, (1936–37)
2. Mimuro, T., Maemura, T. and Fujii, H., 'Development and Application of the Road Profile Measuring System', *SAE Technical Paper No. 930257* (March 1993)
3. Fogg, A., 'The MIRA Proving Ground', *Proc. Auto. Div. I.. Mech. E.,* (1955–56)
4. Lanchester, F. W., 'Some Problems Peculiar to the Design of the Automobile', *Proc. Instn Auto Engrs*, Vol.II, 187–287 (1907–08)
5. Rowell, H.S., 'Principles of Vehicle Suspension', *Proc. Auto Instn Engrs*, Vol. XVII, Pt 2, (1922–23)
6. Jacklin, H. M.. and Liddell, G. J., 'Riding Comfort Analysis', *Engng Bull.*, Purdue University, Vol. 17, No. 3, Research Series No. 44 (1933)
7. Ford Motor Co., 'Vehicle Dynamics' Booklet (1981)

3
Suspension systems and their effects

3.1 AN INTRODUCTION TO SUSPENSION DESIGN

Before we look in depth at the theory and principles of suspension system design and analysis it is necessary to understand some of the basic principles and effects, how the various elements are configured and how they function on the road. Many of the differences between systems are caused by the development of the details rather than the geometric differences in the fundamental layout. In operation the execution of a design is often worth far more than the concept.

Suspension engineers responsible for both production cars and competition machines are highly trained and experienced specialists in a field where the amateur, no matter how enthusiastically he tackles the task, is unlikely to achieve much in the way of satisfaction should he wish to make modifications or improvements. As the reader progresses through this book he will find the mathematics involved in suspension elements and vehicle handling are both complicated and involved. That said, the potential for the development of an advanced suspension system depends entirely upon the original design. Sometimes changes in the emphasis or balance of a standard system can be made effectively, provided the inevitable compromises are acceptable and that no vicous tricks are introduced as a result.

Initial changes to the front and rear suspensions of the Sierra by Ford Special Vehicle Engineering, for example, to increase the handling bias on the first version of the high-performance RS Cosworth version involved replacing the front rubber bushes of the standard design with solid plastic, to take out compliance and improve the steering response. The result was a car so quick to turn that it became 'nervous' on the road, seeming to swing its back end instantly as soon as the wheel was moved. Before production of the 5,000 examples required for Group A competition homologation started, modifications to the bush stiffness and steering ratio were made to reduce this effect.

And there are many other aspects of interrelated characteristics where improvements in one aspect of the design cause severe deterioration in another, with the inevitable compromise between ride and handling being the most familiar. Lower a car's ride height to reduce roll, and the suspension will crash through to the bump stops more readily. Replace standard springs with stiffer rates, and the ride will be firm and harsh. Fit wider wheels and tyres, and there will be heavier steering loads, more kickback on bumps and increased strain on wheel bearings and hubs.

All these conflicting variables weigh heavily in the mind of most suspension engineers when they design and develop original systems. In a way their task is much tougher than that of an after-market specialist because they have a greater freedom of choice, in the initial design stages at least. As a result, suspension systems over the years have shown some very diverse concepts using several different springing media, and a variety of different geometrical links. Lately there has been a more consistent gravitation towards MacPherson front struts and independent semi-trailing links, several examples being shown in Figs. 3.1, 3.2, 3.3 and 3.4.

To cover the full spectrum of chassis and suspension design it is necessary to include all the possibilities for front and rear ends of the vehicle, be it front-wheel-drive, rear-wheel-drive or one of the latest generation of permanent 4 × 4 systems. But for the bulk of conventional cars, suspension can be classified into groups based on their geometric elements, which are explained below.

3.2 SUSPENSION SYSTEMS IN COMMON USE

At the front, most cars use coil springs with either double wishbones or MacPherson struts to locate the wheels and control the geometry of their movement over bumps and in corners. Leaf springs (both front and rear) have become almost entirely extinct due to their high weight, poor location and interleaf friction. There are no passenger cars still in production that use leaf springs except for the classic Morgan sports car (which is a 1930s design) and the Fiat Panda 4 × 4.

Unequal-length wishbones or slightly-inclined struts are preferred now because, apart from separating the effects of the springs and dampers more effectively, they control wheel movement better. Ever since camber angle changes began to play such an important part in handling characteristics, systems that could be designed to use

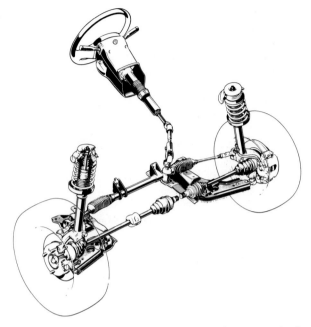

Fig. 3·1   The Ford Fiesta front suspension is a typically modern strut and coil spring system that uses pressed-steel lower arms mounted on two inboard pivots

camber to the best advantage took over. Wheels which move up and down through a vertical path (such as those controlled by sliding pillars, equal-length wishbones or pure leading or trailing links) take up the same degree of positive camber in corners as the body roll, reducing cornering power in the process.

Struts are usually preferred to wishbones because they spread the load inputs to the body better, eliminating the need in most cases for a heavy subframe to achieve acceptable insulation from noise, vibration and harshness. Wishbones at the front of rear-drive cars are usually more compact, allowing a lower bonnet line over the wheelarches, but when driveshafts are added for front-wheel drive, the lower spring attachment moves up.

3.3   SPRING FUNCTION AND THEORY

In its simplest schematic form the suspension of a vehicle can be considered as a basic two-mass two-spring system, Fig. 3.6. The

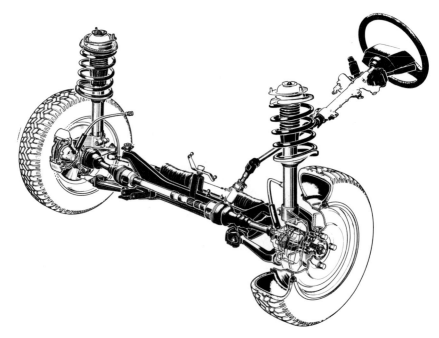

Fig. 3·2   The Peueot 205 system is similar to the Ford design but uses forged lower arms braced by semi-forward-facing tie-bars. Unlike the Ford, the Peugeot has an intermediate drive shaft with equal-length halfshafts to elliminate torque steer effects

primary mass is the bodyshell with all its mechanical components, trim, equipment, occupants and luggage. It is supported by the primary springing medium which today is most often a set of simple helical constant-rate coil springs. The secondary mass is made up of all the individual masses of the unsprung component parts of the suspension, drive, braking and steering system. They are isolated from the road surface by the tyre carcass which acts as a secondary spring.

In reality the primary spring has its own secondary elements such as insulating pads, bump stops and the inherent flexibility in the suspension components, but their effects can be excluded from the analysis at this stage. The dampers also provide a degree of minor secondary springing which can also be ignored. And initially we shall consider the bodyshell to be a perfectly rigid structure, although its flexibility cannot be disregarded if calculated predictions are to be truly representative of real world effects.

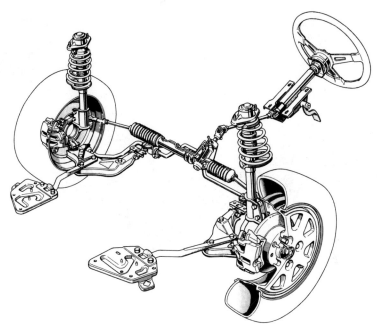

Fig. 3·3   In the Lancia system the lower ends of the front struts are located by wide-based assemblies fabricated from a combination of steel pressings and forged links

The overall rate of a compound spring system can be determined in the same way as for electrical resistances – straight addition for those in parallel ($S_c = S_1 + S_2$) and by adding the reciprocals of those in series:

$$\frac{1}{S_c} = \frac{1}{S_1} + \frac{1}{S_2}$$

(3.1)

The theoretical straight-line relationship between load and deflection of a linear-rate spring is therefore distorted by the other flexible elements in the system into the form of a curve. And to prevent contact between suspension elements or the spring coils at full travel, bump stops are added which distort the load/deflection curve even further.

In dynamic terms the maximum load likely to be fed into a vehicle road spring will be about twice its loading in the static laden condition. If a spring, for example has a stiffness rate of about 30 kN/m, it will be compressed about 0.08 m (3.15 in.) by a typical

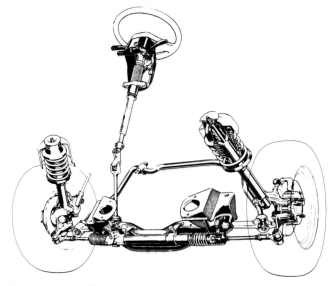

Fig. 3·4   In the Ford Sierra suspension a rear-mounted anti-roll bar provides the fore-and-aft location for the lower links, fulfilling the true definition of a MacPherson strut system

static load of 248 kg (generating a force of 2400 N) but will be displaced a further 0.16 m (6.3 in.) by road inputs. To reduce the clearance needed for suspension movement, therefore, to below 0.16 m some form of supplementary springing is required. This can be in the form of rubber or polycellular cones which progressively distort or variable-rate springs wound from tapered wire. In a typical installation bump rubbers would first come into operation at about 0.1 m dynamic travel and restrict the total movement to about 0.127 m (5 in.). The mean linear stiffness needed to do this would be 37.8 kN/m and the bump stop stiffness therefore from the parallel rule quoted early needs to be only 7.8 kN/m.

Coil springs in effect act as torsion bars, conveniently wrapped up into a more efficient package which is easier to install, especially in the confines of a car's wheelarch area. Because of the twisting of the bar into the helical coil, shear stresses are greater than for a plain torsion bar but quite easy to design for with modern manufacturing and heat treatment methods.

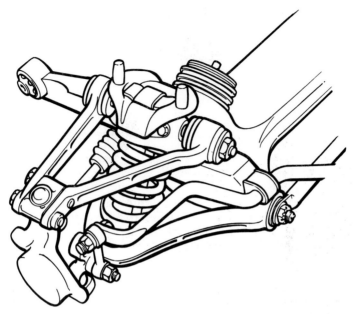

Fig. 3·5   Jaguar has used double-wishbone front suspensions for many years. The design provides a very compact layout with minimal installed height but involves extra complexity and cost over simpler strut systems

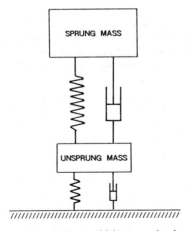

Fig. 3·6   The simplest way to consider a vehicle suspension is as a two-mass system with the body as the primary sprung mass and the unsprung masses of the suspension and drivetrain components forming the secondary mass

3.4 ENERGY STORAGE CAPACITY

An important characteristic of any spring material and configuration is its energy storage capacity at a stress level and range which will permit an acceptable life before failure. The highest possible value for this is not the primary aim in choosing a spring material. A gas, nitrogen for instance, will give an extremely high value but requires to be enclosed to enable it to provide that value. We are therefore concerned with the total weight of the suspension system to provide the desired suspension characteristics of spring rate and bump movement, plus of course the location and guidance characteristics required. For instance, steel as a leaf spring stores considerably less energy than as a coil spring or torsion bar but, as we have seen, can act as a guiding member as well as a spring and may therefore overall show a weight advantage in certain cases. In addition to weight, the cost aspect must be kept very much in mind. It is not possible to go into this thoroughly here because unit cost is very much bound up with quantities.

The energy stored by the spring is represented by the area under its load/deflection curve whatever shape it takes. Different types of springs have different capacities to store energy at the same stress levels. Their performance characteristics and relative fatigue life depend significantly on this capacity value. As mentioned above, leaf springs generally store much less energy than torsion bars or coil springs stressed to the same level, so are about four times heavier when installed to perform the same task.

Spring media other than steel have completely different characteristics. Rubber, as one example, even when used in conjunction with an inert gas or hydraulic fluid has a much higher capacity to store energy than steel, as does a pure gas.

Accepting these reservations it is still interesting to consider the energy storage capabilities of materials involved as springs in suspension systems. The materials to be considered are: steel, as leaf spring, coil spring and torsion bar; rubber; liquid; and gas (nitrogen or air).

Ignoring the parasitic bits, it is easily established that the energy storage per unit volume is

$$f^2/6E \tag{3.2}$$

for a leaf spring and

$$f^2/4G \tag{3.3}$$

for a coil spring or torsion bar. For steel and equal stresses this gives a ratio of 3.9:1 for a coil spring or torsion bar compared with a leaf spring. For most considerations however we are more concerned with energy storage per unit weight of the spring material. For leaf springs this figure is

$$\frac{f^2}{9.74 \times 10^{15}} \text{ Nm/kg} \tag{3.4}$$

and for coil springs

$$\frac{f^2}{2.48 \times 10^{15}} \text{ Nm/kg} \tag{3.5}$$

with steel as the material and the stresses in N/m^2.

For a stress of 700 MN/m^2 the energy storage figures are: leaf springs, 50.36 Nm/kg and for coil springs or torsion bars 197.58 Nm/kg. The question of possible stresses in service depends upon the type of steel and its treatment, i.e. hardness, pre-stressing or scragging, and shot-peening. The desirability of avoiding surface decarburising in hot coiling springs should by now be well known.

The difference between leaf and coil springs depends upon two things: the ratio of just over 2 5:1 of the two moduli (Young's and shear) concerned; and the proportion of the material subjected to the higher stress. Spring leaves are too thin to make them of I section.

Rubber has a much lower specific gravity than steel, so that for equal energy content per unit weight it would occupy more space. The combination of compression and shear preferred by the rubber engineers when using it as a spring is chosen, among other things, to subject the greatest possible amount of rubber to the highest acceptable stress; it is difficult to arrive at expressions corresponding to Equations 3.2, 3.3, 3.4 and 3.5 above for rubber used in this way.

Although the actual levels are difficult to calculate precisely because of the all variations in design and configuration possible, Table 3.1 gives typical examples.

3.5 NATURAL SPRING FREQUENCIES

Any mass supported by a spring and displaced from its position of equilibrium will vibrate with Simple Harmonic Motion at a constant

Table 3·1   TYPICAL ENERGY CAPACITIES (Nm/kg)

Leaf spring	50
Torsion bar	200
Coil spring	200
Rubber cone	375
Hydrolastic rubber	750
Gas springs	1500*

* This figure is highly dependent on the materials used and the ancillary equipment needed in the form of compressors, reservoirs, sensors and operating valves, etc.

natural frequency determined by the amplitude of the initial displacement, the stiffness of the spring and the mass. This frequency is given by the equation:

$$f = 1/T \tag{3.6}$$

where T is the periodic time (time for one complete cycle) and derived from the equation:

$$T = 2\pi \sqrt{M/S} \tag{3.7}$$

where M is the sprung mass and S the spring rate.

This frequency is a powerful factor in the behaviour of a suspension system on the road, for it determines the rate at which the energy stored by a compressed spring is fed back into the body structure – the residual effects of crossing a bump or pothole.

But the wheel of car on its suspension system is not a simple mass on a linear spring. As already explained, it is a compound system in which the relationships between the sprung and the unsprung masses and between the primary and secondary springs (the tyres) are critical. Such a compound system can vibrate in two distinctly different modes. The sprung mass of the body structure can either be in phase with the unsprung wheel and suspension masses or out of phase with them. In the first case the forces involved work together and in the second case they oppose each other.

If the compound system of this type is represented by an equivalent layout with the two elements considered separately, the true natural frequency of the sprung mass can be determined. This value can then be fed into the compound system to calculate the unsprung natural frequency as well. By traditional methods these values were always derived from successively closer approximations, but all that tedious work can now be shortcut with modern computer programmes (see Chapter 12).

Newton's second law of motion (force equals mass times acceleration) can easily be applied to the unsprung masses of a car's suspension, which act upon the spring seats to generate an acceleration in the sprung mass of the body. Assuming no energy is lost in the system, the accelerations of the two parts of the system therefore will be inversely proportional to their relative masses. The less the unsprung mass is relative to the sprung mass, the less will be the effect of wheel inputs to the structure.

Exciting the wheels at the natural frequency of the system on undulations or washboard surfaces can cause them to resonate and lose contact with the road surface. It can also cause the body structure to resonate on its springs at the same natural frequency with very unpleasant effects on the quality of the ride.

Any input which excites this frequency in a totally undamped system would continue as a resonance for ever. In the real world there is friction damping, which exerts a constant force opposing any movement, air resistance damping of the moving parts (which can reach velocities as high as 5 m/s) and is proportional to their linear velocity squared, and the viscous damping designed into the system through the hydraulic shock absorbers. This damping force is directly proportional to the velocity difference between the sprung and unsprung masses.

3.6 LEAF SPRINGS

The leaf spring has a very long history of use; on the private car it was for many years virtually the only type of spring for front and rear axles, almost exclusively in the form commonly known as semi-elliptic. This name arises from the use on horse-drawn coaches of a pair of leaf springs back to back, the upper being a mirror image of the lower. With the necessary curvature on the spring leaves to provide clearance for deflection the shape is sufficiently close to the ellipse to warrant calling it that. Although leaf springs were almost universal for passenger cars, particularly at the rear, they have now been totally superseded by coil springs for reasons which will be discussed later.

Figure 3.7 shows a leaf spring for a rear axle arranged to give zero roll steer at just under fully laden and with a shackle arranged to give variable rate.

To simulate the movement of the end of a leaf spring a construction can be used giving an equivalent link, see Fig. 3.8. With the spring in the position where the main leaf is flat, and assuming an eye offset above the main leaf centre line of e, the centre about which the equivalent link works is $1/2\ e$ below the centre of the main

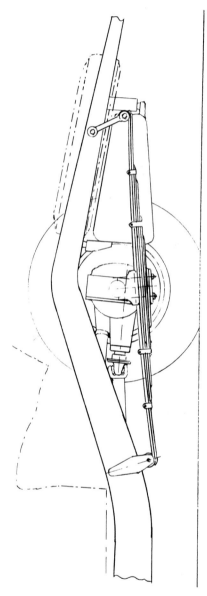

Fig. 3-7 This leaf spring installation uses a rear shackle to modify the load-deflection curve and provide a variable rate

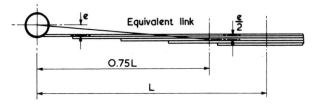

Fig. 3·8   The equivalent linkage to replace a leaf spring

leaf and 3/4 of the effective half-length from the eye. The effective half-length from the eye. The effective half-length L depends upon the clamping conditions: if the spring is clamped between flat rigid abutments L is the protruding length of the spring; if the spring is clamped between rubber L may approach the actual spring half-length, depending upon the rubber hardness and the initial clamping load. The actual value of L therefore has to be estimated.

It is not proposed to give any formulae for leaf spring design; this design is based upon the idea of constant stress in the leaves throughout their length, which gives constant radius for the leaves at any given position; this in turn means a total leaf width proportional to the distance from the eye end of the spring (assuming equal thickness of all leaves) and sufficient to give the desired maximum stress at full bump. The number of leaves is then the total width divided by the width of each individual leaf. The use of a swinging shackle was frequently used to modify the rate of a spring.

3.7   TORSION BAR AND COIL SPRINGS

The torsion bar and coil spring both use a round section in torsion. Rectangular section material in both coil springs and torsion bars has occurred rarely in car suspensions; it is wasteful of material and has only been used when special circumstances have made it desirable.

Torsion bars may be operated directly by one of the suspension arms or by a link and an arm whose sole purpose is to twist the torsion bar. The former is generally the more economical in its use of material overall.

The rate of a torsion bar when the operating arm of length R is at right angles to the applied force is

$$\frac{GI}{LR^2} \qquad (3.8)$$

where L is the effective length of the torsion bar, I the moment of inertia of the bar, $\pi/32d^4$, d being the diameter of the bar, and G the shear modulus of the material (79,300 MN/m^2 for steel). We can therefore simplify Equation 3.8 into the expression:

$$\text{Rate} = \frac{7.785 \times 10^6 d^4}{LR^2} \text{ kN/m} \qquad (3.9)$$

L, R and d being in metres.

3.8 COIL SPRING RATES

Coil springs for suspension are made almost entirely of round section wire. The classic formulae for steel spring characteristics are:

$$f_{uc} = \frac{2.55 W_s D}{d^3} \qquad (3.10)$$

where f_{uc} = uncorrected stress, W_s = spring load, = mean diameter of coils and d = wire diameter.

In the above formula W_s is in lb$_f$ and D and d are in inches then f_{uc} is in lb$_f$/in^2; if however W_s is in N and D and d in metres, then f_{uc} is in N/m^2. The deflection Λ is given by

$$\Lambda = \frac{f_{uc} D^2 n \pi}{Gd} \qquad (3.11)$$

where n is the number of effective coils in the spring and G is the shear modulus, 11.5×106 lb$_f$/in^2 or 79,300 MN/m^2 for steel. If f_{uc} and G are in lb$_f$/in^2 and D and d in inches then the result is in inches. If f_{uc} and G are in the same units, either both in N/m^2 or MN/m^2 and D and d in metres, then the result is in metres.

An alternative formula for the deflection is:

$$\Lambda = \frac{8 W_s D^3 n}{Gd^4} \qquad (3.12)$$

Here too, if W_s is in lb$_f$, G in lb$_f$/in^2, D and d in inches the result is in inches; if W_s is in Newtons, G in N/m^2, D and d in metres, the result is in metres.

Finally we have a formula for the rate of the spring:

$$\text{Rate} = \frac{98.98 \times 10^8 d^4}{nD^3} \text{ N/m} \ (D \text{ and } d \text{ in metres}) \qquad (3.13)$$

Coil spring theory relies upon the wire acting as a torsion bar, coiled into a helix, with the load acting upon it at a radius $D/2$. The line parallel to the wire axis at the inside of the coils is shorter than the corresponding line on the outside of the coils by $2\pi \times$ wire diameter $\times$ number of effective coils. For a given twist in the wire this implies a higher shear stress on the inner surface of the spring coils than that existing on the coil surfaces at the mean diameter of the coils, on which the calculated stress is based; in addition there is a direct shear stress on the wire equal to the spring load divided by the wire cross section. The highest stress in the spring wire must allow for these; Equation 3.10 has to be modified by a correction factor. Several formulae exist to calculate this factor. A convenient one, where c is the ratio D/d, is

$$k = \frac{c + 0.2}{c - 1}$$

(3.14)

Springs and torsion bars are preferably shot-peened to increase their fatigue life. They should be given an anti-rust treatment immediately after shot-peening.

For a given load, outside diameter and compressed length a coil spring will have the minimum stress if the intercoil spaces are minimal; some clearance is generally left to allow for tolerance on the wire diameter and coiling irregularities. An allowance of $1.5d$ to $2d$ must be left for dead coils.

Bars in torsion, whether as torsion bars or coil springs, respond to scragging, a process of overloading in manufacture to take the outer layers beyond the elastic limit. On release there is then residual stress in the spring material. Subsequent loading, not to exceed the elastic limit, results in the maximum stress occurring under the surface of the material and this has been found to give a longer fatigue life in service.

3.9 WISHBONE SUSPENSIONS; EFFECT ON WHEEL RATES

Wishbone suspensions in which the coil spring sits in a pan rigidly attached to one of the wishbones are generally subject to two opposing influences modifying the spring rate at the wheel as compared with the expected value at the end of the arm of $S(R_s/R)^2$, as shown in Fig. 3.9. These two influences are:

(1)   The bending of the coil spring itself, which increases the rate.

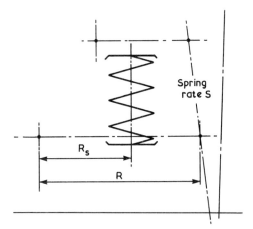

Fig. 3·9 Dimensions necessary to refer the spring rate to the wishbone end

(2) Extra vertical movement of the tyre-road contact point due to its being further out than the end of the wishbone, and the wheel carrier having tilting action as a result of the unequal length of the wishbones and possibly also their splaying out towards their outer ends; this reduces the rate at the wheel.

As mentioned, these tend to cancel each other out; whether they do so or not depends upon the leverage ratio of the spring, (R_s/R), and the extent to which the linkage has any swing axle effect, Fig. 3.10; the greater this is, or the smaller the radius to the linkage instantaneous centre, the greater the difference between wishbone end and contact point travel.

Where a spring has not an integral number of coils the bending stiffness polar diagram does not have a constant radius. The rotational position of the spring in its pan can therefore have an appreciable effect on the suspension rate at the wheel. To avoid variation from this cause it has become general practice to provide a rotational location for the spring by giving the lowest coil a short tangentially projecting end, with a corresponding recess in the spring pan. The spring ends are usually seated in rubber to reduce road noise transmission.

It seems sensible, and is general practice, to arrange for the coil spring to be straight in the full bump position because this will allow the maximum number of coils to be fitted in and will therefore give the minimum stress in the spring.

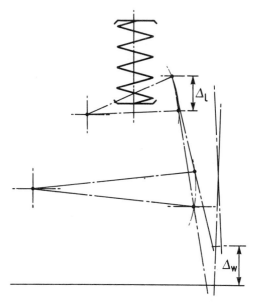

Fig. 3·10   Wheel tilt in an unequal wishbone system leads to different deflection at the ground compared with the link end

3.10   GAS SPRINGS

While there is little point in investigating the energy content of a gas used as a spring, for reasons given earlier, it is appropriate to consider how a hydropneumatic or any other gas spring works.

If a volume of air or any other gas (nitrogen is commonly used in hydro-pneumatic systems) is compressed slowly (e.g. isothermally) the product of its volume and its pressure remains constant. If however the gas is compressed quickly, or fundamentally without heat loss, the relationship is $PV^n = $ constant, n being the gas constant or ratio of the specific heats which is 1.402 for air and for nitrogen almost identical at 1.41.

There are heat losses in practice. Their effect is to reduce the value of n; in the extreme, as we have seen, complete heat loss reduces n to unity. The effective value of n will therefore lie somewhere between 1.0 and 1.4. For what one might regard as static changes, i.e. variations in the load carried, one must make the assumption of $n = 1$. For changes with the car in motion one could reasonably assume that n is unlikely to exceed 1.2. The difference between 1.0 and 1.2 is probably unimportant. For instance, for a reduction in volume of 10 per cent the difference between $n = 1.0$ and 1.2 is a pressure difference of 1.9 per cent.

An unwanted effect of the relationship between volume and pressure is that with increased loading the effective static deflection is reduced, the exact opposite of the usual relationship with steel springs. This can be embarrassing. In the case of the hydro-pneumatic system with a height control, where the liquid displacement is by a piston worked by one of the suspension links, standing height control is achieved by injecting more fluid into the 'push rod' between piston and gas, and there is no leverage change to help with the extra load. A front wheel drive car, likely to be front heavy, may in the extreme have a fully laden rear sprung weight twice that in the one-up condition and therefore have half the effective static deflection. By personal observation this effect is noticeable; an accompanying effect also noticeable is that the damping is relatively less.

For this reason the use of a diaphragm, either to work through a liquid as in the case of the Moulton Hydrogas (Fig. 3.11) or directly on the gas, can be advantageous, because it can be so arranged that its area increases as the suspension moves towards bump. In the extreme, is the area increase were made to equal the increase in load required for the desired load-deflection curve the suspension could achieve that load-deflection curve from the same gas pressure, i.e.

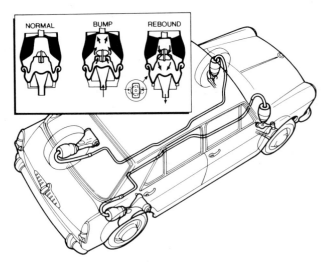

Fig. 3·11   The 'Hydrolastic' and 'Hydrogas' systems designed by Moulton developments for several BMC vehicles used a diaphragm to increase the effective spring area and hence the rate

the gas volume could be infinite. This would be equally embarrassing and there is obviously no need to go to such lengths. In a pneumatic suspension without standing height control the total rate comprises the parasitic or rubber bush rate, the rate due to leverage change and that due to the gas. With a diaphragm area increasing towards bump the final result can be arranged to give nearly constant frequency.

3.11 RIDE HEIGHT CONTROL

There is a considerable difference between the maximum and minimum laden sprung masses of a car. Because most of the additional mass is caused by extra passengers and/or luggage, the greater part of this increase occurs on the rear wheels. The lighter the car, the greater the percentage increases, until the added mass starts to drop because of reduced capacity. Two examples chosen are full five-seaters, one with a conventional front engine, rear-drive layout, the second with front-wheel drive and transverse engine, and appreciably lighter. Table 3.2 shows the sprung mass increases, front and rear, between the two extreme conditions.

With conventional springing there would be three disadvantages to the changes in rear sprung mass. Starting from a rear static deflection of 0.18 m fully laden car, Car A, would have one of 0.112 m, Car B of 0.091 m in the one-up condition. These deflections, particularly the latter, imply considerable changes in natural frequencies: 26.7 per cent higher one-up than fully laden for Car A, 40.5 per cent higher for Car B. They also imply attitude changes: assuming a front static deflection of 0.205 m fully laden for both cars, the attitude change, one-up to fully laden, is 1.23 degrees for Car A and 1.51 degrees for Car B. The head-lamp dip angle is in the range 1.5 degrees to 2.0 degrees. The third disadvantage is that the critical damping force required for the fully laden condition is, for Car A, 26.7 per cent higher than that for the one-up condition. A figure of 0.3 critical for the fully laden condition becomes 0.38 critical for the one-up condition. For Car B the critical damping force for the fully laden condition is 40.4 per cent higher than that

Table 3·2

	Front driver only (kg)	Front fully laden (kg)	Increase (%)	Rear driver only (kg)	Rear fully laden (kg)	Increase (%)
Car A	669.7	696.4	3.99	682.4	1095.8	60.6
Car B	800.65	858.4	7.21	392.8	775.0	97.3

for the one-up condition and a figure of damping of 0.3 critical for fully laden becomes 0.42 critical for one-up. To avoid overdamping in the one-up condition one has to accept underdamping fully laden, unless some means of varying damping with load can be incorporated.

We are however concerned with the other two effects, attitude and frequency changes. To deal with attitude changes, insofar as they affect the headlamp aim, Citroen introduced on the 2 CV model a hand-operated headlamp elevation control; the simplest and cheapest solution on an inexpensive, very softly sprung car with large percentage load variations. Citroen later also, on their DS model, took advantage of hydropneumatic suspension to introduce ride height control on both front and rear suspensions. In their system a piston worked by the suspension arm displaced oil to pressurise the diaphragm compressing the gas. The car had a pump and hydraulic accumulator to provide assistance to the steering and brakes. Each suspension operated a valve which allowed more oil under pressure from this source into the passage between suspension piston and diaphragm, to compensate for extra load on the car, or let oil out back into the system reservoir to correct for reduction of load. This ensured that the average attitude position of the car remained constant.

Effectively the speed response of the correction would be limited by the pump delivery. In practice the valve limits it much more. Too rapid a response would eliminate the suspension completely. This is obviously not desirable. The response is usually too slow even to compensate for braking, accelerating and cornering deflections. This method of height correction reduces the volume of each gas chamber as load is increased and so stiffens the ride.

Rolls-Royce later introduced a height control, also hydraulically operated, which by this means moved the abutments of the coil springs used in the suspensions. To make quite sure that there was no attempt to compensate for normal suspension movements the Rolls-Royce system used the existence or otherwise of open doors to introduce different response speeds. The more rapid occurred with a door or doors open; passengers have to have open doors to get in or out. With doors closed the only mass change is that due to use of petrol from the tank and this is a very slow change.

A simpler scheme providing height correction on the rear only has now become available on a number of models, especially estate cars with high load capacity as both standard equipment and an optional extra. The system uses modified rear dampers incorporating diaphragm and air reservoirs that compensate for extra load by feeding in extra air to the space. In the simplest version this extra air can only be obtained from an external source; while in the more complicated versions a battery operated electric motor drives a pump. Some designs also use the suspension movement to operate a small auxiliary pumping system automatically.

3.12   BUMP AND REBOUND BUFFERS

Suspension movement has to be limited to prevent metal-to-metal contact at the maximum bump limit of available wheel travel and springs becoming unseated at the corresponding rebound limit. The greater the movement that can be allowed, the better the ride can usually be. Depending on the vehicle, the use to which it is put and the spring rate, extending the range of movement becomes progressively less worthwhile in relation to the problems which it involves. Not least of these is the clearance which has to be left for the wheel and tyre in its bump position. In the case of the front wheels this is also complicated by the need to provide acceptable steering lock angles, although the possibility of full bump travel being reached at full lock is so remote that it need not be fully catered for in every case.

The problem however is acute enough as provision for a large bump movement often means either unsightly gaps in the wheel-arches above the tyres when standing at the kerb or a width penalty that increases the overall vehicle size. A reasonable compromise involves therefore using the bump buffer to provide as gradual a transition as possible from the spring rate alone to the final stopping load, likely to be at least three times the laden load and possibly appreciably more. Limitation of downward or rebound movement of the wheels is also necessary for the reason stated above, coupled with the need to limit articulation angles in the steering arm and anti-roll bar ball joints, the driveshaft joints and the suspension arm bushings.

A good design of bump buffer usually comprises a rubber buffer which in its limiting position completely fills the cup which surrounds it while holding the contacting surface clear enough of the cup to avoid metal-to-metal clashes there or elsewhere in the suspension. Loud noises over severe bumps always cause concern and give the impression that the ride is worse than it really is. The contour of the buffer and the range of movement from first contact to final position can be optimised to match the best transition in the load/deflection curve. Figure 3.12 shows one design; further examples in both car and military fighting vehicle suspensions as used on tanks can be seen in Reference 1.

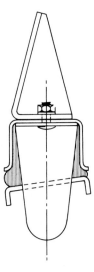

Fig. 3·12   An enclosed bump buffer of this type gives good control of the final position and a progressive build up of load

3.13   INTERACTION OF FRONT AND REAR SUSPENSIONS TO SINGLE APPLIED DISTURBANCES

A car may meet a single bump or hollow affecting one track only, or it may meet a transverse ridge or hollow affecting both tracks. Let us consider the transverse ridge. As a result of passing over it the front end of the car is raised. Then, after an interval depending on the wheelbase and the speed, the back end of the car is raised.

The first effect of lifting the front end of the car is to excite some pitch movement. The subsequent lifting of the back end of the car may mitigate or aggravate that pitch movement, depending on the time interval and the pitch frequency. Because the movement of the sprung weight on its suspension is not critically damped, any movement of the suspensions at each end of the car will persist with diminishing amplitude for a number of oscillations. Depending on the relative frequencies of the front and rear suspensions and the amount of damping, the initial pitching motion may be reduced or increased by the passage of time. We can most easily study this initially by assuming that the natural frequencies of front and rear suspensions are unaffected by pitching motion as opposed to bouncing. The validity of this assumption is discussed in Sections A1.9 and A1.10 of Appendix 1.

With sufficient accuracy for this study the movement of either suspension after its initial impulse can be considered as

$$x = e^{-nt} A \cos(\omega_c t) \qquad (3.15)$$

where t = time in seconds, $n = W/2F_d$ and A = initial displacement.

Figure 3.13(a) shows the front end displacement curve resulting from an initial displacement of 4 cm, a frequency of 1 Hz and $n = 0.8$. Superimposed on this curve are two others for the rear suspension each with an initial displacement of 4 cm but in one case with a frequency of 1.1 Hz and in the other of 0.90 Hz. Both have $n = 0.8$ as for the front suspension. The two rear end displacement curves are shown as starting 0.2 s later than the front. With a speed of 50 km/hr this corresponds to a wheelbase of 2.7 m (109.36 in). Figure 3.13(b) shows the relative displacement of front and rear suspensions, in cm; in curve 1 for the lower frequency rear suspension, in curve 2 for the higher frequency rear suspension. Downward displacements on these graphs correspond to the front end below the rear. To round off the picture, Fig. 3.13(c) shows corresponding 'pitch' curves for a car speed of 100 km/hr, i.e. the rear suspension lagging by 0.1 s.

We notice four things about these curves:

(1)   With the lower frequency rear suspension there is a strongly persisting pitch movement.
(2)   With the higher frequency rear suspension the initial pitch movement is very quickly reduced.
(3)   With the higher frequency rear suspension the initial pitch movement is never so severe as with the lower frequency.
(4)   The initial pitch movement is less severe at the higher than at the lower speed, because the time interval is less. This time interval is at both speeds less than half a cycle of the front suspension.

3.14   EFFECT OF REGULARLY REPEATED DISTURBANCES

Many road surfaces have developed fairly regularly occuring bumps and hollows. For a car traversing such a road the wheelbase filter effect has to be considered. This can be understood from Fig. 3.14. In its simplest form, for condition A, where the vehicle wheelbase equals half the road disturbance wavelength, pitching is excited if the combination of vehicle speed and disturbance wavelength

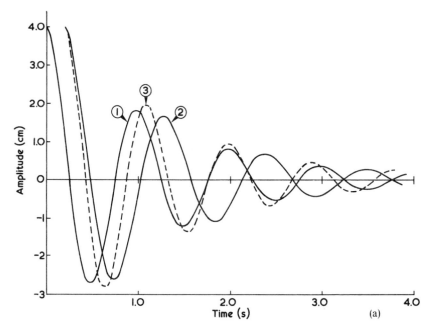

Fig. 3·13   (a) Amplitudes for damped movement of front and rear sprung mass from a single disturbance: Curve 1, front, frequency 1 Hz; Curve 2, rear, frequency 0.909 Hz; Curve 3, rear, frequency 1.11 Hz. Car speed 50 km/h. (b) Resulting pitch movements; Curve 1, slower rear frequency; Curve 2, higher rear frequency. (c) Resulting pitch movements, car speed 100 km/h: Curve 1, lower rear frequency; Curve 2, higher rear frequency

produces a disturbance frequency equal or close to the vehicle's pitch frequency. The extent to which the pitching amplitude builds up depends on the suspension damping factor. Some build up will also occur if the wheelbase is 1.5, 2.5, etc. times the disturbance wavelength and the vehicle speed produces impulses at or close to the vehicle pitch frequency. A similar condition arises for condition B if the disturbance frequency equals or is close to the vehicle's bounce frequency.

These effects considerably influence the vehicle's vertical acceleration spectra at the centre of gravity and rear wheel positions, and the pitch acceleration spectra, as illustrated in Fig. 3.15, which shows the difference between the vertical acceleration at the centre of gravity compared with the pitch acceleration, for the same disturbances.

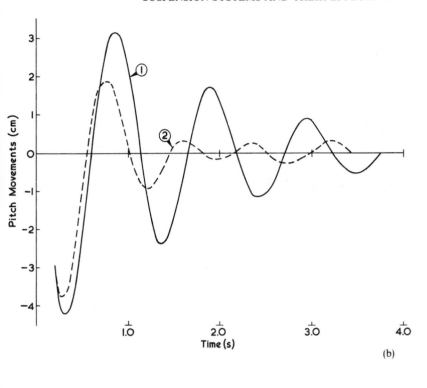

(b)

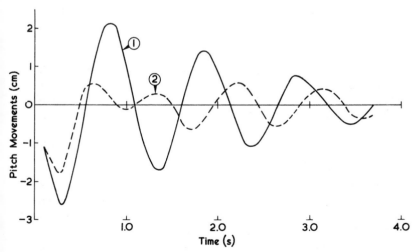

(c)

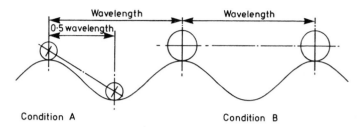

Fig. 3·14 Condition A: For wheelbases 0.5, 1.5, 2.5, etc. of wavelength of disturbances, pitch accelerations are high but vertical accelerations are low. Condition B: For wheelbases 1, 2, 3, etc. of wavelength of disturbances, vertical accelerations are high but pitch accelerations are low

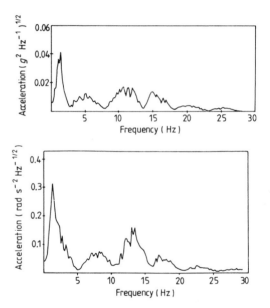

Fig. 3·15 The wheelbase effect is best shown by the juxtraposition of these illustrations taken from Reference 2. The upper shows the vertical acceleration of the centre of gravity, the lower the pitch accelerations. Peaks of the upper curve, at near 5, 10 and 15 Hz, correspond reasonably well with the troughs of the lower curve. (Reproduced from Best, A., *Phys. Technol.*, Vol. 15, 205–10 (1984). *Courtesy of I.O.P. Publishing Ltd.*)

REFERENCES
1. Bastow, D., Chairman's Address to the Automobile Division, *Proc. Auto. Div. I.Mech E.* (1961–62)
2. Best, A., *Phys. Technol.*, Vol. 15, 205–10 (1984)

4

Dampers

4.1 TYPES OF DAMPING

Without damping a vibration once excited would persist indef-
initely. In practice damping exists in three forms: friction, viscous
and that due to the presence of air. Ignoring the generally slight
difference between static and dynamic friction, these types of
damping imply respectively a constant resistance, a resistance
proportional to the velocity and a resistance proportional to the
square of the velocity.

The suspension of most vehicles exists to keep to a minimum the
disturbances of the sprung body due to irregularities in the terrain
over which the vehicle runs. Friction, in the suspension linkage,
means that no movement of the suspension itself occurs for
irregularities below those at which the deflection of the tyre implies
an increase in force equal to the static friction force. Forces up to the
friction force therefore act directly on the sprung mass causing
accelerations and movements of it. With an infinitely small
unsprung weight and no friction, the forces on the sprung weight
would be in the ratio of the suspension spring rate to the tyre rate.
With this ratio, in the examples shown in Section A1.5 of Appendix
1 just over 0.075, it is clear that every effort must be made to
eliminate friction; it should be regarded as a small component only
of the total damping.

Damping due to the air is also small compared to that necessary
to prevent unduly large movements of the sprung weight and can
equally be regarded as insignificant.

The main bulk of the damping is therefore likely to be viscous
damping from the hydraulic dampers which are now universally
used. It is referred to as viscous damping and taken as being
proportional to the vertical velocity between unsprung and sprung
masses because this is mathematically convenient and is reasonably
close to the true state of affairs.

The amount of damping required is, as in so many cases in engineering, a compromise: in this case between that needed to prevent undue persistence of a vibration at natural frequency excited by a single disturbance, which also prevents the build-up of excessive amplitude of a forced vibration due to a series of impulses, and the uncomfortable fact that the higher the damping force the greater the disturbance fed into the sprung mass by any given road irregularity. The damping force is responsible for an additional disturbance on the sprung weight over and above that due to the deflection of the suspension spring

4.2 DAMPING CHARACTERISTICS

Although extra damping in early cars was provided by friction it was eventually realised that this had the wrong characteristics for vehicle suspensions and the hydraulic damper is now universally used and rightly so.

Friction in a suspension is harmful because until a disturbing force exceeds the static friction of the damper and/or the suspension, no suspension movement occurs and the force is passed on to the sprung part of the vehicle. In general this force is a result of an obstruction which deflects the tyre and for a given bump the tyre rate determines the magnitude of the force. Because the static friction force is higher than the dynamic the damping effect on vibrations of friction damping is less than it should be for a given initial static force; moreover there is no increase of damping force with velocity.

The theoretical assumption of viscous damping is that the damping force is proportional to the velocity. To achieve this the flow of fluid from the pressure side of the piston of a hydraulic damper needs to be controlled by a valve with the desired characteristics. In practice fluid flow at small velocities of the damper occurs through 'leaks', partly unavoidable, partly intentional. These leaks are through such small areas that flow through them must be turbulent so that the pressure, and hence the damper load, will vary as the square of the velocity. This characteristic has been found to be unsuitable for suspension damping. The damper characteristic is generally made to be as close as possible to a viscous damping line, as in the bump curve of Fig. 4.1. This can be compared with Fig. 4.2, which although based on actual figures, has been deliberately doctored to show what the curve would look like if the leak, square law, curve had been continued until it met the linear, valve open, curve. Achieving the viscous damping of the

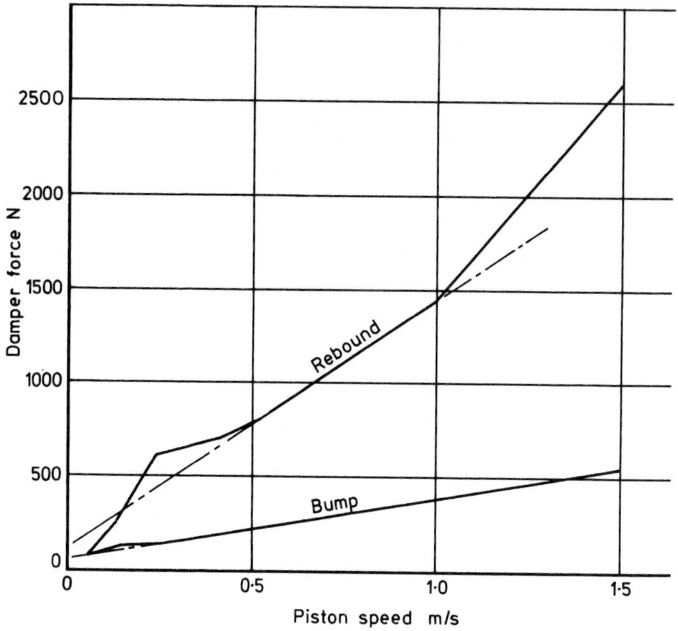

Fig. 4·1   Characteristic curves from a recent model front suspension damper. The bump curve shows how nearly continuous the result can be. The dotted lines show a slope of about four times as much for the rebound line. The divergences from pure viscous on that are probably less important. (*Courtesy Armstrong Patents Co. Ltd.*)

bump curve of Fig. 4.1 requires measures to get a gradual opening for the valve in conjunction with the careful proportioning of the valve and its surroundings.

When a diaphragm rather than a piston displaces the damper fluid there is more control over the initial leak and Fig. 4.3 shows what can be achieved. Further examples of damping force-speed curves are shown in Figs. 4.4, 4.5 and 4.6. In one specific example the rebound damping required a pressure of 3.3 MN/m^2.

Car ride is to a considerable extent a matter of personal preference or prejudice. Damping is an essential part of the ride. It is not surprising therefore that as between manufacturers differences exist as to what is considered a desirable performance curve (force-velocity diagram) for a damper. Figures 4.6(a) and (b) show some of the variations. It will be appreciated that as related to the sprung weight and spring rate of a particular car, lines can be drawn

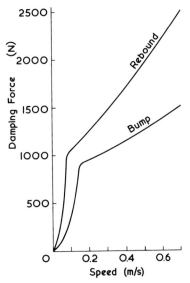

Fig. 4·2   If the two parts of a damper characteristic curve were rigidly separated the result would be as shown here. In practice every effort is made to merge the two parts, as comparison of this illustration with Figs. 4·1 and 4·3 shows

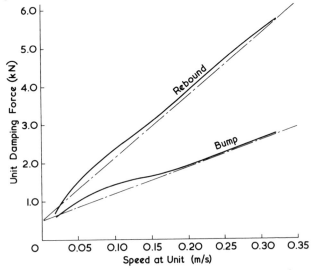

Fig. 4·3   Bump and rebound damper load-speed curves for a 'Hydragas' suspension unit are shown. They are shown for the unit because the leverage ratio between unit and wheel will vary depending on the linkage position. While lines representing a proportion of critical dampling should radiate from zero, they fit the curves better starting from about the 500 N point. Although the existence of some friction is to be expected, one would not expect as much as that, even allowing for the approximate 4:1 leverage ratio. (From information supplied by Moulton Developments Ltd.)

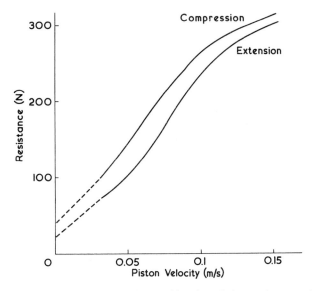

Fig. 4·4   As this diagram shows, the transition from leak to valve control is less clear-cut than the theoretical shapes shown in Fig. 4·2. (*Courtesy Woodhead Manufacturing Co.*)

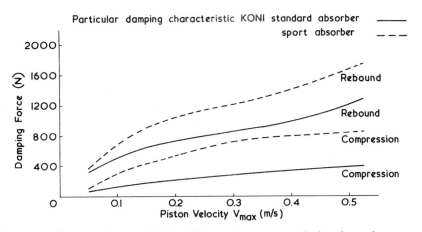

Fig. 4·5   This diagram shows the difference between a standard setting and one intended for competition use. The actual increase on rebound and bump seems about the same but this implies a greater percentage increase on bump. (*Courtesy Koni B.V.*)

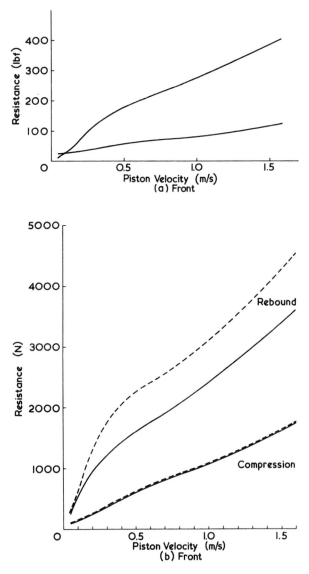

Fig. 4·6   The variation in damper settings between different car manufacturers can be seen from these curves: (a) front and rear of car 'A' are examples of a moderate damper setting, (b) the corresponding curves for car 'B' (the standard or minimum settings; for this comparison the maximum setting can be ignored) indicate much higher damper loads. The two cars are closely related in weight and size and both have rear wheel drive by live axle. (*Courtesy Woodhead Manufacturing Co.*)

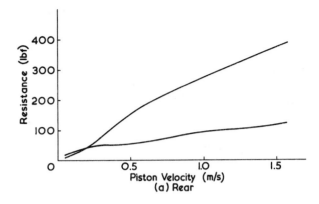

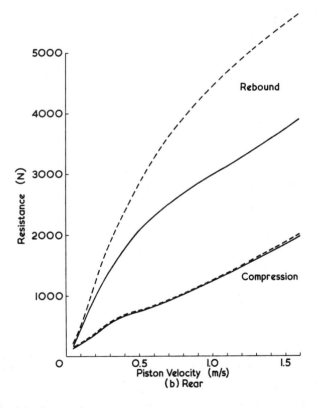

Fig. 4·6 Continued.

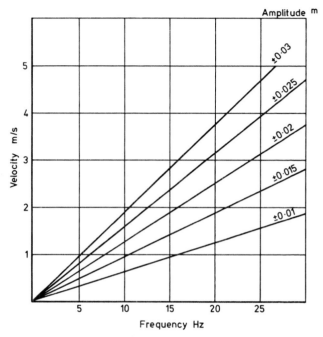

Fig. 4·7   The relationship between amplitude, frequency and maximum velocity in sinusoidal vibrations, $V = r\omega$, allows us to understand the velocities actually achieved

radiating from the origin which represent particular proportions of critical damping.

As will have been seen, Figs. 4.1 and 4.3 illustrate this. In the other examples it will be noticed that it is the bump curves which more closely follow a straight line. Many of the departures are predictably near the leak to valve transition. The wide velocities in piston velocities reflect variations in leverage ratios. Wheel velocities of up to 1.7 m/s are normal; values up to 5 m/s have been recorded. Figure 4.7 relates velocities, amplitudes and frequencies over a wide range, for sinusoidal vibrations, which may be taken as a reasonable approximation.

4.3   HYDRAULIC DAMPERS

F. W. Lanchester patented the idea of using oil as a springing medium, though he records having difficulty in convincing the USA

Patent Office that oil is compressible. In such a use of oil as a spring it is not only the bulk compressibility of the oil which provides the elasticity but also the bulk extendibility of its working envelope. The existence of this elasticity is one of a number of reasons for avoiding the use of high pressures in hydraulic dampers. Reducing the local heating effect in the fluid and keeping seal friction to an acceptable minimum are two others.

The hydraulic damper is a means of extracting energy from a motion; study of the dimensions of the quantities shows that:

$$\text{Pressure drop} \times \text{Fluid displacement} = \text{Work done}$$

We may recognise this more easily by calling the displacement the product of the piston area and the piston travel. The pressure (work done fluid displacement) is therefore a measure of the energy let loose in the working fluid per unit volume and hence of the temperature rise of that fluid. On the basis of a specific gravity of 0.8 and a specific heat of 0.4, a pressure drop of 1 MN/m^2 causes a temperature rise of 0.075 deg C. With the maximum pressure likely to lie in the range 3 to 8 MN/m^2, this implies temperature rises per pass of 0.225 to 0.6 deg C. An indication of the maximum pressure which is likely to be developed is the damper displacement per unit travel per unit sprung weight; this is the effective piston area per unit weight. A survey shows values ranging between 0.5×10^{-3} and 3×10^{-3} $m^2/1000$ kg.

4.4 TYPES OF HYDRAULIC DAMPERS

Apart from hydro-pneumatic and hydro-elastic suspensions, in which diaphragms move the fluid, hydraulic dampers depend upon pistons working in cylinders for developing the pressures necessary to provide the damping forces. These cylinders can be made as either lever-arm devices or telescopic tubes. Vane type hydraulic dampers were also made for a time but have now been abandoned because their ratio of seal length to volume displacement was so unfavourable they had to rely on the use of very thick oil and were particularly susceptible to wear and consequential leaking.

The three main types of the lever-arm dampers have now given way almost universally to telescopic devices. In one, the lever projects downwards from a horizontal pivot shaft with two part-cylindrical surfaces at its working end, each contacting a flat surface on the back of a piston in a horizontal through bore perpendicular to but below the arm pivot axis. Rolls-Royce fitted dampers of this

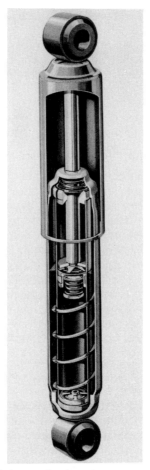

Fig. 4·8   This is a typical example of a telescopic twin-tube damper fitted with separate bump and blow-off valves. (*Courtesy of Monroe Auto Equipment Ltd.*)

type, of their own design and manufacture, for many years. A second design has the arm pivot fixed to a horizontal two-ended rocking lever from whose ends short connecting rods work pistons in parallel vertical bores close to each other; the main example of this type was the Gordon-Armstrong, now known as the Armstrong. The third lever-arm version also used close vertical parallel bores, but with two involute cams on opposite sides of the arm pivot contacting faces on the tops of the two pistons.

4.5 TELESCOPIC DAMPERS

As already described, dampers are hydraulic devices used to restrict the number of cyclic oscillations caused by a bump deflection. Pumping fluid through an orifice converts energy to heat which can then be dissipated in the atmosphere. The objective in damper valve design is to maintain consistent laminar flow characteristics throughout the operating range of loads and input velocities. That usually means incorporating several small nozzles or jets rather than a single large one, arranged to open in stages according to the stroke and internal pressure generated to create a specifically tailored resistance curve.

The most commonly used form of hydraulic damper is now the telescopic double or twin-tube type which combines the action of fluid passing through a piston in a cylinder with the displacement of fluid into a concentric chamber, as shown in Fig. 4.8. It conveniently separates the bump and rebound actions of the suspension movement by the use of separate blow-off valves.

The damper itself takes the form of a piston running in a cylinder, activated by a rod. Within the piston there are the bump valves which open against under pressure against springs to allow the piston to move through the almost incompressible fluid. The blow-off characteristics of these valves can be controlled by the design of their profiles and the spring behaviour.

The substantially vertical cylinder contains a double acting piston operated by a piston rod passing through the top end cover. The piston rod is therefore attached to the sprung mass, the cylinder to the unsprung, this commonly used construction being known as the double or twin tube type. Because there is no balance rod on the lower side of the piston, the collapsed damper has less fluid inside the two ends of its cylinder than the extended damper, by the amount of the piston rod area times its stroke. The oil thus displaced from the cylinder as the damper is compressed (bump movement of the suspension) has to be stored somewhere so in the twin tube damper there is a storage space for fluid between the outside of the cylinder tube and the inside of the second, reservoir, tube. This fluid conducts heat to the outside of the damper and also reduces the temperature rise of the fluid in general so that there are inducements to fill the reservoir as much as possible; the limitation is pressure rise in the gas (usually air) above the fluid as the damper is compressed.

A more developed version, known as the pressurised gas damper is shown in Fig. 4.9. It has the space above the fluid in the outer tube

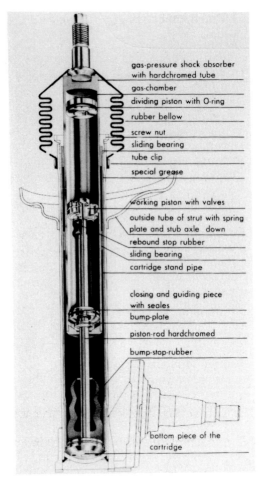

gas-pressure shock absorber
with hardchromed tube

gas-chamber

dividing piston with O-ring

rubber bellow

screw nut

sliding bearing

tube clip

special grease

working piston with valves

outside tube of strut with spring
plate and stub axle   down

rebound stop rubber

sliding bearing

cartridge stand pipe

closing and guiding piece
with seales

bump-plate

piston-rod hardchromed

bump-stop-rubber

bottom piece of the
cartridge

Fig. 4·9   In the more developed gas-filled damper the space above the working fluid
is pressurised to improve control. (*Courtesy of Bilstein GmbH*)

pressurised to around 0.5 MN/m^2. This has been found to improve
control of movements of the unsprung weight. There is a resultant
slight increase in seal friction, and in some cases slight relaxation of
damper settings has been required. The assembly adds some spring
rate and load carrying to the main suspension system.

   In the monotube type damper the usual arrangement is to close
the bottom end of the working space by a floating piston held in
contact with the fluid by gas under pressure below it. One

disadvantage of the monotube damper is its greater susceptibility to damage from flying stones.

On the rebound stroke the effective area of the piston is reduced by the cross-sectional area of the rod driving it, so as well as fluid passing through the piston on bump movement a proportion is forced through valves at the opposite end of the cylinder to compensate. Considerable volumes of fluid flow in and out of the outer chamber where they are cooled quite effectively by the air flow created by the vehicle's forward speed. The limitation of the twin-tube damper performance is usually caused by aeration of the fluid during its passage to and from the outer reservoir or localised temperatures elevated by continuous severe bumps above the fluid's vaporisation point creating gas pockets.

Single or monotube telescopic dampers actually predate the twin-tube variety to patents once held by de Carbon. Instead of a supplementary chamber being used to compensate for the piston rod area, a volume of inert gas under pressure is arranged at the bottom the cylinder, separated from the fluid by a second floating piston. For this reason, single-tube dampers are also known as gas-filled dampers.

As the main hydraulic piston is forced through the fluid under bump movement, the gas is compressed by the increased pressure on the floating piston which moves away to increase the bump fluid volume, effectively decreasing the working area. Unlike the behaviour of the twin-tube damper, the resistance curve for the gas-filled damper increases at a constant rate, instead of tailing off, giving more consistent ride characteristics. There is also no risk of fluid aeration and better overall cooling without the outer supplementary chamber.

To function satisfactorily the damper must be inserted between the moving suspension parts and a relatively rigid part of the main structure which may be either the subframe or the bodyshell directly. Because it provides a resistance to motion, the assembly must be insulated to a degree from acting as a path to the interior of noise, vibration and harshness. The compliance of these mounts forms a critical part of the running refinement.

The telescopic damper was originally associated with pillar type suspensions (Broulhiet, Lancia) but large scale production came much later. With fundamentally different piston areas for movement in the two directions the designer has a choice of what to do about his oil circulation. With the more popular current twin-tube design the working oil level in the outer tube is necessarily below the level of the top of the upper chamber in the damper itself. This means that replenishment in practice has to occur only at the bottom of the damper into the lower chamber; and this in turn means that during damper compression the valve which regulates flow upward through the piston must open at a lower pressure than the valve in the bottom closure of the cylinder, to ensure preferential flow through it. The effective piston area is therefore something over that of the rod for valve controlled damping and the transition from leak to valve control occurs at a lower pressure. The full piston area is available for leak damping. Most of the leak must be in the piston. Damper compression is bump movement of the suspension, during which damper loads tend to be less than on rebound.

On damper extension (rebound suspension movement) the effective piston area is the annulus between piston rod and bore. The generally higher damper loads on rebound suggest a larger piston area. With a damper bore fixed the rod diameter largely determines the ratio of effective bump to rebound piston area.

For reasons already explained, friction in a suspension spoils the ride. The guiding function which the damper performs in the strut and link suspension implies the existence of sideways forces on piston and piston rod bush (Section 5.5). The large piston rod which this encourages tends to upset the area ratio between bump and rebound, Fig. 4.10. The sideways forces are minimised by keeping piston and piston rod guide as far apart as possible, something which is much easier in the twin-tube type of damper.

With the arrangement of monotube damper already described, where the lower end of the working chamber is closed by a floating piston beneath which there is a gas (usually nitrogen) under pressure, the valving is necessarily in the piston. In one example the gas pressure is about 2.5 MN/m^2. The movement of the floating piston is confined to that necessary to absorb the rod volume. The gas pressure times the rod area is responsible for a force which has to be overcome to compress the damper, in addition to the actual damper force. The damper therefore adds some load and proportionately rather less rate to that provided by the suspension spring. The gas pressure should exceed the maximum operating pressure below the rod-operated piston. The full piston area is available for compression damping, which minimises the operating pressures on bump movement.

Woodhead has developed a monotube damper in which the floating piston has been omitted (Fig. 4.11). This means that the working fluid is an emulsion and the valving and restrictions have to be arranged to suit. In practice the fluid above the piston contains more gas than that below. Obviously considerable separation of gas and oil occurs while the car is at rest. With the maximum acceleration of the unsprung weight, to which the damper body is

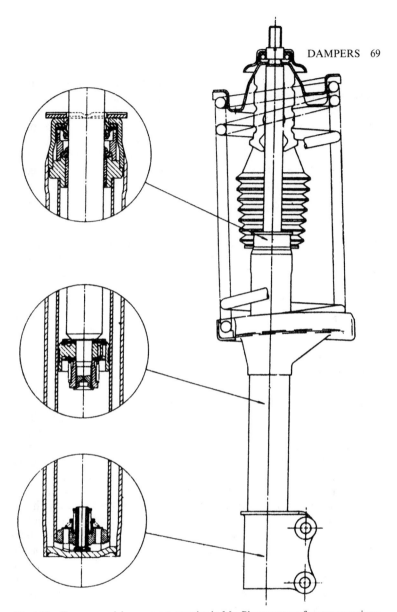

Fig. 4·10   To ease servicing, current practice in MacPherson strut front suspensions is to bolt on the wheel carrier and the associated connection to the bottom link. The welded damper assembly made possible by this divided structure provides the cheapest way of restoring any worn or otherwise sub-standard damper. The sectional details on the left show, from top to bottom: first the top seal, rod bearing and the permanently closed structure; secondly the piston and its valving; and finally the bottom end end structure with the connecting valving to the space enclosed by the outer tube. In the main drawing the two-bolt split clamp embracing the bottom end of the damper outer tube provides the basis of a typical attachment to the wheel carrier; the details of this are likely to vary with the different manufacturers. (*Courtesy Armstrong Patents Co. Ltd.*)

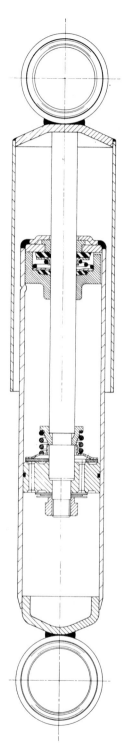

Fig. 4·11   The monotube damper without floating piston clearly enjoys an advantage in the reduced dead length, as well as others mentioned in the text. (*Courtesy Woodhead Manufacturing Co.*)

attached, of the order of 20 to 30 g and with the large flows inherent in the damper design, re-emulsification is very rapid and the performance in practice consistent. The obvious advantages of this type of monotube damper, as compared with the more usual floating piston type, are first the impossibility of jacking up and consequent piston rod bending if leakage occurs past the floating piston and secondly the shorter compressed length.

A logical, but not immediately obvious, extension of this idea suggested by Woodhead is a twin tube damper also depending upon emulsion damping; in its simplest form this has no restriction at the foot of the working cylinder where it is in communication with the reservoir. It has therefore a somewhat shorter dead length than the normal dual tube damper and cannot suffer from cavitation or aeration. As compared with the normal monotube damper it has the advantage of freedom from 'jacking up' which it shares with the emulsion damped monotube and in addition a much reduced dead length, freedom from the possibility of external damage to the working cylinder and the possibility of easy inclusion of a rebound (hydraulic pressure) check on the rebound movement. There is also the possibility of a corresponding bump check and of an increase in versatility by incorporating some kind of restriction at the working cylinder-reservoir transfer. Built in pressures can be less than those of the monotube damper and of course the working cylinder can be considerably thinner. There are manufacturing advantages.

With emulsion damping in general there seems to be less reduction of damping forces with temperature than with normal dampers.

4.6   OTHER ARRANGEMENTS; HYDROPNEUMATIC

Cars with hydropneumatic suspensions have generally used the liquid forming the 'push rod' which moves the diaphragm between liquid and gas to provide the damping. The liquid has to be moved by a piston or diaphragm operated from one of the suspension links and it is logical and economical to push that liquid movement through a damper valve. This feature was a part of the original hydro-pneumatic, the Citroen DS introduced about 1955, and has been perpetuated in more recent models; it is also a feature of the Moulton Hydrolastic and Hydragas suspensions. Fig. 4.12 gives some details of the Citroen DS units.

Where a piston is used to move the liquid, as in the Citroen and more recently some top-end Mercedes-Benz models, it is necessary to use oil as the liquid in order to get lubrication; where a diaphragm

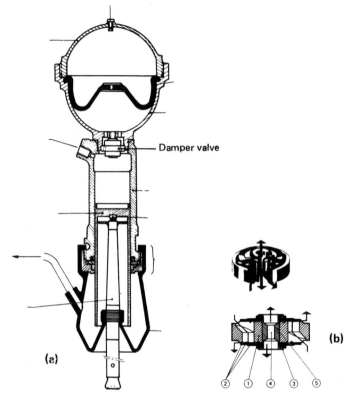

Fig. 4·12   (a) The Citroen gas spring suspension unit shows the location of the damper valve, while (b) shows the simple construction. (*Courtesy Citroen Cars Ltd.*)

is used, as in the Moulton systems, a water based liquid is used. One of the benefits from this is the relative insensitivity of the damping to temperature[1], as Fig. 4.13 shows.

As dampers provide a resistance to movement between the sprung and unsprung masses they also create an additional source of load inputs to the body structure from road shocks. There are limits, therefore, to the amount of damping which is acceptable for a comfortable ride.

In theory at least, a vehicle would be most comfortable if the dampers were designed to provide minimum resistance to suspension movement on bumps and a far greater resistance on rebound. Although distinctly different bump and rebound settings are incorporated into most dampers in practice, their values are always

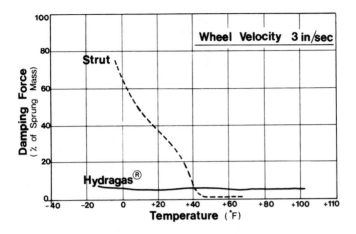

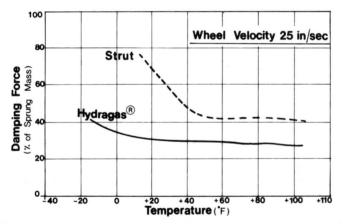

Fig. 4·13 As these two diagrams show, the ability of the 'Hydragas' suspension to use a water based fluid results in less variation in damping with temperature than if an oil based damper fluid were used. (*Courtesy Moulton Developments Ltd.*)

much closer to each other than might seem best because of the inevitable interaction between the two directions of wheel travel.

4.7 CRITICAL DAMPING COEFFICIENTS

Critical damping is defined as the minimum damping effect required to prevent an oscillation passing the static position after a disturbance of the sprung mass[2]. It is a purely theoretical value that is often used as a basis for making suspension comparisons when, for convenience, measured or calculated damping forces are often considered in relation to their critical values.

The critical damping coefficient C_c can be calculated from the following formula:

$$C_c = 2\sqrt{S/M} \qquad (4.1)$$

where S is the spring rate in N/m and M the sprung mass in kg.

In most applications critical damping is far too severe and the best damping for comfort and adequate wheel control falls somewhere in the range of between 15 and 50 per cent of the critical value, depending on the inherent friction in the system and the ride qualities required.

The typical function of the damper in a modern car is to reduce the amplitude of the deflection over a bump to about a fifth of its initial value within two cycle oscillations at the natural frequency of the system.

A more detailed explanation of critical damping and the effects of damping on forced vibration amplitudes, with worked examples, will be found in Section A1.8 of Appendix 1.

REFERENCES

1. Els, P. and Grobbelaar, B., 'Investigation of the Time and Temperature Dependency of Hydropneumatic Suspension Systems', *SAE Technical Paper No. 930265* (March 1993)
2. Newton, K., Steeds, W. and Garrett, K., 'The Motor Vehicle', *Butterworths*, (1989)

5

Front suspensions

5.1 FRONT AXLE: REASONS FOR DECLINE IN USE

The front axle on the passenger car is effectively dead. There are a number of reasons for this. The main ones are:

(1) Single wheel bumps are responsible for gyroscopic torques from both front wheels.
(2) Single wheel bumps produce front end steering effects from both front wheels because of the sideways deflection of the contact patches in relation to the car due to the high roll centre.
(3) Front axles, with front brakes, are liable to tramp.
(4) Front brake torque implies considerable caster angle change unless a parallel linkage is provided to control it.
(5) The narrow spring track implied by half-elliptic springs and front wheel lock clearance imply low front anti-roll resistance and a consequential oversteer effect unless an anti-roll rod is provided.
(6) The limitations (3), (4) and (5) make it in practice impossible to get the front springs soft enough to obtain a pitch-free ride.
(7) Better utilisation for passenger accommodation of the area occupied by the car on the road makes engine and front axle want to occupy the same space.

Some of these limitations can be overcome by a variety of complications. Even if they are, the result is less satisfactory than, and almost if not quite as expensive as, independent front suspension.

5.2 INDEPENDENT SUSPENSIONS

As a result of these limitations, American cars in 1935 generally adopted 'knee action', i.e. independent front suspension. Poor roads on the European continent encouraged Ford and General Motors to transfer this US technology across the Atlantic to their subsidiaries in Germany and Britain. Some European companies such as Lancia and Morgan had anticipated the Americans moves and now all manufacturers have adopted independent front wheel suspension even for light and medium commercial vehicles.

Over the years many types of independent front suspension have been tried. Many of them have been discarded for a variety of reasons, with only two basic concepts, the double wishbone and the MacPherson strut, finding widespread success in many varied forms.

The geometry of any independent front suspension should be devised to meet certain requirements:

(1) It must allow the roll centre height to be arranged at a desired level.
(2) It must allow cross steering connections to be made to each wheel knuckle that induce minimal variation of toe settings with vertical wheel movement.
(3) It should allow anti-brake dive geometry to be incorporated if this is required.
(4) It must allow coil springs, torsion bars or other springing means to give a desired load-deflection diagram.
(5) It should be possible to incorporate telescopic dampers.
(6) It should allow an anti-roll bar to be added if necessary.
(7) It should not prevent some overlap of the engine with the front suspension to allow the driver's pedals to be installed with minimum offset from the steering centreline position.
(8) It must withstand all the forces imposed on it by braking, accelerating or cornering with the ability to isolate the body structure from noise, vibration and harshness.
(9) It should restrict the inertia, gyroscopic or other forces produced by vertical movement of the wheels.
(10) It should create the minimum amount of friction associated with its vertical movement.
(11) It should operate without noise throughout its full range of travel and reach its limits progressively.

5.3 SIGNIFICANT OBSOLETE SYSTEMS

The following front suspension systems can be regarded as significant in the evolution from early rigid front axles to modern independent designs:

Pillar type

Early examples of this were used by Morgan (on the three wheeler) Lancia Lambda and Broulhiet. The latter and the post-World War II Invicta 'Black Prince' relied upon ball splines to transmit steering movement from a sprung steering linkage to the unsprung wheel (Fig. 5.1, Broulhiet). Without splines, ball or otherwise, i.e. on Morgan and Lancia Lambda, and later model Lancias, it is not possible to avoid toe-in changes with up and down wheel movement. In practice this means that suspension movement has to be drastically limited, generally more so on rebound than bump. Certain models, because of this, have suffered from excessive understeer at higher sideways accelerations when the limited suspension movement has been used up by roll and practically all further weight transference is concentrated on the front wheels.

Dubonnet type

The characteristic of this is that kingpin bearings and steering linkage are on the sprung part of the car and the suspension movement occurs between the kingpin bearings and the wheel, typically with a casing containing springs operated through a lever from a transverse horizontal pivot. An arm on the pivot either had at its non-pivot end the wheel stub or formed a part of a parallel linkage whose side remote from the arm pivots carried the stub axle. Several of the about 1935 American cars used this type of suspension; all eventually discarded it in favour of the double wishbone system which was cheaper and had other, mechanical, advantages. Opel in Germany and Vauxhall in the UK had a form of it in the middle to late 1930s which had several interesting and ingenious features, including the first application of anti-dive geometry using what was called the 'strong arm' short single arm, which lifted the car front end under braking.

Trailing links parallelogram

The first example of this was probably on the Auto-Union racing car designed by Porsche in the early 1930s. The suspension comprised two parallel trailing arms with transverse horizontal axes; the rearward end of each arm had an outwardly projecting ball. These two balls allowed the steering movement and defined therefore the kingpin axes. One of the levers each side was connected to a torsion bar providing the springing medium.

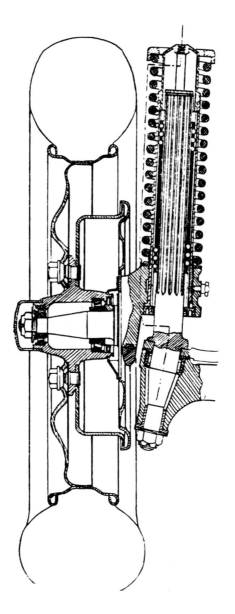

Fig. 5·1   The Broulhiet is an example of a pillar type suspension; the use of ball splines allows the steering to be sprung and so avoids the bugbear of earlier pillar types. (*Courtesy Institution of Mechanical Engineers*)

In its usual form with parallel horizontal axes and equal and parallel links this suspension gives the wheel straight up and down movement in end elevation. There is therefore no gyroscopic action and the roll centre of the suspension is at ground level but there are inertia torques associated with this layout. Any change in caster angle is confined to that due to attitude changes of the car.

Swing axles

In these suspensions the front wheel was carried by a single transverse arm whose outer end incorporated either the kingpin anchorage or bearings for it to pivot on. Some means of taking braking torque was also provided, usually with a roughly fore and aft arm whose frame anchorage was often arranged to lie on the pivot axis of the swing axle. If this is the case then as in the previous section, caster angle changes are confined to those due to car attitude changes. There is however considerable gyroscopic action and therefore torque. With the usual swing arm length slightly less than the half track, the roll centre is somewhat above the arm pivot axis and this leads to high weight transference in cornering. This, at the front end, is not necessarily a disadvantage and may be helpful. Changes in wheel camber in corners tend to induce positive angles on the more heavily laden wheel, reducing the cornering power available especially from wider section tyres. This factor plus the effects of the gyroscopic torque generated led to swing axles being abandoned in favour of systems where the laden wheel could be induced to adopt a negative angle.

Transverse leaf springs

The more or less transverse double lever suspension is one of the two majority types of front suspension in production. In the early days of independent front suspensions leaf springs were sometimes used to combine the functions of spring and locating lever. There are two major disadvantages of this practice: first the stress caused by high fore and aft loading resulting from braking forces; and secondly the impossibility of getting adequate up and down movements without thin leaves or high stresses or both. Interleaf friction also made it extremely difficult to provide an acceptable ride quality as cars became lighter. Modern transverse leaf systems have been proposed and built experimentally using advanced composite materials, but there is no suspension of this type on a current production car.

5.4   RECENT INDEPENDENT SYSTEMS

The two types of independent front suspension that account for practically all the private cars in large scale production are the transverse double lever or wishbone, Fig. 5.2, and the MacPherson strut and link, Fig. 5.3. In fundamental principles of operation these are the same, since the strut merely gives motion equivalent to an arm of infinite radius whose centre lies on a line perpendicular to the strut and starting from the strut top anchorage pivot point.

In both cases the axes of the transverse levers can be straight fore and aft or inclined in plan view. Initially those of the upper and lower levers on one side of the car were always made parallel to each other.

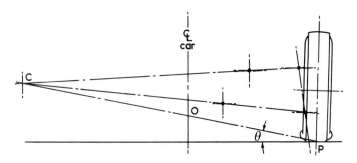

Fig. 5·2   The roll centre derivation for a double wishbone suspension, in this case arranged to give some swing axle effect, is shown

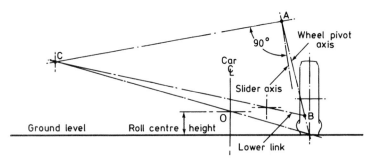

Fig. 5·3   The derivation of the roll centre height for a strut and link type suspension is shown. The 'kingpin' axis is defined by the pivot-attachment point of the slider, *A*, and *B*, the outer end of the lower link. The slider axis could, but more often does not, lie along this axis. *C* is the instantaneous centre of the linkage, the intersection point of the perpendicular to the slider axis from its attachment point and the centre line of the lower link continued

Double wishbones

There are several ways in which pairs of parallel arms can be arranged to control suspension geometry. There can be two upper and lower trailing arms each side, used with transverse torsion bars as on the now classic VW Beetle layout, transverse tubular symmetrically arranged A-frame links or angled derivatives and hybrids. Parallel motion from equal-length links maintains wheel camber angles at their static value over bumps, but causes track changes and positive camber angles to be generated by body roll, to the detriment of cornering power.

The way to control camber better is to fit shorter upper links than lower ones, so that the top of the wheel moves in as the suspension is displaced from the mean travel position. In many applications dating from the time when lever-arm hydraulic dampers were popular, the short upper link was formed by the damper-actuating lever.

If a substantial front sub-frame forms part of the inherent vehicle design, double wishbones can be designed to attenuate road noise better. For precision control of the system, close manufacturing tolerances are vital for any layout and it is usual to machine the attachments after subframe assembly. On the Jaguar XJ6 (shown previously in Fig. 3.5), which is a classic example of how well a wishbone system can be developed, the dampers are attached directly to the body structure to ensure that the damping forces on the body are not depleted by the insulation of the sub-frame mounts.

The first design to depart from this was the post World War II 2.6 litre Lagonda. It had become fairly general practice for the axes to be splayed out towards the front of the car; if the lower lever was longer, either to get or approach straight line motion of the tyre-road contact point up and down or to be able to use a two-piece cross steering tube with central idler with reasonably correct up and down geometry then the desire to shorten the distance from the front wheels to 'back of dash', which would place the engine as far forward as possible, would make it convenient to splay the axes of at least the longer lower levers so as to keep these out of the way of the engine. The Lagonda layout sprang from a realisation that the shorter upper levers were outside the space occupied by the engine. Associated with this was a desire to use a double piston and lever type hydraulic damper actuated by a rod up the middle of the coil spring operated by the lower triangle lever. The upper lever was swung round towards the back far enough to clear this damper operating rod.

An even greater divergence from parallelism was incorporated in the Rover 2000 introduced in 1963 where the upper lever was fore and aft, the transverse axis making it possible to couple an anti-roll rod directly to the levers.

In the Nissan multi-link front suspension[2], double wishbone geometry has been ingeniously incorporated within the confined packaging restraints of wide tyres and low bodywork by adding an extra curved upper part to the hub carrier, as shown in Fig. 5.4 (a). This allows a much longer upper wishbone to be used and greater freedom in the arrangement of the wheel geometry, independent of the king pin axis.

Another example of the double wishbone suspension is seen in Fig. 5.4, as used on the Renault 25. In this instance leaving room for the front wheel drive shaft forces the spring and damper to be placed above and operated by the upper wishbone.

The Citroen CX suspension also has to leave room for a drive shaft. The operation of gas spring and the location of the bump and rebound buffers are the interesting features here (Fig. 5.5).

MacPherson struts

The most commonly used design of front suspension on modern cars is known as the MacPherson strut. It is named after a Ford suspension engineer called Earle S. MacPherson who in America nearly 40 years ago first patented the idea of locating the lower end of an inclined strut system by means of the anti-roll bar link. Although strictly speaking a description of only this composite system, the term is generally applied to all kinds of strut suspensions.

Construction of a MacPherson strut[3] is based on an outer tube, fixed to the hub carrier at its lower end and welded to a seating cup for the suspension spring at its upper end. Inside the tube is a telescopic damper with its piston rod attached to a thrust bearing in the centre of a turret formed in the inner wheelarch area of the car body, which also carries as the upper spring seat. Location of the lower end of the strut is triangulated, usually by a transverse link (or track control arm) and a tie-bar or the lever arm of a transverse anti-roll (or stabiliser) bar.

The advantages of a MacPherson strut are that the suspension inputs to the body can be fed to inherently stiff areas and well spaced. Like the alternative unequal-length wishbone systems, struts allow considerable design flexibility, but with the significant

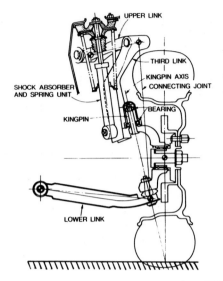

Fig. 5·4 (a) The multi-link front suspension for the 1990 Nissan 300ZX allows a much longer upper wishbone to be used, offset to clear a low-mounted coil spring and damper unit. (Courtesy Nissan Motor Co. Ltd.)

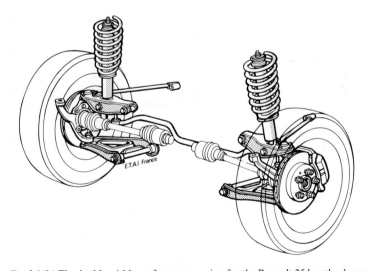

Fig. 5·4 (b) The double wishbone front suspension for the Renault 25 has the damper and spring above the top wishbone to make room for the driveshaft to the front wheel. Press steel links are used with an additional tie-bar to brace the upper wishbone to a stiff part of the integral body. (*Courtesy Renault SA*)

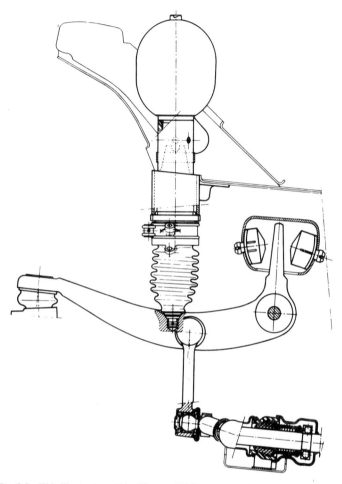

Fig. 5·5   This illustration of the Citroen CX front suspension is included to show the operation of the height controlled gas spring, the connection to the anti-roll bar and the bump and rebound buffer operation. (*Courtesy Automobiles Citroen*)

advantage that a front sub-frame is not usually required to ensure adequate close tolerance for the location points.

Several examples of a typical strut and link suspensions systems are shown in Figs. 5.6, 5.7, 5.8 and 5.9. Only in the case of the Audi 100 in Fig. 5.6 does the anti-roll bar operating arm provide the fore and aft tie for the lower link.

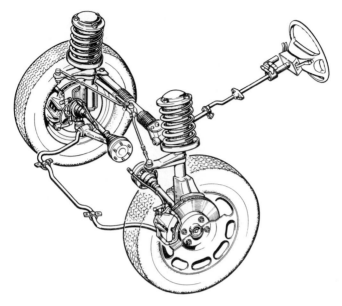

Fig. 5·6   For the Audi 100 front suspension the anti-roll bar locates the lower links according to the description in the original MacPherson patent. (*Courtesy Audi AG*)

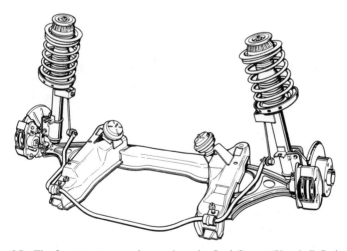

Fig. 5·7   The front strut suspension used on the Opel Omega (Vauxhall Carlton) features wide-based lower links and a separate anti-roll bar system. It is designed to provide a self-stabilising system through the inner wishbone bushes. (*Courtesy Adam Opel AG*)

Fig. 5·8   The Volkswagen Golf system shown here is typical of front suspensions used on current front-wheel drive family cars. It has wide-based lower links and a separate anti-roll bar. (*Courtesy Volkswagen AG*)

5.5   FRICTION IN STRUT AND LINK TYPE

We have seen, Section 4.5, that friction damping is undesirable, although some inherent frictional forces obviously cannot be entirely eliminated. Those pivots in a linkage which have rubber bushes tend to reduce friction, but pivot friction in a linkage is unimportant compared with sliding friction at the full suspension movement velocity. The piston and rod seals in telescopic dampers are not detrimental because their friction is proportional to the damper force itself. Fully lubricated frictional forces from piston and rod sliding will also be proportional to velocity.

It is when the damper performs a guiding function that harmful friction can occur. This applies particularly in the MacPherson type strut and link suspension. The forces on piston and rod are greatest when cornering, braking and, dependent on the layout, possibly when driving. Care can be taken in design to minimise these forces and low friction materials such as PTFE can be used to minimise the

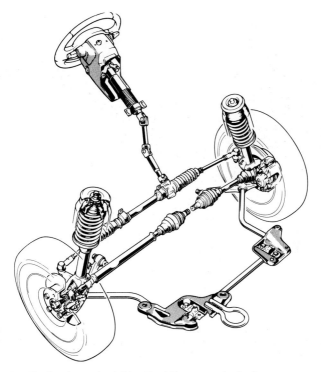

Fig. 5·9 The first front-wheel drive Ford Escorts used a basic strut system with a forward-running tie and no anti-roll bar. (*Courtesy Ford Motor Co.*)

friction resulting from them. Nevertheless these friction forces remain considerable and from a suspension aspect form a fundamental disadvantage of strut type suspensions. This is likely to become more obvious as improvement continues to be made in the quality of the ride.

5.6 SUSPENSION ROLL-CENTRE HEIGHT DETERMINATION

To determine cornering weight transfer the height of the roll centres for both front and rear suspensions must be determined, see Sections A1.15 and A1.16 of Appendix 1. Figure 5.10 shows one method by which the car roll-axis can be experimentally determined, by photography from both ends of the car, of a vertical line at each end; different amounts of roll torque are applied to the sprung part

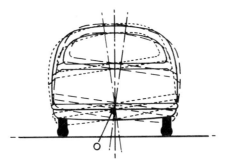

Fig. 5·10   Applying a range of rolling torques to a car, in both directions, which has had fitted at each end screens with vertical central lines on a contrasting colour and photographing the different positions, locates the roll axis at each screen position. The sketch indicates what the result is likely to be and the resulting position of the roll axis

of the car in any convenient way. The common intersection of the lines, for different roll angles, is obviously the point about which the sprung part of the car rotates in relation to the unsprung and therefore defines the roll axis at two points. The height of this axis at the front and rear wheel centre planes is a matter of interpolation.

The experimental determination of the roll axis and suspension roll centres in this way is the final answer but is not possible when the suspensions exist only as designs on paper. With independent suspensions the roll centre is the intersection with the car centre line of the perpendicular to the path of the contact point between tyre and road, with bump and rebound movement, taken from the actual contact point position at the state of load with which we are concerned. Figure 5.11 for instance shows a suspension with two initially parallel but unequal links at an angle θ to the ground. We know that the instantaneous centre of the contact point P lies on a line parallel to the two links so that the roll centre is at the point O where a line at an angle ψ to the ground, from the contact point, intersects the car centre line.

A more general solution appears in Fig. 5.2 where again two transverse links provide the suspension; in this case they are not parallel and their centre lines meet in C. Here the roll centre is at O, on the line joining the contact point to C and of course by symmetry on the car centre line.

The two links forming the suspension may have axes which are not parallel to the car central plane. In this case, the path of each link end, viewed from the front or rear of the car, will be a part of an ellipse; one of the known constructions for an approximate

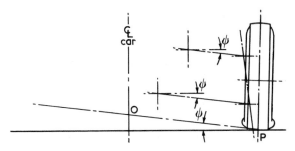

Fig. 5·11   Initially parallel upper and lower wishbones can give a roll centre above the ground with the minimum of gyroscopic action

ellipse will give a centre for the part of the ellipse in question and the line joining the point on the curve to that approximate centre can be regarded as the link in the diagram Fig. 5.2.

As we have already mentioned the strut and link suspension, Fig. 5.3, is a special case of the two-link suspension with one link of infinite length. There is therefore a link intersection point C and as before a roll centre O.

To be strictly accurate, tyre deflections in roll will very slightly affect the roll centre position; so will deflections under cornering loads at the link ends if flexible bearings are used there; these effects are unlikely to affect the results sufficiently to be practically important.

With upward deflection of one suspension and downward of the other as the car rolls the two suspensions will almost certainly give different heights of O and the defining lines from the two contact points will not meet on the centre line of the car. At first sight one might imagine that where they meet is the roll centre for the complete suspension and that as a result of this there has been some raising or lowering of the front of the car, with a corresponding modification of the anti-roll rate. In practice however the raising or lowering of the end of the car is not determined by the linkage characteristics we discussing but by the load-deflection curves of the left and right suspensions, the existence or otherwise of fore and aft weight transference, the sources of that weight transference and the anti-dive or squat geometry of the suspensions. As a first approximation one can assume no height change with roll and a roll centre mid-way between the centres resulting from the two suspension positions, left and right.

5.7   SUSPENSION GEOMETRY FOR ANTI-DIVE AND ANTI-SQUAT

To determine car fore and aft attitude changes under braking (dive) or acceleration (squat) we need to know either the effective pivot points of the suspensions in side view or at least the paths, in that view, of the tyre-road contact points – see Sections A1.15 to A1.19 of Appendix 1 – so that we can determine the angles θ_f and θ_r.

Figure 5.12 shows one way in which the double wishbone type suspension with axes parallel to the car central plane can have anti-dive; the two wishbone axes in side elevation are no longer parallel; the lines parallel to them from A and B, the outer ends of the upper and lower links respectively, meet at O. The line joining the tyre-road contact point to O is at an angle θ to the ground.

A related situation exists in Fig. 5.13, where both wishbone axes are parallel to each other but not to the ground. The angles of

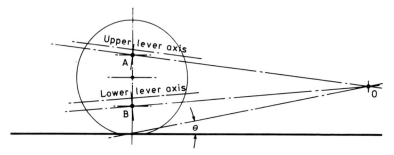

Fig. 5·12   A double wishbone suspension whose axes are not parallel in side elevation can provide anti-dive under braking. If the lines parallel to these axes, from the outer ends of the wishbones, A and B, meet in O the relevant angle θ is shown

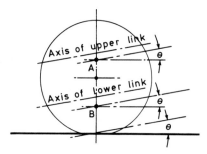

Fig. 5·13   Analogous to the case of roll centres, the use of parallel axes not parallel to the ground can also produce a relevant angle θ. Point A and B are the outer ends of the wishbones

wishbone axes to the ground, θ, are also the angle θ defining the anti-dive characteristics.

As in the case of the suspension in front view, wishbone axes not parallel to the car central plane will produce paths at the outer ends of the wishbones and at the tyre-road contact point which are arcs of an ellipse in side elevation. Perpendiculars to these ellipses can be approximated with sufficient accuracy by aiming at the centre of the radii for the construction giving an approximate ellipse; the lines so produced will either give a meeting point such as O in Fig. 5.12 or an angle θ as in Fig. 5.13. The construction for a strut and link suspension is given in Fig. 5.14(a), for an angled axis of the link; the strut also may be angled, as in Fig. 5.14(b).

Strut suspensions can also be given anti-dive by using non-parallel links or pivot axes. By this means also the inertia torque affecting the steering can be reduced – see Section 8.9.

For axles generally, in braking, and live axles for acceleration, we are concerned with the path of the tyre-road contact point. We shall see that offsetting the axle on semi-elliptic springs gives an effective

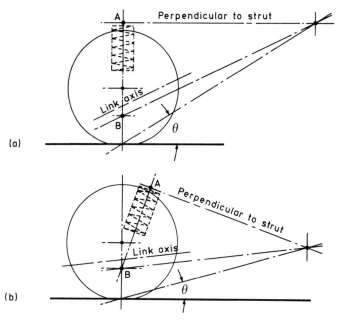

Fig. 5·14 Two variations in the strut and link suspension to produce relevant angles θ. The link axis for both is preferably not parallel to the ground. Points A are the anchorages/pivots of the struts; Points B are the outer ends of the lower links

centre about which the axle rotates, Section 6.2. Three- or four-link axle location systems (as used by Mazda and on the latest Ford Mondeo) can also be arranged to have an instantaneous centre about which an axle rotates (Fig. 6.6). A torque arm or tube on an axle provides an obvious centre about which it rotates.

Reference is sometimes made to the percentage of anti-dive or anti-squat of a particular suspension or car. If we are thinking in terms of braking we can only consider it in relation to the complete car and refer it to the proportion of the complete elimination of attitude change which has been achieved. Further details are given in Appendix 1.12. If the centre of gravity is a distance H above the ground and a distance a behind the front wheels and a distance b in front of the rear wheels (so the wheelbase $L = a + b$) and the front braking proportion is p, this percentage of anti-dive is given by the equation

$$100 \times \frac{pa \tan \theta_f + (1 - p)b \tan \theta_r}{H} \tag{5.1}$$

If we are interested in how that correction is subdivided between front and rear we have to compare θ_f and θ_r with the ideal angles θ_{fi} and θ_{ri} which as we have seen are $\theta_{fi} = \tan^{-1}(H/pL)$ and $\theta_{ri} = \tan^{-1} H/(1 - p)L$.

The percentage correction of the front is therefore

$$100 \times \frac{(\tan \theta_f)}{(\tan \theta_{fi})} \tag{5.2(a)}$$

and of the rear

$$100 \times \frac{(\tan \theta_r)}{(\tan \theta_{ri})} \tag{5.2(b)}$$

We can do a corresponding exercise for four-wheel drive by substituting p_d, the front torque proportion in driving, for p, the front braking proportion, if there is a fixed torque ratio between front and rear drives. Because p_d is never likely to be the same as p the proportion of anti-squat will differ from the proportion of anti-brake-dive.

Total avoidance of attitude change is highly improbable because of the bad effect of such an angle θ_f on the front suspension reaction to road bumps. We must therefore expect a vertical reaction at the centre of gravity as well as an attitude change. The vertical reaction at the centre of gravity will be shared out between front and rear suspensions in the proportion of their sprung masses. Because, as we have already said, there are ideally differences between front and rear suspension effective static deflections such a vertical reaction at the centre of gravity will result in a very slight attitude change. This attitude change has been ignored; it is considered likely to be small compared with the other attitude changes to be expected. It is easily calculated if we know the front and rear spring rates, S_{cf} and S_{cr}. To include this effect in the formulae would be an unnecessary complication likely to cloud our recognition of the fundamentally important requirements.

If the drive is confined to one end of the car the major attitude change can be avoided if $\tan\theta_{fi}$ for front end drive, and if $\tan\theta_{ri}$ for rear wheel drive, satisfy Equations 5.2(b) and 5.2(a) respectively. The percentage correction is generally $100(\tan\theta)/(\tan\theta_i)$.

Moulton and Best[4] have preferred to relate the percentage correction, with front wheel drive, to the condition which produces zero deflection of the front suspension, i.e. $\tan_{fi} = H/L$. This is a matter of personal choice; we must understand and state which criterion is being used as a reference.

5.8 COMPLIANCE; EFFECT ON ROAD NOISE AND HARSHNESS

Section 7.2 shows that fore and aft compliance is necessary to reduce vibrations and harshness, more particularly with the radial tyre which is then superior to the cross-ply. In the front suspension care has to be taken to provide this longitudinal compliance without introducing an unwanted degree of flexibility in the steering linkage. With front suspensions virtually confined to the double wishbone and the strut and link, the bottom link is the obvious place to provide this longitudinal compliance. Many suspensions have used a bottom link consisting of an arm and an additional diagonal tie whose inner and generally forward end is at least approximately in line with the arm and pivot axis. This tie is usually anchored to the car structure through rubber, sometimes to the arm through rubber. One construction which has been particularly used in strut and link suspensions is for the anti-roll rod arm to provide the tie. The bearings for the anti-roll rod are rubber; the connection to the suspension arm in this construction is also through rubber which has to be able to swallow the anti-roll bar arm angularity due to the total up and down movement.

It has long been realised that road noise finds its way into the car through the suspension system and that rubber in each of the paths from wheel to car structure could provide a barrier whose effectiveness appears to depend on the hardness difference between the rubber and its surroundings. The present concern with compliance is probably another way of expressing the same requirement but more precisely.

An alternative to incorporating the compliance in the lower link is to mount the whole suspension on a sub-frame consisting primarily of the front suspension cross member. This sub-frame is then attached to the car structure through rubber. One advantage of this is that the steering gear can be mounted on the sub-frame with the suspension and this can be helpful if the cross-steering tubes are at an appreciable angle to the perpendicular to the car centre line. A cross-steering tube angled in that way would introduce steering errors if there were relative fore and aft movement of the wheel and the steering tube inner end.

If such a front suspension sub-frame exists it is usually an advantage to mount at least one end of the engine to it; with a transverse engine it may be possible to have all the engine mountings on the sub-frame. Too much flexibility in the suspension linkage has been known to encourage brake judder.

REFERENCES

1. Lanchester, F.W., 'Motor Car Suspension and Independent Springing', *Proc. Instn Auto. Engrs.*, Vol. XXX (1935–36)
2. Murakami, T., Uno, T., Iwasaki, H. and Noguchi, H., 'Development of a New Multi-Link Front Suspension', *SAE Technical Paper No. 890179* (1989)
3. Aigner, J., Goegel, E. and Cayless, G., 'The new Escort: The European Version of Ford's Worldwide Pinto-Escort Concept', *Int. J. of Vehicle Design*, Vol. 2, No. 4 (November 1981)
4. Moulton, A. E., and Best, A., 'From Hydrolastic to Hydrogas', *Proc. Auto. Div. I. Mech. E.* (1978–79)

6

Rear suspensions

6.1 CLASSIFICATION OF TYPES

The considerations governing the choice of rear suspension design are highly dependent on the drive configuration (see Chapter 10). In general terms, the case for independent rear systems with rear wheel drive is easy to prove, whereas its justification with front-wheel drive is not. A live rear axle system, using a conventional rear axle, coil springs and proper multi-link location by double links each side and a transverse Panhard rod, typically provides about twice the unsprung mass of an independent arrangement. In between is the undriven dead beam axle and the semi-independent de Dion system.

We can divide rear suspensions therefore into three main types:

(1) Live axles, with the final drive and differential incorporated.
(2) Dead axles, either as the back end of a front driven car or as the embodiment of a de Dion axle with driven rear wheels and a frame-mounted final drive and differential.
(3) Independent rear suspension.

We shall see later that the dividing line between (2) and (3) is possibly difficult to draw with one type of suspension.

One attraction of types (2) and (3) over (1) is a considerable reduction in unsprung mass, which both theoretically and in practice improves the ride and also avoids or at least minimises a variety of agitations of the driven rear axle which have proved troublesome[1]. Another is the elimination of the propeller shaft torque effect on wheel loading while driving.

The idea that a rigid axle always holds the wheels associated with it perpendicular to the road surface is obviously incorrect, as soon as a single wheel bump occurs. The departure from perpendicularity on both wheels, say 1.0 degrees to 1.2 degrees for 0.025 m lift of one wheel, is the same as would occur on one wheel only with an independent rear suspension whose instantaneous centre was at the other wheel plane.

6.2   LIVE REAR AXLES

With the almost complete design shift from rear wheel to front wheel drive, especially on small cheap cars, the live rear axle no longer survives. Larger cars with rear wheel drive now require some form of independent rear suspension to provide competitive standards of ride comfort and handling. For many decades the live rear axle was a universal design that proved cheap, robust and very efficient. Its main disadvantage was the fairly considerable extra unsprung mass due to the final drive and differential and its enclosure, plus part of the propeller shaft taking the drive to the axle. This unsprung mass compromised the ride and made the back axle more prone to hop and tramp, especially when it was transmitting high torque. Torque control for a live axle, to resist both braking and driving torques took many forms. As this type of rear suspension is no longer used, except for some commercial vehicles, it is not proposed to dwell on it here.

6.3   DEAD AXLES

The dead rear-axle is a simple lightweight tubular assembly used to locate undriven rear wheels with a constant track. Because it does not have the complication of a drive system it can be designed and manufactured much more simply and cheaply than a live axle. With outboard brakes and no drive to worry about it can have an instantaneous linkage centre which will completely avoid any lifting of the car back end under braking and still give no roll steer. This can be done either by a three- or four-link control system or by a torque arm each side. The main types of sideways location are the Panhard rod and the Watt linkage. A third is the use of a triangulated upper link; as on the Renault 12 and 18 in Fig. 6.1 which has its base pivoted to the car structure so the roll centre therefore always remains at the same height above the ground.

A variation of the Watt linkage which can be useful is shown in Fig. 6.2, where the swinging links are of unequal length. The connecting link of length L then has to be split up as shown, the part connected to the shorter link of radius r being of length $LR/(R + r)$, R being the length of the longer swinging arm. Watt used several

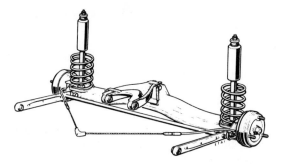

Fig. 6·1 (a) The dead axles once used by Renault on the 12 and 18 were located by two lower links at the sides acting in the longitudinal direction and an upper link to resist torque reactions and provide lateral location. (*Courtesy Renault SA*)

Fig. 6·1 (b) The dead axle used on the first model Ford Fiesta was located by two longitudinal links and a Panhard rod. (*Courtesy Ford Motor Co.*)

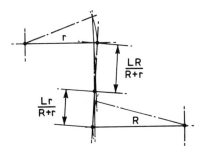

Fig. 6·2 The Watt linkage can have unequal arms as shown here

types of straight line motion apart from the more generally known one.

The torque arm location each side was originally used with a tubular axle beam; this had to have a rotationally free joint somewhere along its length to avoid the suspension being impossibly stiff in roll. One solution frequently used is to make the beam of channel section which is flexible in torsion but extremely stiff in bending and compression. This design incidentally demonstrated to us that the position of the axle beam could be used to produce a camber angle on both wheels in roll. This effect depends upon the connection between axle beam and wheel carriers being rigid and gives a camber thrust that reduces the rear tyre slip angles. Torque arms of the type shown have to be torsionally flexible to permit car roll. Some sideways flexibility is also required. The torsional stiffness of the axle beam and the torsional and sideways stiffnesses of the torque arms all contribute to the anti-roll rate of the rear suspension.

[This design concept[2], with which Donald Bastow was involved as

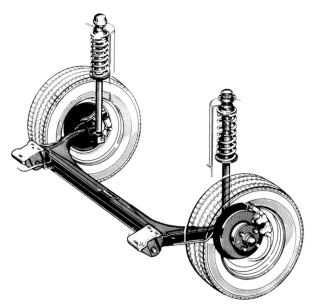

Fig. 6·3   The twist beam axle as shown here on the Volkswagen Golf has become almost an industry standard for rear suspension systems on small front-wheel drive cars. (*Courtesy Volkswagen AG*)

early as 1948, became the basis of the modern 'twist beam' axle now found almost universally on modern small FWD saloons. GPH]

The use of a twist or compound-beam system[3] was pioneered by Volkswagen on the Golf and has been widely copied ever since. It is a typical example of how the control of engineering characteristics is developing as a new science with significant efficiency benefits that will undoubtedly be the subject of much further development in the future.

Modern compound beam rear axles consist of an assembly with two trailing arms interconnected by a cross-tube rigidly attached to them each side. It depends on large elastic deformations of the structure to perform the essential roll functions or for single wheel deflections, but remains unstressed when traversing a uniform ridge. There are no flexible links in the axle assembly, although on some applications a small section Panhard rod is used to control lateral axle movement.

One attraction of the compound beam from the designer's viewpoint is that it provides a versatile degree of fine tuning the handling in development from the position chosen for the cross-tube location. Placed at the trailing arm pivots, it acts only as conventional torsion anti-roll bar, while moving it rearwards to the wheel centres subjects it to a variety of conical and axial displacements as well, and adds bending loads to the torsional strain. It is also extremely compact, as can be sen from the cross-section in Fig. 6.4.

The optimisation of a compound beam design[4], where the trailing arms must be laterally and torsionally elastic as well, cannot be achieved by manual techniques and depends heavily upon Finite Element stress analysis (see Section 11.2) of the complete welded assembly. The selection of the geometry for bump steer, roll steer,

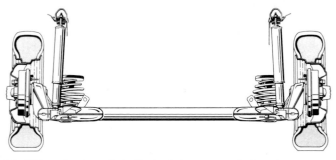

Fig. 6·4   This section through the Opel twist beam rear axle shows how compact the design can be with minimal intrusion into the passenger and luggage space

roll camber, deflection steer and the roll centre height also requires the use of advanced dynamic computer modelling.

The existence of camber change with roll implies that the dividing line between axles and independent rear suspensions is rather indeterminate. An axle beam, torsionally flexible, located on the torque arm-trailing arm pivot centre, with torsionally stiff arms, is an example of a trailing arm independent rear suspension. That same axle beam located at the wheel centre, with torsionally flexible torque arms, is an example of an axle. Any other beam location is a mixture of the two types of suspension.

6.4 DE DION AXLES

Another type of dead rear axle which has lost favour in recent years is known as the de Dion type, named after its inventor, a French car builder from the very early days of motoring. De Dion axles are a kind of compromise between live and independent systems, with less unsprung mass than a live axle and the same kind of rigid wheel geometry as a live axle assembly. In basic concept, a de Dion axle has the differential and final drive mounted on the chassis with the two wheels connected rigidly by a lightweight transverse dead tube axle, often curved to clear the axle housing and hollow at the ends to provide driveshaft access to the hubs. Because it is not fully independent, the de Dion system is often referred to as semi-independent.

De Dion axles were often considered as an effective design because they maintained the rear wheels at right angles to the road. This claim became a fallacy as soon as a single wheel bump occurred, when an important disadvantage of the design manifested itself as a rear-end steering effect. Most rear axles have a sideways location whose height is not far from that of the wheel centres. It is certainly not possible to get it very close to the ground. Whenever one end of the axle rises there is a sideways movement of both wheel contact points which is equal to (wheel lift x roll centre height)/ track. This is likely to be between 0.2 and 0.25 of the wheel lift. It produces a steering effect on the back of the car which is resisted only by the inertia there and the self-aligning torque of the rear tyres. As compared with an independent rear suspension, even a swinging half-axle type, which would produce about as much sideways movement of the contact point, produces that movement only at the wheel which is lifted by the bump and the steering effect is resisted by the other wheel as well as by the inertia.

6.5   INDEPENDENT REAR SUSPENSION SYSTEMS

Variety in driven rear suspension design used to be more diverse, with many different live axle layouts and fully independent systems located by many different kinds of geometric links. The simplest, but notoriously tricky kind of independent system is the swing axle. This type was used by Volkswagen on the original Beetle (and all of its later derivatives until the last Super Beetle version in 1972 when a semi-trailing arrangement finally took over), Renault on the 750 4CV, Dauphine and all the later rear-engined designs, Chevrolet on the rear-engined Corvair, Porsche on their rear-engined dynasty, Mercedes-Benz on the classic 300SL Gullwing, Triumph on the Herald, and many more besides. Swing axles were particularly favoured with rear engines on cheaper family cars because they eliminated the need for costly outboard universal joints.

The problem with the swing axle was that the roll centre was relatively high, causing the cornering forces acting at ground level to twist the system, lift the rear end and flick the wheels into positive camber, reducing their grip dramatically in the process. With the tyre sections available at that time, swing axles usually displayed very unpredictable cornering behaviour.

Mercedes-Benz started a significant trend when they finally turned away from the swing axle concept in 1972. Prior to the S-Class launch that year, Mercedes-Benz had stuck resolutely to various designs of swing axle rear suspension. They liked the way swing axles helped large, front-heavy cars negotiate tight curves. It was a heritage derived from the early cars of racing, when the fastest way through a turn was a four-wheel drift.

Slowly they were weaned away from the swing axle characteristics, first by lowering the pivot point to reduce the roll moments and hence the camber changes, then to a totally different suspension geometry in 1972. By the time they reached this stage of development, they had tamed the swing axle to the point where it functioned extremely well under normal road conditions. But it always had a vicious final sting literally in its tail, when the unexpected happened and the driver was forced to brake in the middle of a bend.

Of the many different types of independent rear suspension very few indeed are still examples of swinging half-axles; other types are trailing and semi-trailing arms, double link or wishbone (sometimes with the drive shaft acting as one of the links or a part thereof) and strut and link.

The origin of the swinging half-axle was to get independent rear suspension in the simplest possible way by putting a universal joint in each half-shaft as far inboard as possible and providing coaxially with that universal joint pivots between an arm on the wheel carrying member and the final drive casing or vehicle structure. Porsche was responsible for fitting this type to an Austro-Daimler in the early 1920s; he clung to variations of this type to the end of his working life. One might argue that the later variations, such as that on the VW Beetle, are really semi-trailing arms. That suspension however still has virtually the same wheel tilt with bump and rebound as a half-axle and because of the very high mass transference in cornering due to its high roll centre is very liable to oversteer.

Daimler-Benz were also early in the field with this type; they too clung too it, with variations and refinements, until 1968. These variations were a number of means of reducing the anti-roll rate of the rear springing and the 'low pivot' arrangement where the two arms pivoted together below the final drive casing. Because the common pivot was on the car centre line it slightly reduced the wheel camber changes on bump; and the pivot below the final drive casing lowered the roll centre considerably. Even this version still suffered from the 'tuck under' effect. One version of this at least restored the propeller-shaft torque induced mass transfer between rear wheels on drive because the final drive casing was integral with one of the half-axles.

The symptom of the driving 'tuck under' effect is that if in hard cornering, road surface irregularities (e.g. a hump across the road) produce a condition in which the wheels drop far enough in relation to the car, the back end of the car will break away and lead to control problems.

Figure 6.5, with what may be considered reasonable proportions, shows that for actual 'tuck under' to occur, even with allowance for

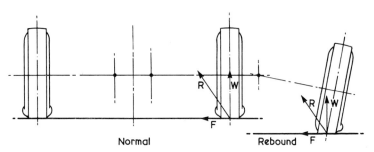

Fig. 6·5   The so-called tuck-under effect of a swing axle can introduce adverse handling characteristics, as explained in the text

a considerable rebound of 0.1 m, the side force would still have to be about 1.5 times the vertical load to get a reaction under the pivot point and so hold the back end up or even raise it. It seems probable that what happens is:

(1) On the rebound position attained, the load carried by each tyre is reduced; in the rolled state of the car, the inner wheel may be actually lifted.

(2) If it is, the full sideways force required to maintain the car in its previous attitude would have to be provided by the outer wheel only; with its reduced load this becomes impossible and the back end therefore slides out. The sideways slip angle is so high that the sideways force has become insensitive to slip angle.

(3) When recovery begins, i.e. settling of the car on its springs, its first effects are to increase the sideways slip angle and of course the load carried by the outer wheel. The two effects tend to cancel each other out.

(4) As soon as the inner wheel touches down the direction of motion of the contact point is such as to reduce its slip angle. With an extreme slip angle the slightly less slip angle of the inner wheel will help it to provide some sideways force and so reduce the total slip angle. With a smaller slip angle we can progress towards, and reach, the condition where the inner wheel has no slip angle at all and so contributes no sideways force, again leaving the outer wheel to provide it all. At an even smaller slip angle, less than that whose tangent is the outward velocity of the inner wheel contact point divided by the forward velocity of the car, the inner wheel is pushing the car outward and so increases the total outward force which the outer tyre is being asked to provide.

Without attempting to put actual values to the slip angles and forward velocities concerned, it is at least clear that this succession of events will tend to delay the recovery of the car from the outward slide initiated by the reduction of vertical force due to the wheels going to rebound in the first place and will therefore prolong the period when the car is effectively out of control.

6.6 TRAILING AND SEMI-TRAILING ARMS

The fundamental difference between trailing and semi-trailing arms is that the axis of the former is at right angles to the car centre line; this implies that there is no change, in end view, of the angle of the wheels with suspension movements. The semi-trailing arm, so far confined to examples where in plan view the axis of oscillation of the arm meets the vertical plane of the wheel axes towards or beyond the other rear wheel, necessarily introduces some swing axle effect. Although it is generally considered that the instantaneous centres are where the arm axis intersects the vertical planes of the rear wheel axes across the car and fore and aft, this is not strictly true. The actual path of any point on the wheel, in side or end elevation, is an

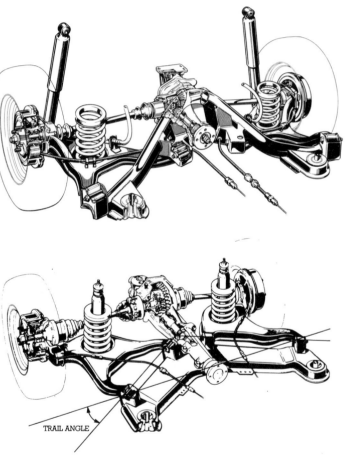

TRAIL ANGLE

Fig. 6·6   The Ford Sierra rear suspension (top) uses semi-trailing arms with a trail angle of 18°. It was reduced from the 23° used on the previous Granada system (below) to improve transient handling in power on/power off conditions. (*Courtesy Ford Motor Co.*)

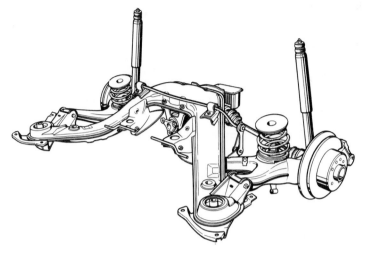

Fig. 6·7 The Opel Omega/Vauxhall Carlton design of semi-trailing arms rear suspension has effectively even less trail angle and incorporates self-stabilising articulation. (*Courtesy Adam Opel AG*)

ellipse and the instantaneous centre for that part of the ellipse can be found by known methods.

The knowledge that roll-steer effects are at a minimum when the semi-trailing arm axis is parallel to the ground is useful but we need to know more. For this we must study how toe-in changes on bump and rebound vary with changes in position of the semi-trailing arm axis, in plan view and in the angle which the axis makes with the ground. A basic case has been chosen in which the semi-trailing arm axis is at road wheel centre height, meets the rear wheel axis of the car at one wheel plane, point 2, and intersects the plane of the wheel whose movements are being studied 0.4 m forward of its centre, point 1. Figure 6.8 shows this. An alternative plan position shows the semi-trailing arm axis meeting the rear wheel axis at twice the car track from the wheel being studied, point 2A. Points 3, the wheel centre, and 4, 0.1 m away along its axis, are for calculation purposes to obtain the toe-in changes. The heights of points 1 and 2 in Table 6.1 define the axis changes studied, in height and inclination to the ground: rising to the front, dropping to the front, high or low; and parallel to the ground but above or below the original position. The resulting roll centre heights are also shown; they indicate the amount of sideways 'scrub' of the contact patch with bump and rebound movements.

Anthony Best Dynamics Ltd. computed the results summarised in

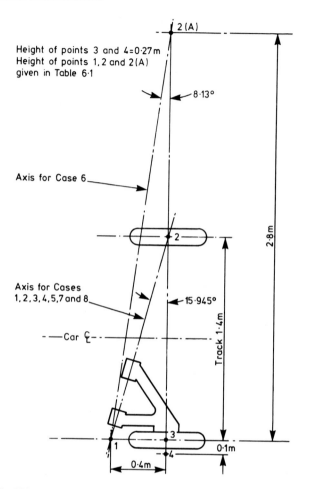

Height of points 3 and 4=0·27m
Height of points 1,2 and 2(A)
given in Table 6·1

Fig. 6·8   This is the plan view of the semi-trailing arm suspension for which the calculations were made. For all except one of the cases the semi-trailing arm axis intersects the rear wheel axis plane at the opposite wheel; for the remaining case the intersection point is twice as far away from the affected wheel

Fig. 6.9(a). Figure 6.9(b) shows the camber changes. Within the limits studied, i.e. axis height ±20 mm parallel to the ground, and a height change of 20 mm in sloping axes, nose high and nose low, and bump and rebound movements each of 75 mm, axis height does not affect the results (to two significant figures). The nose high axis position favours bump movements, and vice versa. Camber changes depend only on the distance from the studied wheel to the

Table 6.1 EFFECT OF CHANGES IN SEMI-TRAILING ARM AXIS POSITIONS ON ROLL CENTRE HEIGHT. AXIS POSITIONS FOR ROLL-STEER EFFECT STUDY

Case number	Heights above ground of points on axis, mm 1	2	Roll centre height, mm	Remarks
1	270	270	135	Basic case
2	270	250	125	Axis rises to front — low position
3	270	290	145	Axis drops to front — high position
4	290	270	135	Axis rises to front — high position
5	250	270	135	Axis drops to front — low position
6	270	270	67.5	Reduced angle of axis to rear wheel axis
7	250	250	125	Axis dropped — parallel to 1
8	290	290	145	Axis raised — parallel to 1

Axis when tilted is at angle to ground of 0.787°
For location of points 1 and 2 see Fig. 6.19

intersection of the semi-trailing arm axis, point 2, with the transverse vertical plane containing the undeflected rear wheel axes. From the trends within the range studied, we see that a sufficiently large nose-high axis angle will give toe-out on bump and toe-in on rebound; and again vice versa.

If the distance between wheel arches is important it must be remembered that the introduction of any swing axle effect has to be accompanied by an increase in the track to maintain that distance between wheel arches.

Partly to handle the extra power of the largest-engined versions and partly to avoid any risk of the handling-related product liability issues in the USA around another swing-axle car, the Mercedes-Benz S-Class rear end developed in 1972 became the standard design of semi-trailing arm system that most other manufacturers have since copied.

For road and axle noise insulation, it was mounted on a large-section fabricated steel sub-frame, vee shaped and supported on three large diameter rubber bushes. Wide-spaced pivots for the angled rear wishbones had little compliance, but the upper spring and damper attachments were through thick rubber insulators. Half-shafts were fully articulated with constant velocity plunging joints at each end, and there was a two-piece prop-shaft with centre steady bearing. Linear-rate springs were near vertical, concentric with the telescopic dampers, and there was a cranked anti-roll bar mounted above the wheel centre-line.

Careful arrangement of the rear geometry introduced an anti-

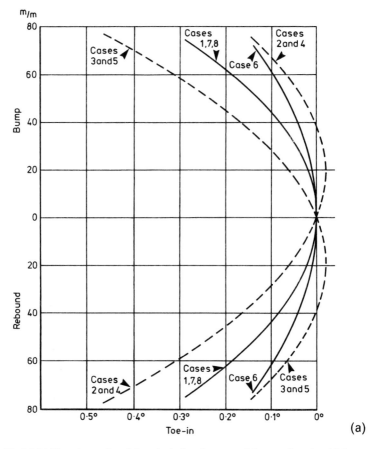

Fig. 6·9 (a) Here the results of the calculations in terms of change of toe-in with bump and rebound movement are shown. There are effectively no differences between cases 1, 7 and 8 where the axes are parallel to the ground but at different heights. Cases 2 and 4, axes up towards the front but at different heights, are also effectively the same as each other but now favour bump at the expense of rebound. The converse applies to cases 3 and 5, where rebound is favoured. Case 6, axis parallel to the ground and more nearly so to the rear wheel axis, halves the toe-in changes.

squat feature, to resist weight transfer under hard acceleration, while at the front there was an equally clever new system of anti-dive, also described as anti-lift when referenced to the rear. In both systems the torque at the wheels is arranged to generate vertical suspension control by angular displacements of the suspension pivots, countering the effects of dynamic mass transfer. The harder the driver

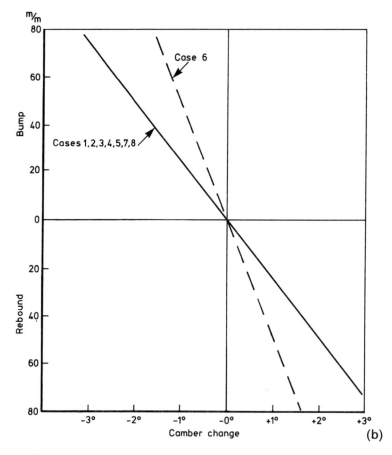

Fig. 6·9 (b) The chamber changes depend only on the distance from the affected wheel to the intersection of the axis and the vertical transverse plane containing the wheel axes

accelerated or the more the effect, giving a very reassuring feel to step off under full power or emergency stops without resort to stiff springs.

But it is the packaging advantages of semi-trailing arm systems as much as their dynamic control of wheel geometry which has made them a firm favourite since, with only a few specialists like Jaguar sticking undeterred to their traditional double wishbone designs.

The fundamental deficiencies of semi-trailing geometry are mostly concerned with the changes that occur in camber and toe setting (steer angle) with wheel travel. The need to make the wishbone bushes soft enough for acceptable primary compliance also causes some secondary problems of throttle steer (toe changed caused by power on/power off transients). Reaching the optimum for the disturbing effects of squat and lift is a more difficult task.

Independent rear suspension through a semi-trailing arm system does not provide as much design flexibility in selecting the amount of wheel camber change and toe change that occurs during roll in corners, and hence the amount by which the rear cornering power is increased. For each trail angle chosen there will be a specific amount of toe change, the effects of which must be considered in association with the length of arm required, the inclination of the pivots to the horizontal plane and the various influences of compliance in the bushes. Trail angles of around 23 degrees on the Ford Granada, were reduced to 18 degrees on the Ford Sierra to give optimum handling in terms of power on/power off response, steady state cornering and transient behaviour.

6.7   OPEL'S SELF-STABILISING SYSTEM

Suspension engineers working on the new Opel Omega (Vauxhall Carlton in the UK) devised some extremely advanced new characteristics for the fully independent system that cause it to react automatically in severe conditions to stabilise the handling and improve safety levels. In many ways it comes close to being an 'intelligent' suspension that thinks for itself and initiate its own corrections. The design is shown in Fig. 6.10.

The concept employs a whole series of special kinematic features front and rear, extensively developed over several years, first using advanced computer simulations and then prototype vehicles under controlled conditions at the proving grounds and then under more severe circumstances on the Nurburgring Grand Prix racing circuit.

Basic elements of the concept at the front are a strut and wishbone system incorporating a unique combination of negative scrub-radius geometry and compliance steer, for a self-stabilising effect under uneven braking forces. When a front wheel tries to turn out, the geometry of the insulating bushes 'steers' it back to the true running angle.

At the rear, the live axle used on the previous Rekord range was replaced by a fully independent semi-trailing arm system with a compound trail angle (inclined in two planes) designed to improve handling and cornering power, operate more consistently over the

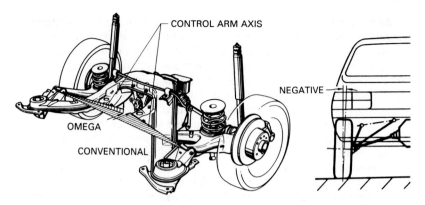

Fig. 6·10 The Opel Omega/Vauxhall Carlton rear suspension employs a compound trail angle (in two planes) to steer the rear wheels slightly to maintain stability better in a turn. (*Courtesy Adam Opel AG*)

full range of load conditions, reduce tyre wear and introduce a small amount of rear wheel steering when required to improve stability in extreme conditions.

The system uses independent kinematic control to provide high cornering power combined with automatic compensation for the normally unsettling changes that occur during transient manoeuvres. For maximum grip in a turn a tyre should ideally lean in at the top of the wheel to give negative camber. The problem with a semi-trailing independent system on a car is that the camber angle changes with the suspension movement under both dynamic roll forces and the static laden condition, affecting the handling and increasing tyre wear. And the need for softer suspension bushes at the rear to improve ride comfort and reduce the harshness of modern low-profile tyres also introduces compliance steer effects induced by the forces at the wheel when decelerating or braking. These conflicting effects were reduced on the Omega by arranging the rear suspension arms to pivot at a compound angle (displaced from the longitudinal axis of the car in both the horizontal and vertical directions). The effect is to increase toe-steer when lifting off to maintain a constant rear roll height (the point about which the body rolls) under all conditions.

Opel pioneered a new trend towards lower rear trail angles with the independent suspension system first introduced on the Senator in 1977. The Omega system is a new-generation development of the same concept with the trail angle in the horizontal plane reduced still further from 14 to only 10 degrees and combined for the first time with a 1.35 degree vertical inclination as well. This allows consistently higher negative camber angles of the wheel to be maintained throughout the full range of suspension travel for improved stability and handling without increasing tyre wear.

While most conventional trailing arm systems can be designed to perform adequately under typical two-passenger load conditions, they are restricted in practice by the need to stay within the tyres' durability limits at the maximum rated gross vehicle mass. And the height of the rear roll centre varies with the load as well, tilting the roll axis (the line joining front and rear roll centres about which the whole car rolls) from a stable downward inclination to a less stable upward inclination when fully laden.

On the Omega, rear camber angles and the rear roll height stay virtually constant at all times, while the front roll height reduces slightly with load, increasing stability under conditions when most conventional cars start to feel unsteady. In addition, the vertical trail angles induce a small degree of toe-in under deceleration and braking, to counter the normal tendency for the tail to swing out when lifting off in a corner.

These combined characteristics provide a measure of 'response steer' that automatically stabilises the Omega at the rear with the same kind of artificial kinematic intelligence as that applied at the front. Other benefits derived from the new design include reduced unsprung masses, for better wheel control, multi-axis front cross-member support brackets and double-isolated anti-roll bar attachments for improved noise suppression, minibloc progressive-rate coil spring design that prevents metal-metal contact at full bump and optimised damper mountings positioned where they operate at the best leverage ratio.

6.8 WISHBONE AND STRUT-AND-LINK TYPE REAR SUSPENSION

Double independent wishbones and multi-link locations systems of the type shown in Fig. 6.11, provide total flexibility of static geometry and geometry changes with wheel travel, they offer the possibility of full squat and lift compensation and their unsprung mass is relatively low, especially if component economies are made (as on the Jaguar where the drive shafts provides wheel location).

As in the front suspension, the strut and link and double wishbone suspensions can be regarded as being of the same fundamental type. The embodiments can be very different. Figure 6.12 is an example of the strut and link as used on the first design of

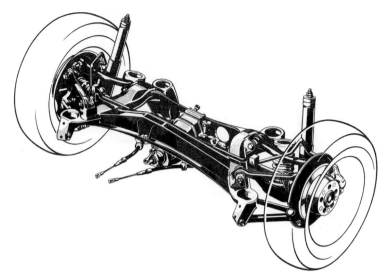

Fig. 6·11 The multi-link rear suspension of the Mercedes-Benz 190 provides freedom of design for wheel geometries but is more complex and costly to produce. (*Courtesy Daimler-Benz AG*)

front-wheel drive Ford Escort; while Fig. 6.13 is an example of a variation used on the Mazda 323.

In the first design of Jaguar rear suspension a forward facing radius arm was used each side to assist in the control of pitch and yaw of the unsprung masses and the subframe assembly. The wishbone pivot points and the positioning of this link allowed little possibility of controlling the anti-squat and anti-lift characteristics. In the development of the new XJ6 system, the pivots were inclined, but the resultant path locus of the hub with wheel travel was incompatible with a simple horizontal radius arm. Substituting a Watts linkage, which could handle the geometry, was ruled out on cost and complexity grounds.

Several other advanced rear systems were also attempted before the final solution was selected. It is a double wishbone system much like the previous one but with the key difference that the inner pivots for the lower arms are mounted on what is described as a pendulum, or hanger yoke, at the front of the differential casing and a straight cross-tie at the rear. It provides inboard compliance that is independent laterally from the longitudinal stiffness, so that bump shocks can be absorbed independently from the transverse control of the suspension arms.

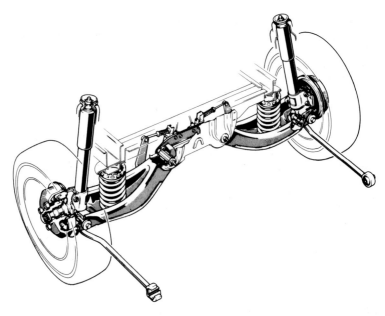

Fig. 6·12   The strut and link rear suspension for the front-drive Ford Escort used a fabricated transverse arm and a tubular forward-facing tie bar. The coil spring were inboard of the telescopic dampers. (*Courtesy Ford Motor Co.*)

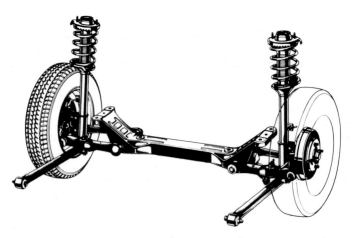

Fig. 6·13   The Mazda 323 strut and link system put the coil spring on top of the dampers and used separate transverse arms in front of and behind the rear wheel centres. (*Courtesy Mazda Cars Ltd.*)

Fore and aft compliance is necessary to reduce road noise; introducing this without at the same time incorporating flexibilities which would result in undesirable steering deflections from the assorted braking, driving and cornering loads is a difficult problem. Rolls-Royce were one of the first companies to provide compliance by mounting of the rear suspension assembly to the body structure. The actual suspension, using semi-trailing arms, was relatively rigid.

The original Jaguar double-link rear suspension also relied on the mounting of the rear suspension unit, which had a relatively rigid linkage, for its compliance. It was notable for its use of the drive shaft as the upper link, flanked front and rear by the twin spring-damper units, while the torsionally stiff lower link dealt with fore and aft loads. There were flexible rubber mountings to the body structure, high up each side, with compliance controlled by fore and aft links from the wheel carrier, connected to the body through rubber. The disc brakes are inboard to keep unsprung mass to a minimum. In its latest form (known as the XJ-40), this has been supplemented by flexibility in the linkage.

Chronologically between the two Jaguar designs, the latest Mercedes-Benz independent rear suspension relies upon both the mounting of its five link (each side) suspension assembly and some flexibility in the linkage itself. The compact assembly comprises a complete unit flexibly mounted at four points to the body structure. The spring abutment each side and the damper upper attachments are also through rubber.

The novelty of the Mercedes system[5] will be better appreciated by study of Fig. 6.14 which represents the linkage in skeleton form. Each upper and lower triangle comprises two links, rubber ball jointed at both ends, with two exceptions: one is the rear lower link, which at its inner end has a rubber bush to provide some stability for the operation of the spring and damper and at its outer end has a steel ball in a plastic socket; the other exception is the outer end of the fifth, steering, link which also has a metal ball in a plastic socket. This link provides a stabilising influence and is an essential part of the linkage.

If the links forming the upper and lower suspension levers were arranged along the sides of triangles with apices on the vertical from the middle of the tyre-road contact patch, the flexibility in the ball joints would allow some fore and aft movement. In the case of a drive force, applied at the height of the wheel axis, there would be loads applied at the intersection points of the triangles pushing them forwards; the compression in the front link and the tension in the rear would induce some steering action on the wheel carrier, giving

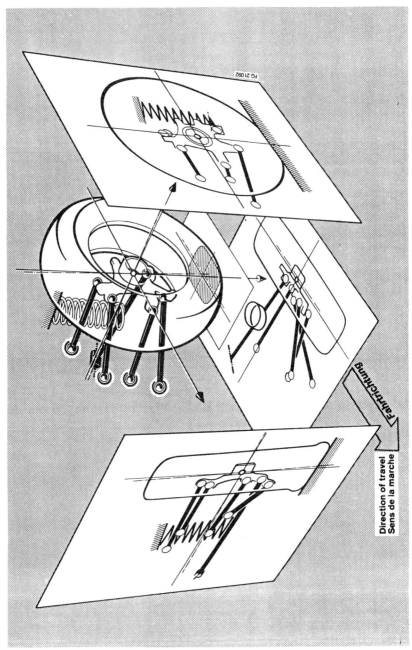

FIG 21 092

Direction of travel
Sens de la marche

Fahrtrichtung

Fig 6:14   The skeleton view of the linkage in perspective requires the corresponding front and side views and plan to be fully understood

toe-in. This is undesirable; if however the apices of the triangles are outside the vertical from the middle of the contact patch there is a tendency for forward movement to give toe-out steering deflection. The positions of the apices are chosen so that these tendencies cancel each other. Fore and aft compliance is therefore obtainable without any tendency to steering deflection. The task of the fifth link is therefore eased.

A further refinement is that in sideways elevation the 'axis' for the meeting points of the triangle links rises from the point of action of sideways forces, i.e. allowance is made for pneumatic trail. Because the rearwards links in the upper triangle lie directly above the wheel axis and the lower ones almost so, they take respectively all or the bulk of the sideways forces.

Figure 6.15 has indications of bump and rebound movements marked on the skeleton linkage drawing. These show no steering deflections with such movements, some raising of the roll centre and appreciable anti-dive and squat, said to be 60 per cent.

The Jaguar suspension[6], designed to provide even further reductions in road noise than the first generation system, has been simplified, Fig. 6.16. The drive shaft still acts as the upper link and the suspension is still a complete unit in itself, based on an A-frame that rigidly supports the final drive housing. The legs of the A diverge to the two front mounting points to the body, as widely spaced and as low as possible. There are diagonal ties from close to these mounting points to the top of the rear flange of the drive unit, to make reinforce the assembly. A single spring-damper unit each side lies forward of the drive shaft and its top abutment to the body, through rubber, lies on the line joining the wheel centre to the middle of the line across the car joining the two front mountings. The rear attachment of the unit to the body is by two links, with rubber at each end, rising from the A-frame to brackets, again well spaced sideways, on the body structure. The instantaneous centre of these links is also low down.

The lower link is a very rigid boxed assembly made from two pressings welded together with rubber bearings at its inner end; their axial flexibility provides some of the compliance. The rear ones are located by a cross tie fixed to the A-frame through rubber at two points. More compliance for fore and aft forces on individual wheels is gained by mounting the front bearing of each lower link in a distorted ring surrounding the drive pinion bearing housing. This ring is mounted through rubber at two points to the top front of the drive unit. The flexibility of these upper mountings allows some sideways movement of the lower part of the ring. The disc brakes, not shown, are now outboard. The lower frequency of the heavier

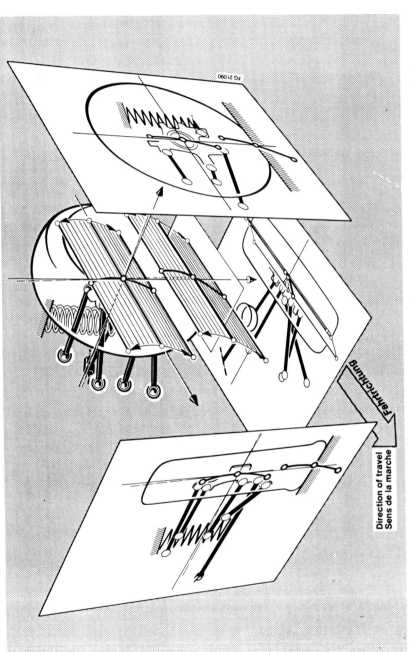

FG 21 090

Direction of travel
Sens de la marche

Fahrtrichtung

Fig. 6·15   In this repeat of the skeleton space linkage, the bump and rebound movements of link ends, contact point and wheel centre are indicated. The front view of the contact point shows that the roll centre is above ground level; the side view that there is anti-dive and squat, by the movement traces of contact point and wheel centre

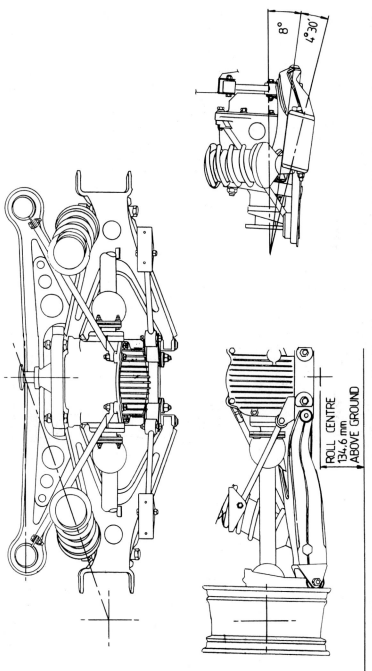

Fig. 6·16   The Jaguar XJ-40 rear suspension is an improved version of that previously fitted to cars of this make; it retains the use of the drive shaft as the upper link of a double suspension. The lower link still has to provide the torsional stiffness to take braking loads from the outboard brakes at ground level and driving loads at wheel centre height. Although much of its compliance comes from the rubber mountings of the suspension assembly to the body, some is now provided by the lower arm pivots and their attachment to the suspension assembly. (*Courtesy Jaguar Cars Ltd.*)

unsprung mass on the tyre rate is convenient in allowing the drive unit mass to act as a harmonic damper to the unsprung vibrations, the spring and damper unit providing a flexible fulcrum.

In side view the lower link inboard axis rises at 8 degrees towards the front, to provide 69 per cent anti-squat and 17 per cent anti-brake dive. The outer end bearing of the lower link rises upwards to the front at an additional 45 degrees, to avoid steering effects from the vertical wheel movements.

In all of these basically wishbone suspensions it is possible to put the instantaneous centre, in rear view, wherever you want it, with two considerations. These are: (1) the height of the roll centre, and (2) the amount of swing axle-effect that is desired. The considerations involved in fixing the height of the roll centre are the amount of total mass transference required at the back and the extent to which this is to be attained by anti-roll stiffness of the suspension (see Sections 7.9 to 7.11 and Appendices 2.10 to 2.12). The total mass transference required is also affected by the swing-axle effect. With swinging half-axles body roll leaves the wheels very nearly vertical to the road; the position of the pivot centres somewhat out from the car centre line tends to give each wheel an inward lean on the corner but in each case the tyre deflection changes, due to mass transference, tend to reduce that helpful camber. With no swing-axle effect, the wheels will lean with the car and there will be outward camber thrust generated by both. (The effect of swing axles themselves as a result of road irregularities in cornering has already been discussed.)

To resolve this compromise it helpful to study Fig. 6.17 which indicates the locus lines of linkage instantaneous centre positions to give calculated equal understeer angles for a particular car layout. This diagram was prepared with data from cross-ply tyres and

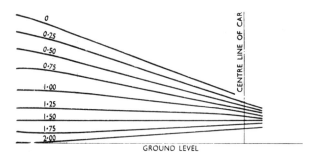

Fig. 6·17   Loci of the instantaneous centre of an independent rear suspension to give equal understeer angles are shown. (*Courtesy Institution of Mechanical Engineers*)

though the tendencies would be similar for radials, the actual positions and the separation of the lines for given differences in understeer will vary with tyre and car characteristics.

REFERENCES

1. Polhemus, V. D., 'Secondary Vibrations in Rear Suspensions', *J. Soc. Auto. Engrs.*, July (1950)
2. Bastow, D., 'Independent Rear Suspension', Proc. Auto. Div., I. Mech. E. Pt. II (1951–52)
3. Satchell, T. L., 'The Design of Trailing Twist Axles', *SAE Technical Paper* No. 810420 (February 1981)
4. Horntrich, H., 'Rear Suspension Design with Front Wheel Drive Vehicles', *SAE Technical Paper* No. 810421 (February 1981)
5. Enke, K., 'Improvement in Ride Handling by Compromise in the Elasto-Kinematic System of Wheel Suspension', C117/83, *Road Vehicle Handling*, I. Mech. E. Conference Publications (1983–85)
6. Cartwright, A. J., 'The Development of a High Comfort, High Stability Rear Suspension', *Proc. I. Mech. E. (Transport)*, Vol. 200, No. D5, S57-60 (special issue The Jaguar XJ40 Project) (1986)

7

The Wheel and Tyre

7.1 PNEUMATIC TYRE AND WHEEL

The wheel consists of a rim on which the tyre is placed with a demountable means for locating that rim in relation to the hub so that the two components can only rotate together as an assembly. Figure 7.1 shows in section a typical pressed steel rim and wheel. The rim is defined by its width and the contours of its lips or sides which are rounded to minimise damage to the tyre sidewalls when meeting bumps or cornering. It is also defined by the size and position of the well, provided to allow the inextensible tyre bead to be coaxed over the rim sides, and by the existence and nature of any taper tyre bead seat modifications to discourage unwanted bead movement when the tyre is deflated. The most common types of wheel rim profile are shown in Fig. 7.2 with the so-called 'double hump' type being the most secure.

If a tyre can be coaxed off a rim for refitting it is also possible for a deflated tyre to be forced off. This can provide an added hazard for the driver when the tyre goes flat. To resist this occurrence Avon developed a ring for filling in the well after fitting the tyre so that it could not come off involuntarily. With the almost universal adoption of self-sealing tubeless tyres, the system was never exploited commercially.

As already mentioned earlier, the tyre in suspension terms should really be considered as a secondary spring working in series with the main road spring. Later in this chapter the physics of tyre behaviour in the vertical plane will be explained in detail. But the tyre is far more complex than a simple spring and plays a vital part in the dynamic handling behaviour of the vehicle.

The elements of a tyre's construction are simple. The working medium is the air chamber which converts input loads and forces into stresses applied to the carcass, or flexible framework, to which

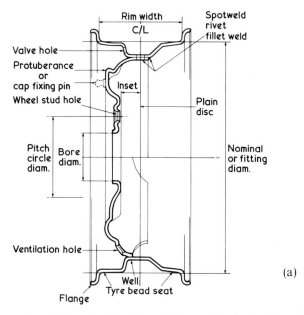

Fig. 7·1   This section through a typical pressed steel wheel shows the key features

the rubber is bonded. In the analysis of the tyre's behaviour the factors to consider are the design of the carcass, the composition of the rubber and the pattern of the tread ribs and blocks[1]. Each will be dealt with separately before total tyre designs are discussed.

7.2   TYRE CONSTRUCTION TYPES

There are three main types of tyre construction in use now. The oldest is the cross-ply; next in order comes the radial-ply, with two sub-divisions, steel belt and fabric belt; the latest is a compromise between the first two, the bias-belted, which has a cross-ply carcass supplemented by a fabric belt. Fig. 7.3 shows the differences in construction.

In a cross-ply tyre, which was the first design to be adopted, several layers of cords are laid diagonally across at alternating angles between the beads (stiff multi-stranded wire rings moulded into the open carcass lips each side to hold the inflated tyre against the wheel rim). The beads prevent the lips stretching and slipping

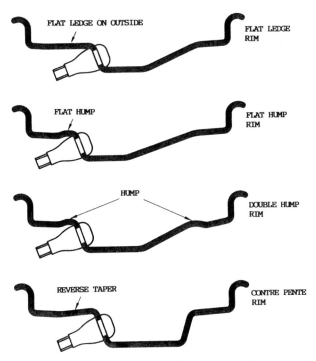

Fig. 7·2   Wheel rims can be made with several different profiles. The 'Double Hump' type provides the best defence against a deflated tyre leaving the rim. (*Courtesy Michelin Tyre plc*)

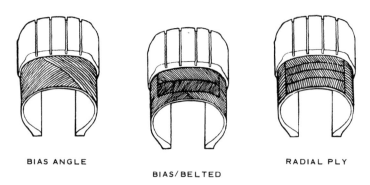

BIAS ANGLE   BIAS/BELTED   RADIAL PLY

Fig. 7·3   The construction of the three main types of tyres in use today. (*Courtesy Goodyear Tyre and Rubber Co.*)

over the upturned flange of the rim, except when mounting or demounting the tyre with the aid of levers.

The angles of the plies to the plane of the wheel set the balance between directional stability and ride comfort, because they control the way in which the tyre can distort. In most cross-ply tyres the most acceptable compromise is obtained when this angle is 45 degrees, although there are some designs where it has been reduced to as little as 30 degrees for specific stability or speed requirements.

For the past 20 years however there has been a long-term trend towards radial-plies, or separate cord layers laid in the same direction as the wheel plane and at 90 degrees to it. Fig. 7.4 shows the details of the carcass construction. This type allows the two conflicting design requirements to be handled separately, although the interaction of one ply against the other can never be eliminated totally.

In both cross-ply and radial-ply tyres the number of layers and the material they are made from are the factors which decide how the tyre will perform. In addition to these two main tyres, there are variations which cover the area between them with a number of hybrid permutations. Basically the plies can be of flexible fabrics like

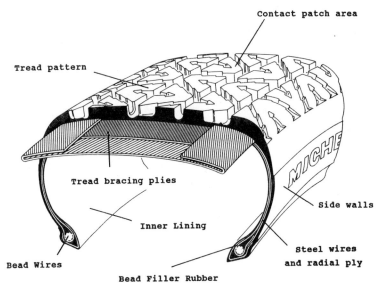

Fig. 7·4 This shows the various elements of a modern steel-braced radial tyre (*Courtesy Michelin Tyre plc*)

rayon, nylon and other members of the polyester family or more rigid materials such as glass fibre, steel or graphite.

The main physical characteristic that affects ride the most is the sidewall stiffness, although road inputs also contain a horizontal vector derived from the forward motion of the wheel. Soft sidewalls, on the other hand, delay the response between the wheel and the tread footprint and usually lead to unstable handling in extreme conditions.

The mechanism of the rolling tyre is complicated and not always as predictable as might be expected or desirable. As the distortion caused by the static mass of the vehicle in effect passes along the tread, a compression wave is formed across the contact patch which causes a shuffling and abrasive action on the rubber compound in contact with the road. When this wave is distorted by bumps, tractive effort from the driving wheels or braking forces, the situation becomes very confused indeed. Cornering loads and steering inputs add further to the pattern of distortion and the complexities

It would be extremely difficult and inappropriate to enter here into all the details of modern tyre design. That part of suspension engineering is best left to those involved in the tyre industry where there are many well-versed and experienced specialists. Suffice it to say at this point that all carcass designs have their own individual characteristics which need to be allowed for in the development of the total vehicle.

As already mentioned, the carcass of the cross-ply tyre consists of a number of layers of parallel cords held together by rubber, the cords in adjacent layers being at an angle to each other but each at the same angle to the car centre line, though on opposite sides. The exact angle of the plies to the central line is a compromise between tyre sideways stiffness and ability to swallow bumps, with an interest in rolling resistance and tyre wear as well. It varies between 25 and 45 degrees.

The carcass of the radial-ply tyre, Fig. 7.5, consists primarily of one, two or three layers of cords arranged radially; in addition there is under the tread a belt or breaker strip of steel or fabric cords which still have the adjacent layers arranged at an angle to each other, like the cross-ply tyre, at between 10 and 30 degrees to the tyre centre line. As compared with the cross-ply tyre the walls are much more flexible and the enveloping ability of the tyre is improved by this; the reinforcing belt under the tread increases sideways stability and by reducing movement between tread elements and road in the contact patch reduces both rolling resistance and tyre wear.

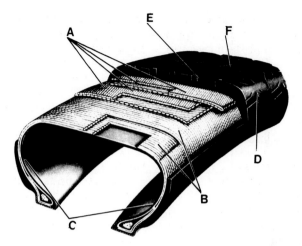

Fig. 7·5   Construction details of the typical radial tyre show here reveal four diagonal rayon plies (A) and two radial plies (B), wrapped round a 70-series inner lining (C). The tread rubber is moulded well round the shoulders (D) with deep drainage channels (F) in the large tread blocks (E). (*Courtesy B.F. Goodrich*)

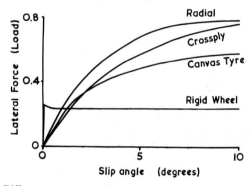

Fig. 7·6   Different tyre constructions cause slip angles to develop in different ways, as this illustration from work undertaken in 1976 clearly shows (*Courtesy Dunlop Rubber Co. Ltd.*)

The third variety shown in Fig. 7.3 has a cross-ply carcass to which has been added a circumferential belt. The carcass cords are generally at an angle to the tyre centre line of 25 to 45 degrees; the belt plies have greater angles than those of the radial tyre belt and lie between 20 and 45 degrees. The belt ply angle is usually about 5 degrees less than that of the carcass.

The differences in various properties of the first two types of tyre can be seen by reference to graphs. Figure 7.6 shows that the radial

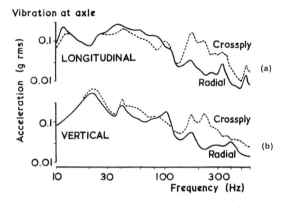

Fig. 7·7   These graphs compare the attenuation of vertical and horizontal vibrations by different tyres of tyres. (*Courtesy Dunlop Rubber Co. Ltd.*)

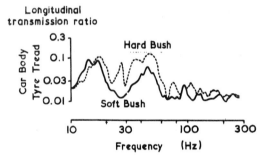

Fig. 7·8   Different types of tyres also require different stiffnesses of suspension bush, as these plots of longitudinal compliance show. (*Courtesy Dunlop Rubber Co. Ltd.*)

ply tyre develops given side force figures initially at much smaller drift angles than the cross-ply. Figures 7.7 shows the attenuation of vertical and horizontal vibrations, in the range 10 to 600 Hz. On vertical vibrations the radial tyre is superior almost throughout this range and particularly so at the higher frequencies. On the longitudinal vibrations the radial-ply tyre tends to be worse up to 100 Hz and noticeably better thereafter. Figure 7.8 shows that the longitudinal transmission efficiency can be considerably above about 18 Hz by the provision of suspension compliance. With this provision therefore, horizontal compliance, the radial tyre transmits noticeably less vibration, both vertical and longitudinal, to the car than the cross-ply. It therefore reduces both road noise and harshness.

In general, as would be expected, the bias-belted tyre has characteristics between the two earlier types, as far as cornering properties and tread wear are concerned. It is also worse than both earlier types in transmitting vertical vibrations.

7.3   ASPECT RATIOS

The vast majority of tyres are made to fit rims of 13, 14 and 15 in bead diameters, though 10 and 12 in rim sizes are also made in reasonable numbers and some high performance cars now use 16 in or even 17 in rims.

Tyres are now made in several aspect ratios[2]; as defined in Fig. 7.9, typically 0.83, 0.78, 0.70, 0.65, 0.60 and 0.50; the aspect ratio is section height/section width. Normal load deflections lie in the range of between 18 and 24 per cent of the section height. Aspect ratios have been diminishing but have now probably reached their practical minimum limit. The general choice of section width and depth and rim diameter needs to be made in conjunction with the tyre manufacturer and extensively investigated for its affects on ride and handling during the vehicle development stage. As the area of the contact patch is constant (approximately equal to the load carried divided by the inflation pressure), increased section width, for instance, will reduce the length of the contact patch and therefore allow less time for the tread blocks to remove the film of water on wet roads. The importance of this aspect in the car's operation must therefore be balanced against other factors. In some cases the tyre manufacturer may be able to offer a tyre with better

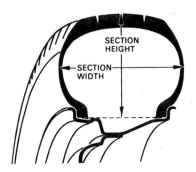

Fig. 7·9   Tyre aspect ratio is defined by the proportion of section width to height. (*Courtesy Michelin Tyre plc*)

escape routes for the water. The wider the tyre, the less reliance can be placed on sideways venting of water.

7.4 TUBELESS TYRES

Originally all tyres had inner tubes whose function was to hold under pressure the air which provided the cushioning of the pneumatic tyre. Over the years improvements were made in the material of these inner tubes and today they are usually made of butyl rubber which has remarkable air retaining properties, holding pressure for months. Most tyres however now dispense with inner tubes. This has meant that the rims must be airproof, that there must be a seal between tyre beads and the rim, that provision must be made in the tyre itself to reduce its permeability to air and that a tyre valve must be fitted in the hole in the rim previously used to permit the inner tube valve to pass through and be accessible for inflation and pressure testing.

The advantages of the tubeless tyre are:

(1) It is, even if only marginally in some cases, lighter than the tyre-tube combination.
(2) It is much easier to fit and replace, though care must be taken not to damage the tyre beads in handling.
(3) It has the property of not deflating suddenly; avoiding sudden deflation is a considerable move towards primary safety, by avoiding the swerve which can accompany it.

7.5 RUBBER COMPOUNDS AND TREAD PATTERNS

Probably more significant than the design of a tyre's carcass in ultimate handling terms is the nature of the compound used for the surface of the tread in contact with the road. Although the pure laws of physics governing sliding motion state quite clearly that the frictional forces (F) can never exceed the vertical loading (R), a rolling tyre does not behave in a theoretical way. As long as the wheel keeps turning, friction coefficients ($\mu = F/R$) will at the limit be greater than 1.0, especially on a coarsely dressed surface. Studies into this behaviour show that the rubber cogs into the macro features of the surface to generate a kind of rack and pinion effect.

By virtue of its origins, natural rubber is naturally a very gummy substance. Modern tyre treads are made from a mixture of natural and man-made materials which are blended together to form what is called a polymer.

When several molecules of a material combine together to form a larger, more complex molecule (often referred to as long molecules or macro-molecules) with the same empirical formula as the simple molecule, the process is known as polymerisation and the resultant structure is a polymer. Various different polymers of the same material can be formed by chemical reactions that result in the joining together of the basic chemical building blocks in different ways.

There are two major classes of polymers – plastics and elastomers (with different physical properties, as the names suggest) – while some polymers can also be formed into sheets of film or strands of synthetic fibres.

Plastics are formally defined as a large and varied group of materials that consist of, or contain as an essential ingredient, a substance of high molecular weight which (while solid in the finished state) at some stage in its manufacture is soft enough to be formed into various shapes – most usually through the application (either singly or together) of heat and pressure. These materials are then sub-divided into two distinct classes according to their fundamental behavioural characteristics.

One class, known as thermoplastics, become soft when exposed to heat and harden when cooled, regardless of how often they are subjected to this cycle. That means they do not work-harden or become brittle in any way. By alternately heating and cooling they can be reshaped many times over. When heated, they are mouldable; when cool, they are hard and rigid, but on reheating become soft and pliable again.

The other class, known as thermosetting plastics or thermosets, are set or cured into a permanent shape by heat. Once they have set they cannot be remelted or returned to their original state. Most materials of this type do not retain all their hardness at extreme heat, but they do maintain their manufactured shape. Elastomers are really synthetic rubbers and, like rubber, display various degrees of elastic properties. They are similar to plastics only insofar as they are composed of long molecular polymer chains. They cannot be moulded under pressure alone as they behave elastically when strained and try to recover most of their original shape when loadings are relaxed.

Elastomers differ from plastics (which have a rigid or crystalline structure) by having an essentially mobile (or colloidal) structure of their molecules. With difficulty elastomers can be moulded into forms that do retain their shape, but they normally allow considerable levels of distortion without plastic yielding or fracture. There is no sharp dividing line between plastics and elastomers. In fact, the transition between the two categories is so close that a new intermediate group of polymers known as thermosplastic elastomers has recently been developed.

Both categories of plastics and elastomers can be further sub-divided into materials commercially available in bulk as general purpose commodities and materials of a more specialised engineering nature where properties are tailored to the operating environment or load conditions. Man-made (synthetic) fibres form the basis of most modern clothing materials in the general commodity bracket. In the speciality group one class is known as the aramids, of which Kevlar is probably the most famous. Fibres are used to reinforce various plastics (such as epoxy resin), usually in the thermosetting category.

From that slight diversion into the field of chemical engineering it can be seen that almost every part of the tyre can be tailor made to provide the best engineering compromise for its performance requirements. What matters to the suspension engineer is how well the tread compound stands up to wear, how well it absorbs small amplitude vibrations and how it behaves as it approaches the ultimate limits of its frictional grip.

Excessive heat is the major enemy of materials like elastomers, but their characteristics also change at low temperatures and they can be seriously degraded by acids, chlorine, hydrogen, sulphur, oxides of nitrogen and even exposure over long periods to atmospheric oxygen. The tyre designer is committed to making sure there is plenty of useful life in every tyre long before any of these effects becomes a matter for concern.

Tread patterns today have developed a long way indeed from the simple circumferential grooves of 30 or even 20 years ago. The prime function of the tread is to provide drainage for water. On a clean, dry road the smooth slicks of a racing car or dragster place the most compound on the surface and give the best grip. When there is a film of water between the two, the tread must clear it away so that at least some of the compound can come into contact with a relatively dry part of the surface. The ability to disperse water rapidly is a critical feature in tyre tread design[2].

If there is too much water for the tyre to cope and an unbroken film remains, what starts as a simple lubrication layer builds up, allowing a wedge of water like a standing wave to force itself under the tyre and all control of the vehicle is lost. All tyres will eventually reach this stage, known as aquaplaning, if the water is deep enough or the speed is too high for the drainage available from the tread

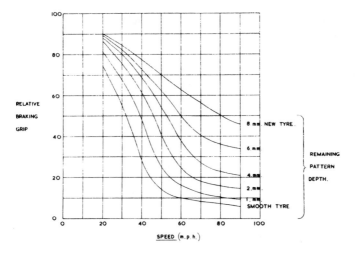

Fig. 7·10 This shows how wet road grip reduces with tread wear and speed on a typical motorway road surface in heavy rain (2.5 mm water depth) (*Courtesy Dunlop Rubber Co. Ltd.*)

pattern. Fig. 7.10 shows the deterioration that occurs as a tyre wears.

Other considerations in tread design are mostly concerned with the noise generated by the wind resistance of each separate block and the acoustic effects of their rhythm as they beat against the road. Computers are now used to design patterns which are randomly spaced to avoid natural resonances.

7.6 TYRE PROPERTIES AND CHARACTERISTICS

Recent advances in vehicle safety as demonstrated by reductions in road traffic accident statistics are largely attributable to improvement in tyre performance. To achieve the best combination of tyre and vehicle characteristics we need to know the various properties of the tyre. Many of these are associated with grip between tyre and road. In braking, for instance, Fig. 7.11(a), we see that on a wet road the major influence on the braking force coefficient is speed, with rate of slip the secondary item. On a dry road, Fig. 7.11(b), the differences due to speed are much less and up to between 16 and 20

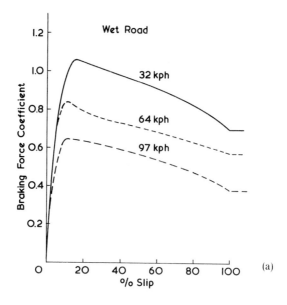

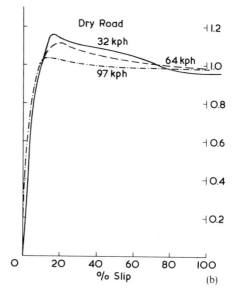

Fig. 7·11   These charts show how braking performance is affected by speed on (a) wet surfaces and (b) dry roads

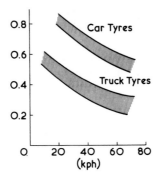

Fig. 7·12   Cross-ply car tyres sized 5.90-13 in. and inflated to 0.15 MN/m² and loaded with 300 kg each are compared here with 10.00-20 in. truck tyres at 0.55 NM/m² loaded with 2400 kg each

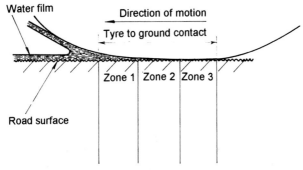

Fig. 7·13   The three zone concept of wet tyre grip suggests that Zone 1 is a region of unbroken water film, Zone 2 is a region of partial breakdown of the film and Zone 3 is a region of dry contact. (*Courtesy Dunlop Rubber Co.*)

per cent slip, the rate of slip is the most important factor. The locked sliding friction coefficient is one likely to interest the average driver in panic braking.

Figure 7.12 shows that there is a considerable size effect in the braking force available from car and truck size tyres, possibly due to the difference in inflation pressures and the types of compounds used for the tread rubber.

The reason for the sensitivity to speed is that on a wet road the contact patch can be divided into three sections: or zones, Fig. 7.13[3]. Zone 1 is where tyre and road surfaces are separated by an unbroken water film; zone 2 is where some of the water has been squeezed out and some contact occurs between tyre and road, and zone 3 is where all the water has been squeezed out and contact is general. According to work described by V. E. Gough in his discussion contribution to a paper by Tabor[4] as long ago as 1959, the coefficient of friction given by a tyre in a particular set of wet road conditions may be approximately represented as

$$\mu = \frac{A_1(a + b) + A_2(c + b) + A_3(d + b)}{W} \tag{7.1}$$

where A_1, A_2 and A_3 are the areas of the three zones, a is the hydrodynamic drag per unit area of unbroken water film, b the tyre hysteresis loss, c the drag per unit area of partial breakdown of lubricant film and d the frictional force per unit area of dry contact. W is the vertical load on the tyre.

If the whole of the contact patch falls into category (1) above there is no directional control, no braking force and the condition is referred to as aquaplaning.

Removing the water between tyre and road is a matter of providing drainage. It is easier to achieve satisfactory drainage if an open-textured road surface is a part of the tyre-road combination. The main responsibility for drainage however falls on the tyre designer and the tread elements must be disposed to provide transverse and circumferential channels for the escape of the water. Sipes, i.e. cuts across the tread pattern, are also provided because their wiping action helps to dry the tyre-road contact. The need for drainage is the reason for the British regulation forbidding the use of tyres with groove depths less than 1.5 mm. The road engineer, by providing an open texture surface, aggregates with reasonable coefficients of friction and proper surface drainage, can make important contributions towards minimising danger in wet conditions. Some road authorities are better than others in this respect. The inability of the human foot in combination with the car braking system to maintain peak braking coefficient is responsible for the desire to incorporate anti-lock devices into the braking system. The pioneer of these, the Dunlop 'Maxaret', developed for aircraft application and useful as much to avoid tyre destruction in a single landing as to obtain maximum retardation, measures the rate of wheel deceleration and lets off the brakes momentarily if this exceeds a design figure. More recent anti-lock systems (ABS) depend upon electronics and are becoming considerably cheaper and even standard in some cases as electronic components costs continue to fall.

The so-called circle of friction as shown in Fig. 7.14 has been used to explain the reduction in retarding ability while cornering force is

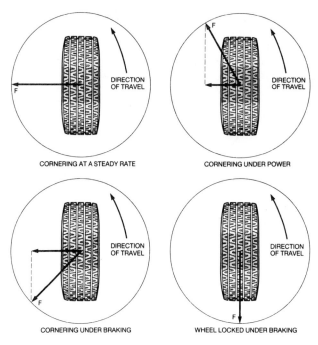

CORNERING AT A STEADY RATE

CORNERING UNDER POWER

CORNERING UNDER BRAKING

WHEEL LOCKED UNDER BRAKING

Fig. 7·14 The circle of friction suggests that the force available from the tyre has a limit *F* that takes no account of direction so that less braking is available when cornering and less cornering power is available when braking or accelerating

being developed, and vice versa. This is an oversimplified explanation; the relative availability of sideways and longitudinal forces depends upon the parts of the contact patch where actual sliding first develops with the development of the different forces. The curves showing this interdependability are given in Fig. 7.15, at two different speeds.

Another characteristic which depends upon speed is the rolling radius of the tyre. We need to differentiate between the rolling circumference of the tyre and the height of the centre of the rim. Figure 7.16 shows the latter for equivalent sizes of cross- and radial-ply tyres. The further difference between these two types of tyre is that the rolling circumference of the cross-ply tyre increases considerably more with speed and inflation than that of radial-ply tyre, in which the constricting influence of the belt makes itself felt.

Rolling resistance also varies considerably with speed and again there is noticeable difference between cross- and radial-ply tyres.

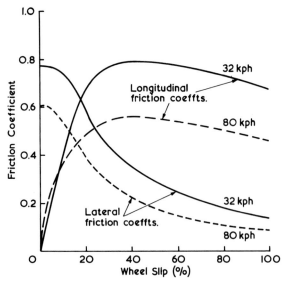

Fig. 7·15   Longitudinal and lateral friction coefficients vary with speed and wheel slip

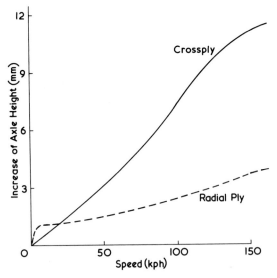

Fig. 7·16   Radial-ply tyres are much less prone to 'grow' in diameter with speed than cross-ply tyres, as shown by these measurements of wheel centre height. Both tyres were loaded to 300 kg at an inflation pressure of 0.15 MN/m². The radial tyre was size 155SR-15 in and the cross-ply 5.60-15 in

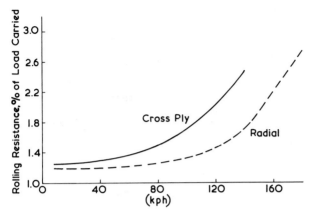

Fig. 7·17   The rolling resistance of cross-ply tyres tends to increase with speed earlier than for radial tyres

Figure 7.17 shows comparative figures for the two, for a particular load and inflation. The major cause of the considerable increase in resistance, above characteristic speeds for the two types of tyre, is the setting up of standing waves in the tread.

There is a difference between the effective rolling resistance of the non-cornering tyre and that subjected to sideways force. As we have already mentioned, the major reason for this is the component of the sideways force, normal to the tyre plane, which acts in the direction of movement of the wheel. The relative importance of this can be seen in Fig. 7.18, which shows how little of the increase is due to increased resistance in the plane of the wheel.

The effect of braking and traction on rolling resistance can be seen in Fig. 7.19. The difference between the two lies in the part of the contact patch which first develops actual sliding.

The most important tyre characteristic from the control or handling aspect of the car is its relationship between cornering force and slip angle, Fig. 7.20. The figures in this case are taken to much higher slip angles than we have considered before.

Steering feel depends far more on the self-aligning torque of a tyre as it develops sideways force than on caster angle of the kingpin axis. Figure 7.21 shows how this varies with load and slip angle; it has diminished noticeably at 10 degrees slip angle and is entirely negative at 20 degrees.

Inflation pressure, by changing tyre deflection under load and hence the length of the contact patch, affects both self-aligning

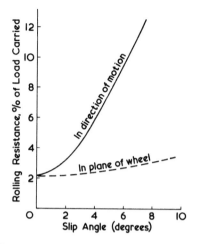

Fig. 7·18   The difference between the true increase in rolling resistance with slip angle and the effect of the slip in providing a component of sideways force in the direction of motion is shown here. The tyre is a 7.50-14 in cross-ply carrying 400 kg at 0.17 MN/m² inflation pressure

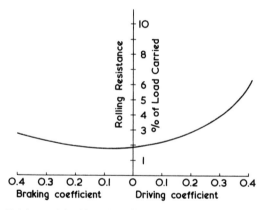

Fig. 7·19   Driving and braking also affect rolling resistance but not to the same extent. The tyre here is size 8.20–15 in carrying 650 kg at 0.17 MN/m² inflation pressure

torque and cornering force[5]. Figure 7.22 shows how self-aligning torque at a given load varies with inflation pressure through a range of slip angles. Figure 7.22 shows how cornering force varies with load carried and inflation pressure at two slip angles.

One of the components of the outward force at each end of the car

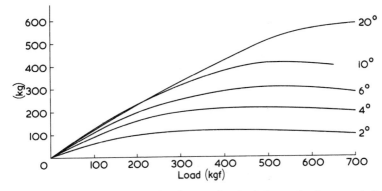

Fig. 7·20   This graph of cornering force against load shows what happens at slip angles up to 20°. The tyre size used in these tests was 8.00–14 in. with an inflation pressure of 0.14 MN/m² at a speed of 30 km/h

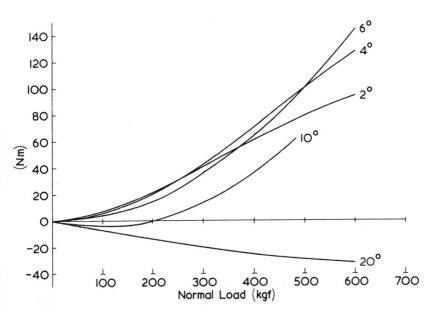

Fig. 7·21   By the time the slip angle reached 20° in this test the self-aligning torque had become completely negative. Tyre size was 8.00–14 in at 0.14 MN/m² and a speed of 30 km/h

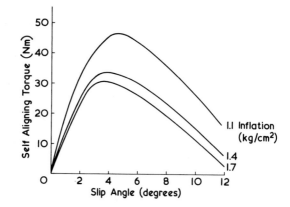

Fig. 7·22   Self aligning torque decreases with higher inflation pressures. Tyre size was 5.20–13 in. carrying 250 kg at 40 km/h

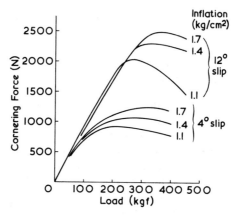

Fig. 7·23   Cornering force at given slip angles is reduced by lower inflation pressures and the peak also occurs at a lower load carried

while cornering is camber thrust. Figure 7.24 shows how this varies with the load carried and the camber angle of the wheel.

7.7   NON-DIMENSIONAL TYRE DATA

Various methods have been used to obtain the tyre data required for handling calculations, the principal variation being between the use of a drum and testing on a flat surface, either the road itself or a

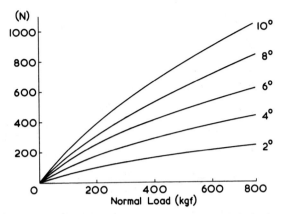

Fig. 7·24   Camber thrust is a somewhat smaller proportion of the load carried as load increases. Tyre size was 6.40–13 in. inflated to 0.2 MN/m²

moving belt offering a flat surface. If drums are used corrections should be made for the drum-induced distortion; flat testing surfaces are obviously desirable.

For sideways forces the effects of load carried, steer or slip angle, and camber angle need to be found; the friction coefficient of the surface also affects the results; and the existence of braking or traction forces will certainly reduce the maximum sideways forces available. Whatever the method used, finding all the information needed is time consuming and expensive; and because the results depend on the extent of tread wear, and its type, a lot of tyres are required for any particular size and construction. The possibility of being able to deduce all characteristics as a result of simple tests on a static tyre is so attractive that any possibility of it must be studied theoretically and the results of such study checked by tests. That possibility may still be remote, but Radt and Milliken[7] suggest methods of non-dimensionalising tyre data which considerably reduce the tests required. The resulting test programme suggested by them comprises three types of tests:

(1)   Cornering stiffness, defined as the slope of the cornering force-steer angle curve, and pneumatic trail, defined as the slope of the aligning moment-slip angle curve, as functions of load at small steer angles (say 1 degree, 2 degrees and 3 degrees).

(2)   Maximum side force at a single large value of non-dimensional steer angle, at several loads over the desired range.

(3)   All forces and moments over the full range of steer angles at one intermediate load.

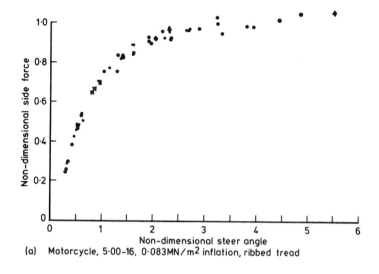

(a) Motorcycle, 5·00-16, 0·083MN/m² inflation, ribbed tread

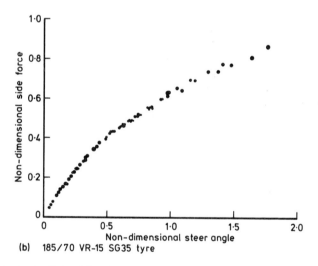

(b) 185/70 VR-15 SG35 tyre

Fig. 7·25 Section 7.7 explains about the much reduced tests required to make use of the non-dimensionalising technique. It is interesting that the tests represented by (a) were taken over a load range from 45 kg to 358 kg, and those for (d) over a load range from 182 to 909 kg, without too much scatter in either case. The technique is aimed at getting enough information to carry out handling calculations without too great an expense or delay. (Reproduced from Radt and Milliken[7]. *Courtesy of the Council of the Institution of Mechanical Engineers*)

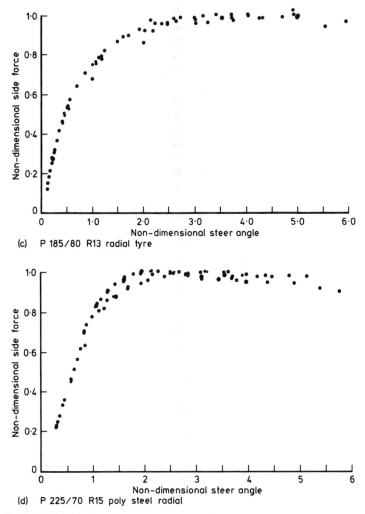

(c) P 185/80 R13 radial tyre

(d) P 225/70 R15 poly steel radial

Fig. 7·25   *Continued.*

Figure 7.25 (Fig. 1 of Reference 7) with results from four different types of tyre explains the need for these tests: to establish the slope of the low steer angle end, the final limit and a point on the curve near the 'knee'. It ought eventually to be possible to establish the low steer angle end by static tests to arrive at load deflection curves to sideways forces alone and to combinations of sideways force and torque about a vertical axis. This should also give pneumatic trail.

Fitting a curve to the results of the any of the tyres of Fig. 7.24, having obtained end conditions and an intermediate precision point, suggests the polynomial equation and experience will show whether sequential orders can be used or a more complicated selection of orders is necessary.

Proposals are made by Radt and Milliken[7] to relate the braking force to the slip ratio, to combine cornering and braking, and steer and camber angle effects. A study of this reference is recommended to those interested.

7.8   TWIN TYRES AND RUN-FLAT TYRE SYSTEMS

Tyres mounted in dual formation have been used on rear axles of commercial vehicles for over 50 years, to increase the load capacity easily and cheaply, with a degree of extra safety in the event of an unexpected and sudden deflation. Twin rear wheels also featured on pre-war competition cars for a spell to improve traction in short sprints.

The use of double tyres on single rims front and rear for cars is a relatively new and controversial idea that has varied in its success. In 1978, Dunlop tried fitting two slim cross-ply motor cycle tyres to a Jaguar to assess the potential of such a system, but their test results were not encouraging and they abandoned the idea quite quickly. Towards the end of 1983 a Geneva-based inventor, Juhan, revealed a fully engineered system as shown in Fig. 7.26 with more significant effects.

The rationale behind twin narrow section tyres is quite simple. If a very large drainage channel is cut around the centre tread of a high performance 50-series tyre, it dramatically reduces the possibilities of aquaplaning on deep standing water. This effect was proved by various comparisons performed by car manufacturers and consumer magazines. The results of regular tyre tests conducted in Germany are reproduced in Fig. 7.27. By separating the two halves into their own air chambers for safety, two relatively narrow tyres were mounted side by side, making manufacture much easier and the costs significantly lower. More importantly, the system then offered a valuable and unique back-up against the dynamic effects of a sudden blow-out at speed and the means to continue the journey with minimum disruption.

In his first experiments Juhan tried mounting two very narrow steel-belted radial tyres – size 125/85SR-15 in as used in the Citroen 2CV - on specially made wheels which he fitted to a Lotus Esprit. On its standard 235/60VR-15 in tyres in heavy rain the Lotus proved

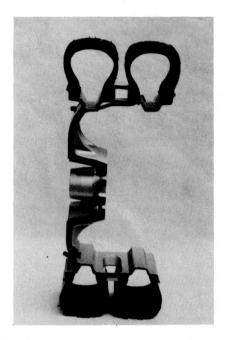

Fig. 7·26   The JJD twin tyre system comprises two narrow tyres mounted on a single rim

very prone to aquaplaning, but on the twin tyres the problem disappeared. The space between them acted as a gutter; and the narrow tyres themselves cut through the standing water more easily and cleared away the water beneath their treads, as shown in Fig. 7.27.

The safety benefits were fully proved. If one tyre was deflated, stability was retained and the car could still be driven (at higher speeds and for longer distances than competitive run-flat systems) without too much effect on its handling, provided the remaining tyre on that rim was inflated to a considerably higher pressure to compensate for its higher loading.

Negative factors of twin tyres, apart from their higher cost which can be offset against the deleted spare wheel, include a deterioration in ride comfort on some cars and heavier steering. The same problems tend to exist in cars using ultra-low aspect ratio conventional tyres and could doubtless be resolved by detail development and power assisted steering.

Before the JJD system appeared there had been several previous

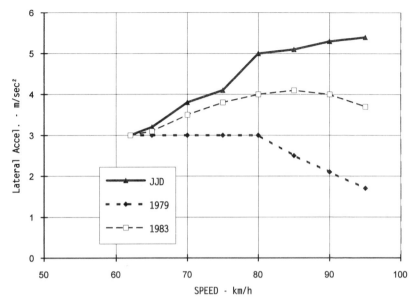

Fig. 7·27   Regular wet road tyre tests show the improvements in tyre performance and the advantages offered by the JJD twin system

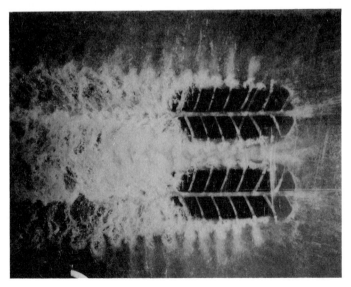

Fig. 7·28   The benefits of twin tyres in action are shown clearly in this view taken from the underside of a glass road surface at 100 km/h

ideas on eliminating the dangers and inconvenience of a punctured tyre to varying degrees. The Dunlop Denovo launched in the late 1960s as the first real run-flat design was intended to dispense with the spare and allow the driver to continue at reduced speed for up to 100 miles with the carcass running against the rim. It relied on a ring of small capsules of sealant/lubricant carried inside the air chamber being ruptured by the weight of the vehicle on the deflated tread and positive bead location to prevent the tyre running off the rim.

Although the Denovo was offered for a while as optional equipment on the BL Mini and the Rover SD1 range, it was comparatively expensive and failed to make much impact.

In 1983 Continental Gummi-Werke released details of their revolutionary new tyre system, which was under development until 1990. It failed to reach the market because of the manufacturing difficulties of providing the smooth inner surfaces it required to operate on low cost wheel rims and the inevitable market forces of a unique system in a highly competitive commercial environment.

The ContiTyreSystem (CTS) concept as shown in Fig. 7.29 was a run-flat design that uses a kind of 'inside-out' wheel rim and bead: The tyre bead wraps round the outside of the wheel rim and is retained by a hollow-section insert. This does several things for the car designer and for the vehicle operator in step. It saves space in the spider/rim area of the wheel, where conventional rims have their well, allowing bigger brakes to be installed with more air around

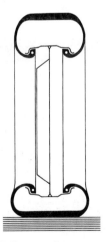

Fig. 7·29   In the Continental CTS system the tyre seats on the area of the wheel rim internally so that it cannot leave the rim when deflated

them. It takes the S-bend out of the carcass sidewall, allowing it to flex more easily for improved ride comfort (or for lower sections to give the same ride comfort as before).

Removing most of the rigidity in the bead area allows the footprint area to develop more freely, with more uniform pressure distribution on the ground and more effective use of the tread area. The energy wasted in the distortion of a conventional stiff bead area is saved, which aids fuel economy. But the real claim for the CTS is its ability to stay wrapped round the rim when deflated. It is so firmly locked on the rim, say Conti, that it is possible to maintain full control and drive for several hundred miles on a flat CTS tyre, eliminating the need for a spare wheel.

The arguments for and against spare wheels have been raging for many years and were all voiced when the Dunlop Denovo was first launched. Most drivers when they get a puncture want to fit the spare as quickly and easily as possible and get motoring again, without restrictions. The space-saver wheel and tyre now supplied with Audis, Porsches, Golf GTis, Saabs and many US models has conditioned quite a large section of the motoring public away from that ideal. And tyres are now so resistant to punctures that the statistical average incidence is only one puncture every five years.

In 1990 after seven years' development CTS disappeared from the technical scene in much the same way as the Dunlop Denovo had before it. Apparently, it could not function effectively without the high-precision polished alloy wheels on which it had been developed.

7.9   TYRE CHARACTERISTICS: EFFECT OF SIDEWAYS FORCES

The sideways flexibility of a tyre arises partly from the deflection of the tread elements and partly from the carcass deflection. A new tyre, with full depth tread elements, is therefore more flexible sideways than one which has worn and thereby reduced the depth of the tread elements. An observant driver is most likely to notice this if he goes from worn to new tyres on a given car. Some cases have been reported of increased sideways flexibility as the tyre wears; this must be due to the increase of carcass flexibility with use.

Tyre characteristics in cornering are best understood by thinking of the sideways flexibility being the result of the separate tread elements and carcass flexibilities. The following explanations are only approximately correct but help to fix the tyre behaviour in our minds.

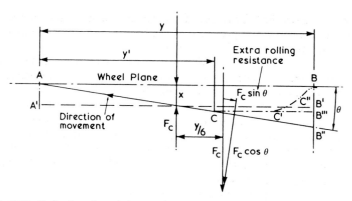

Fig. 7·30   Deflection of tread elements in contact patch; stationary tyre, dotted line, area ABB'A'A: rolling tyre (or stationary tyre with appropriate applied torque about

steering axis), full line, area ABB"A, self-aligning torque $= \dfrac{F_c y}{6}$. The reasons for the

extra rolling resistance of a drifting tyre and for its self-aligning torque can be seen. If the tread element reaches its limit of adhesion at a distance y' from the front of the contact patch, the chain dotted line, an approximate idealised solution, shows how the modified tread element deflection pattern will affect the sideways force for a given

drift angle, and also the self-aligning torque $\left(= F_c \dfrac{y'(3y + 2y')}{6(2y + y')} \right)$, area ABB'"CA. It is

likely that the actual trend element deflection pattern will depart from the ACB'" boundary as indicated by the double chain dotted line ACC'C"B due to the reduction in vertical force on the tread elements as they approach the end of the contact patch

Applying a sideways force to a static, load carrying, tyre and wheel will produce a sideways deflection x, dotted line in Fig. 7.30, in those tread elements which are in contact with the ground. Accepting the broad division of tyres into cross-ply and radial ply, the latter with rigid or semi-rigid breaker, we would expect the cross-ply carcass deflection to be much more local to the contact patch than that of the rigid breaker tyre, in which the sideways stiffness of the breaker under the tread will spread the sideways deflection over a greater length of carcass. We would therefore, correctly, expect the cross-ply tyre to be more flexible sideways than the radial ply tyre; and of the radial ply tyres the rigid breaker, steel band, to be stiffer than the semi-rigid, fabric band, tyre.

We are, however, mostly concerned with the behaviour of the rolling tyre. There cannot be sideways forces between the tread element and the road until they are in contact, so that the pattern of tread element sideways deflection is broadly that of the full line in Fig. 7.30. There is still an average deflection of x but this implies an extreme deflection of $2x$ on the rearmost element. To achieve this deflection pattern the wheel must move in a direction at a slip angle θ to the plane of the wheel, where $\varpi = \sin^{-1}(2x/y)$, y being the length of the contact patch.

The greater sideways stiffness of the radial ply tyre means that x is less and therefore the slip angle is less; it is of the order of half that of the cross-ply tyre.

The full line deflection pattern of Fig. 7.30 can be applied to a static tyre by the application of (1) a sideways force, and (2) a torque sufficient to deflect the plane of the wheel by an angle θ from its original position.

Since sideways deflections of tread elements are approximately proportional to the forces involved we can say that the area of the rectangle AA′B′B in Fig. 7.30, corresponding to a given sideways force F_c, must be equal to that of the triangle AB″B. The resultant force from this triangle will act through its centre of area $2y/3$ behind the front of the triangle or $y/6$ behind the wheel axis. The torque required to turn the static wheel to the position of Fig. 2.25 will therefore be $(F_c)y/6$ and there will be a self-aligning torque of this magnitude trying to straighten the rolling wheel.

With the force F_c perpendicular to the plane of the wheel but the direction of motion of the wheel at an angle θ to this there will be a component F_c, of amount $F_c \sin \theta$, resisting the forward movement of the wheel. This accounts for the apparent increase in rolling resistance of car when cornering.

The relationship of the sideways force F_c, the extra 'rolling' resistance $F_c \sin \theta$, and the self-aligning torque $(F_c)y/6$ is indicated in Fig. 7.30.

If we consider the case of the wheel with camber angle φ, Fig. 7.31, we see that the tread portions within the contact patch are constrained to lie along a straight line joining the two ends of the contact patch rather than the portion of the ellipse which in plan view represents the path of the centre of the tread of an undeflected tyre. If the tyre vertical deflection under load is x_v the maximum deflection of a tread element is $(x_v) \sin \varphi$ and the sideways force or camber thrust about 2/3 of that which would occur with a deflection $(x_v) \sin \varphi$ over the whole length of the contact patch.

In the days when front wheels had generally larger camber angles than are customary today, it was usual to provide those wheels with a toe-in which resulted in zero sideways force on the rolling tyre. This was judged likely to give minimum tyre wear.

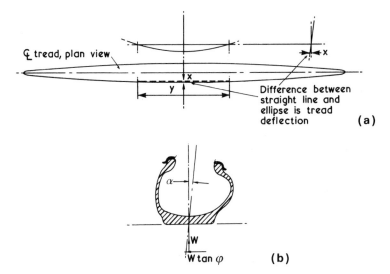

Fig. 7·31.(a) Origin of camber thrust. (b) Relationship of camber angle, load carried and force developed

7.10   TYRE SLIP ANGLE NEARING LIMIT OF ADHESION

The behaviour pattern so far described refers to a tyre and wheel carrying a given constant weight and with tread element deflections dependent on no slip between them and the ground over the whole length of the contact patch. This is only the beginning of the story.

As the total sideways force increases, and therefore the force per tread element and its corresponding deflection, there must come a time when the tread element towards the back end of the contact patch is asked to provide (by virtue of its growing sideways deflection) a sideways force higher than can be expected from the vertical load carried by that tread element and the coefficient of friction between it and the road. If this happens, Fig. 7.30, at a point y' behind the front of the contact patch, the element should ideally maintain its deflection $y' \tan \theta$, at the point where it starts to slip, until the back end of the contact patch at B‴. This reduces the sideways force developed in relation to a given angle θ in the proportion

$$1 - \frac{(y - y')^2}{y^2} \qquad (7.2)$$

and the moment arm is also reduced in the proportion

$$\frac{y'(3y - 2y')^2}{y(2y - y')} \qquad (7.3)$$

The self-aligning torque is the product of these two; in order to put a value to it we have to relate F_c to the area yx or to $y \tan \theta$. Expressed as simply as possible this means that above a certain level of sideways force depending on the load carried and the coefficient of friction between tyre and road the slip angle will increase more rapidly than the sideways force and the moment arm of that sideways force behind the kingpin axis will diminish also.

7.11   TYRE CHARACTERISTICS: EFFECT OF LOAD AND INFLATION PRESSURE

The behaviour pattern described is oversimplified. The carcass deflection, especially with rigid breaker tyres, will spread beyond the

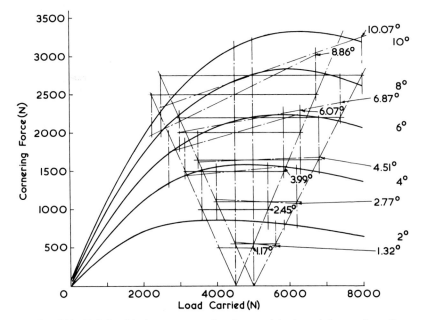

Fig. 7·32   Relationship between cornering force and load carried at various slip angles showing the effect of tyre loading

length of the contact patch, so that the tread element will already have some sideways deflection before it touches down.

Moreover, towards the end of the contact patch the load carried by the tread element will tend to diminish and the pattern of deflection will follow the line CC'C"B rather than CC'B"'B in Fig. 7.30. As one would expect, the pattern of slip angle and sideways force is also affected by the load carried by the tyre and by its inflation pressure. For a given inflation pressure the sideways force – slip angle characteristics of a given size tyre are shown in Fig. 7.32. We see that for each slip angle there is an optimum load carried at which the sideways force is highest; loads above or below this optimum imply smaller sideways forces for a given slip angle. One way of explaining this is that for higher loads, although the length of the contact patch is increased and therefore more tread elements are in contact and have to be deflected, the greater vertical deflection of the carcass implies more sideways flexibility and there is an overall loss of stiffness. Correspondingly for lower loads, with reduced vertical deflection making a carcass stiffer, the shorter contact patch means fewer tread elements in contact and an overall loss of stiffness.

In looking for typical tyre behaviour one tends at first to think of

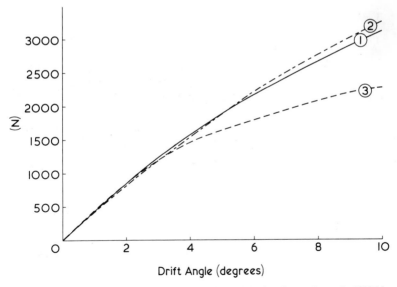

Fig. 7·33 Relationship of load transference on cornering force. Curve 1: 4500 N load, Curve 2 outer wheel, Curve 3 inner wheel

plotting the slip angles against the sideways forces for a given load carried by the tyre, as in Fig. 7.33 where Curve (1) is in effect a section on the 4500 N load line. This is interesting and we observe how towards the upper limit of sideways force the slip angle increases progressively more rapidly and eventually, for reasons which we have seen above, with the tread elements beginning to slip sideways closer and closer to the front of the contact patch, the slip becomes a slide and control is lost.

When a car turns a corner, the loads on its outer wheels increase and the loads on the inner wheels reduce. If there is a linear relationship between sideways acceleration and weight transfer we can construct, for the front and rear of a given car at a given state of load, a diagram shown in Fig. 7.32 which show the loads on inner and outer wheels at given sideways accelerations and so deduce the slip angles. The behaviour characteristic for these is effectively another section through the original diagram, giving the other curves of Fig. 7.33. Sliding off obviously occurs at lower sideways forces; but this is what we get in operation.

REFERENCES

1. Setright, L. J. K., 'Automobile Tyres', *Chapman & Hall* (1972)
2. Kovac, F. J., 'Tire Technology', *The Goodyear Tire and Rubber Co.* (1973)
3. Allbert, B. J., Walker, J. C. and Maycock, G., 'Tyre to Wet Road Friction', *Proc. Auto. Div. I. Mech. E.* Vol. 180 Pt. 2A No.4 (1965–66)
4. Tabor, D., 'Friction of Rubber on Lubricated Surfaces', *Rev. Gen. du Caoutchouc.* 36 (No.10), 1409 (1959)
5. El-Gindy, M. and Ilosvai, L., 'An Experimental Investigation into Vehicle Response During Steering and Braking Manoevres', *Int. J. of Vehicle Design*, Vol. 2, No. 4 (November 1981)
6. Clark, S. K. (edited), 'Mechanics of the Pneumatic Tire', *U.S. National Bureau of Standards*, Monograph No. 122 (1971)
7. Radt, H. S. and Milliken, W. F., 'Non-Dimensional Tyre Data for Vehicle Simulation', C133/83, *Road Vehicle Handling*, I. Mech. E. Conference Publications (1983–85)
8. Dinkel, J., 'Comparison Test: Radial Tires For Your Car', *Road & Track* (August 1972)

8
Steering

8.1 DYNAMIC FUNCTION OF THE STEERING SYSTEM

The suspension system of a car is intended to allow the vehicle to accept vertical irregularities in the roads on which it travels with as little disturbance as possible. In the same way, the steering system allows the wheels to follow horizontal irregularities in those roads without directional disturbances. But at the same time its primary function is to give the driver directional control with sufficient accuracy to choose his best course round corners, to avoid other vehicles and stationary obstructions and to manoeuvre the car efficiently at low speed when parking.

The main conflicts entering into the design of steering systems concern the isolation from feedback of road shocks, while retaining sufficient road feel for positive control, and striking an acceptable compromise between light steering efforts when parking and sufficient 'weight' at speed. Much of the dynamic effects attributed by customers to the steering system are the result of suspension geometry and wheel control factors, especially in regard to toe settings and dynamic toe changes either at the front or rear.

8.2 UNDERSTEER AND OVERSTEER

Under some conditions of steady state cornering the rear end of the car hangs out to the extent that the rear tyre slip angles exceed those of the front tyres, giving rise to what is known as an 'oversteering' characteristic. Under other conditions, the rear tyre slip angles may be less than at the front, in which case the car is considered to be 'understeering'. The condition when front and rear tyre slip angles are the same is a state of equilibrium known as 'neutral'. In this case the actual centre about which the car is rotating is half way along the

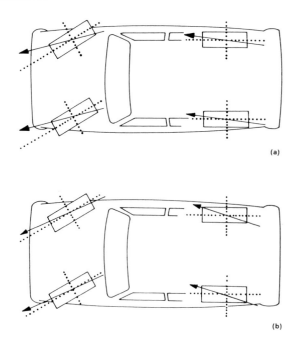

Fig. 8·1 (a) In understeer the slip angles of the front tyres are greater than the slip angles of the rear tyres, loading the steering against the driver's input for maximum stability. (b) In an oversteering car the rear slip angles are greater, effectively unloading the driver's input and eventually requiring corrective steering action

wheelbase, i.e. $x = L/2$, Fig. 8.2. For an arbitrary figure of slip angle 5 degrees and a wheelbase of 2.75 m this implies a radius R_o of some 15.75 m. At 25 km/hr this means a sideways acceleration of 0.31 g, reasonably appropriate for cross-ply tyres. For radial-ply tyres a slip angle of 2.5 degrees would correspond to $R_o = 31.5$ m and a sideways acceleration of 0.3 g at a speed of 35 km/hr. It follows that for this condition of coinciding front and rear wheel tracks the effective front steering angle has to equal the rear tyre slip angle, i.e. 5 degrees or 2.5 degrees, depending on the type of tyre, in the conditions chosen above. To achieve this the actual steering angle must be the sum of the front and rear slip angle. Higher speeds at these radii will cause the tail of the car to swing out relative to the path of the front axle.

In terms of avoiding impacts with other objects, stationary or otherwise, the driver has to remember that he must allow for the effective width of the rear of the car when turning being greater than

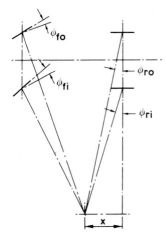

Fig. 8·2   When sideways forces produce slip angles in a tyre, the centre about which the car turns in relation to the wheelbase moves forwards by the distance *x*. This diagram shows the condition where front and rear slip angles are equal and the car is handling with so-called neutral characteristics. As the steered angles for the inner and outer wheels are slightly different, the slip angles are different in proportion

the actual static distance between its two sides, possibly by an embarrassing amount. Although this has assumed front wheel steering it is effectively universal for the reasons given in Appendix 1.12, unless the car has an all-wheel steering system such as that referred to in Section 8.10.

8.3   LOCK ANGLES: EFFECT OF TYRE SLIP ANGLES

Simplifying again for the sake of an easy understanding and making the assumption that front and rear slip angles are the same, we see from Fig. 8.3, given that the angle subtended by a secant at the circumference of a circle is a constant, that the locus of intersection of the radii of the outer wheels, when allowance is made for slip angles, is on a circle from centre A. The corresponding locus for the inner wheel radii intersection lies on a radius from centre B, A and B both being half way along the wheelbase and on lines perpendicular to and bisecting R_{ro} and R_{ri} respectively. There is a slight discrepancy between the two loci. Moreover, it is clear that equal slip angles on both rear tyres will produce parallel lines from the two rear tyre contact points. Also, equal slip angles on both front wheels will maintain a constant angle at the intersection of R_{fo} and R_{fi},

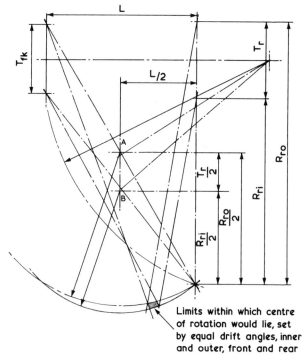

Fig. 8·3 Aiming for as nearly as possible equal inner and outer slip angles front and rear gives us an area within which the rotation centre of a car in a turn should fall. The reasoning is explained in the text

which again will lie on an arc of a circle whose centre is the intersection of the bisecting perpendiculars of R_{fo} and R_{fi}, which also by definition must lie on the car centre line. The net result of all this is that equal slip angles give an area, an irregular quadrilateral with two straight and two radiused sides, rather than a point intersection. What we do also see, however, is that within the normal range of steering angles, and even at full lock, very small differences from the no tyre slip angle lock angles would be required to achieve equal slip angles on the front wheels. It seems reasonable to accept the desirability of the relative lock angles calculated from the assumption of no slip angle and swallow the small differences in slip angle which this will imply, especially as the rear tyres will have slightly unequal slip.

The purist might aim for equal front slip angles at an average front slip angle, if one could determine what that might be. The differences would probably lie well within the expected range of tyre tolerances. This characteristic is often referred to as the 'Ackermann effect', Ackermann was merely the patentee of a communicated invention, not the inventor of the arrangement he patented.

8.4   FORCES IN STEERING SYSTEM: STATIONARY CAR

The highest forces in a steering system occur when the wheels are turned with the car stationary (Gough[1], discussion) gives a formula for the approximate value of the static torque to turn a non-rolling tyre as:

$$T = \frac{\mu W^{3/2}}{3P^{1/2}}$$

(8.1)

where T = torque (Nm), μ = coefficient of friction, W = load (N), and P = tyre pressure (N/m^2). On dry concrete or tarmac μ can be taken as 1.0. So long as the kingpin axis meets the ground within the contact patch the torque T is hardly affected by kingpin offset from the middle of the contact patch.

With many cars now fitted with power-assisted steering and human effort no longer the limiting factor there is more probability of steering systems being subjected to forces greater than those resulting from turning the wheels of the stationary car. The vehicle for instance may be parked or manoeuvred close to a kerb; more rarely there may be off-highway operation in which the tyre tread pattern may sink into the ground. The former may result in kingpin torques 1.5 to 1.75 times the static torque itself; the latter may give values of twice the static torque. Consideration should be given to such possible torques in stressing the steering system parts; the stress level permitted can be chosen in relation to the estimated frequency of occurrence to lie somewhere between the fatigue and elastic limits of the materials.

8.5   THE MOVING CAR: SELF-ALIGNING TORQUE

As a rough guide, the maximum steering torque with a moving vehicle is one third of the static torque. An example of the way self-aligning torque varies with cornering force is shown in Fig. 8.5. The load carried by the tyre is 5340 N (544 kg). The inflation pressure is not known; on an assumed 207 kN/m^2 inflation pressure (30 lbf/in^2) the static torque by Equation 8.1 would be 286 Nm which is 3.4

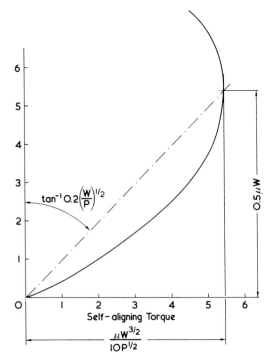

Fig. 8·4 This is Dr. Gough's construction for arriving at a typical curve of the type shown in Fig. 8.5. (*Courtesy Institution of Mechanical Engineers*)

times the maximum value in Fig. 8.5. Gough in fact suggests a maximum value for the self-aligning torque of $0.1 \ \mu W^{3/2}/P^{1/2}$, which is 1/3.3 of the static torque. The approximate form of the self-aligning torque-cornering force curve is that of Fig. 8.5.

8.6 EFFECT OF CASTER ANGLE

The effect of caster angle on total torque about the kingpin[2] is shown in Fig. 8.6, where the three curves are self-aligning torque for 3 degrees negative, zero and 3 degrees positive caster angle. Gough points out that the torque curve for 3 degrees negative caster has the disadvantage that over the middle part of the range of cornering coefficient it remains relatively constant and therefore gives no indication of sideways acceleration. Negative caster also has the disadvantage of possible instability of the wheels in low μ

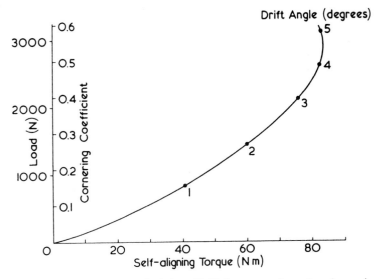

Fig. 8·5   This is another way of relating self-aligning torque, slip angle and cornering coefficient, used by the late Dr. V. E. Gough. (*Courtesy of Mechanical Engineers*)

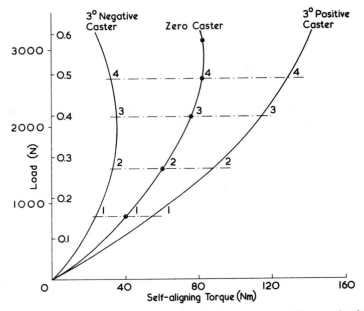

Fig. 8·6   The influence of caster angle on self-aligning torque while cornering is shown here. (*Courtesy Institution of Mechanical Engineers*)

conditions. Zero caster has the advantage of still retaining the slight reduction in kingpin torque before reaching the limit of adhesion which to the driver is a useful indication of when that limitation of adhesion is near. This would seem to be a disadvantage of the curve for 3 degrees positive camber, however, where the only indication of approaching sliding of the front wheels is a reduction in the rate of increase of kingpin torque with increasing sideways acceleration. The question of what caster angle is finally preferred would seem to depend on the type of car, the tyre characteristics, the use or otherwise of power assistance for the steering and the nature of that power assistance. Figure 8.6, or more correctly a similar diagram for the actual tyres being used in the conditions applying, is useful to the development engineer by reminding him of what is happening and helping him to understand his observations.

8.7   STEERING BALL JOINTS

The relative movements of steering levers and rods, especially track rods, demand the use of joints capable of moving, fortunately within limited angles, in any direction. These movements are most easily accommodated by the use of ball joints. The ball pin is usually made of case-hardened or possibly through-hardened steel. The thread on the end of the shank is generally left unhardened. If the taper, its length and diameter and the engaging load (usually by way of a recommended tightening torque on the nut) are correctly chosen in relation to the overhang of the ball centre and the loads applied in service there will be no tendency of the shank to loosen even if the nut should subsequently slacken or be removed.

8.8   CONSTANT VELOCITY DRIVESHAFT JOINTS

One of the key components vital to the success of front-wheel drive systems is the constant velocity (CV) joint, first introduced on the BMC Mini in 1959. Details of this joint are shown in Fig. 8.7. It allowed the steered front wheels to be driven by the engine and has played a key role both in the upsurge of front-wheel drive designs and the steady growth of four-wheel-drive transmission systems ever since[3]. Neither configuration would have penetrated world markets so effectively without joints capable of transmitting torque efficiently, reliably and smoothly through relatively large angles of articulation.

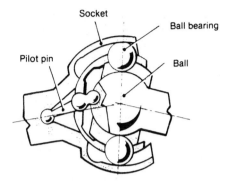

Fig. 8·7   The Rzeppa constant velocity joint in its original form used a pilot pin to guide the ball cage

Although CV joints have been used as drive-line components in the automotive industry ever since, they still have considerable potential for development in the future. Increased working angles, reduced plunge resistance, increased joint efficiencies, greater damping properties and lower production costs are all design goals that are already being achieved in the latest new designs.

The driving wheels of a vehicle do much more than turn to apply the tractive effort. They also move vertically up and down with suspension deflections and, in the case of front-wheel drive, are steered in the horizontal plane to provide directional control in corners, when manoeuvring or simply to maintain stability under external influences such as crosswinds. This means that the drive shafts between the transmission and the wheels have to be articulated to allow free movement in all directions.

Typical angular changes caused by vertical suspension movement at the inboard (transmission) end of a driveshaft range between 5 and 11 degrees during acceleration to as much as 22 degrees between the limits of suspension travel. At the outboard end of a steered driveshaft, horizontal angular changes are over twice as great, sometimes reaching as much as 50 degrees on a car with a particularly compact turning circle. It is vitally important in front wheel drive designs that the CV joints prevent snatch and surge and also help reduce powertrain noise, vibration and harshness being transmitted to the body structure.

In contrast to Cardan or Hooke joints, which comprise a simple cross-shaped spider between two pairs of connecting forks, CV joints transmit angular forces uniformly at constant torque and speed, known as homokinetic motion. To accommodate geometric

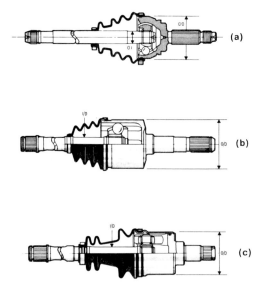

Fig. 8·8   Three types of constant velocity joint in general use are (a) the fixed type developed from the Rzeppa design with a maximum angle up to 47 degrees (b) the balls-driven plunging type with a maximum angle of 22 degrees combined with, typically, 55 mm of telescopic freedom and (c) the tripod type driving through needle-roller supported spherically-contoured bushes with the same range as (b). (*Courtesy GKN Automotive*)

changes in wheel movements created by most suspension systems, plunging CV joints also absorb axial driveshaft displacements without the need for separate sliding telescopic splines.

Plunging CV joints are designed according to several basically different conceptual principles, three of which are shown in Fig. 8.8. Each type has its characteristics closely optimised to the application. Three of these are plunging tripod (three-armed spider) joints and two are ball-driven joints, all capable of accommodating various amounts of free plunge movement. Several other new joint designs have also been developed recently, while others are under development for future applications.

Over the past few years the rapid increase in new front-wheel drive vehicles has led to almost universal adoption of CV joints in transverse driveline systems that use the sliding tripod arrangement. The robustness, reliability and free sliding properties of this type of joint under load have been universally accepted by vehicle manufacturers as the best design solution.

Increased package constraints and a growing demand for greater comfort levels have shown up the limits of this technology, however. CV joint manufacturers led by GKN, who dominate the market worldwide, have responded to this challenge with new products designed to reduce the pulsed axial vibrations (or 'shudder') generated in tripod joints working at severe angles under load.

A recent new GKN tripod joint development, known as the GIN design, incorporates smaller rollers on a larger radius and special features to reduce internal friction. It reduces the axial forces present by around 40 per cent and can now be connected to large diameter drive-shaft tubes without compromising the capacity of its angularity or sliding performance. Another new GKN design extends the performance capabilities by carefully proportioning the gradient of the axes of the tulip and journal paths to improve both the constant and maximum working angularities.

An example of one of the latest angular adjusted roller (AAR) CV joints is shown in Fig. 8.9. It has been developed from previous tripod joint technology but use an original double roller design linked to the tripod by a spherical joint. The assembly is guided within the tube by ramps that constrain the rollers so they operate within the axis of a predetermined path no matter what position or angle the tripod has adopted. This arrangement considerably reduces internal friction and mechanical losses without compromising sliding freedom. It also generates very low levels of axial forces, even at operating angles as high as 12 or 16 degrees (the limits for this type of joint). The AAR joint is particularly effective in improving refinement levels in operation by eliminating 'shudder' phenomenon and insulating the vehicle structure from transmission derived engine vibrations.

The working life of all CV joints depends on an efficient long-life seal being provided in the form of a moulded thermoplastic elastomer boot around the total assembly. This boot is required to

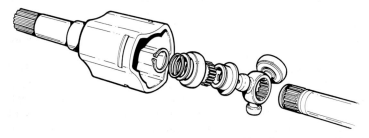

Fig. 8·9   The latest type of tripod CV joint uses a double roller system to adjust the angular rollers. (*Courtesy GKN Automotive*)

keep the lubricant complete and uncontaminated without attention for the life of the car. Advanced engineering of the boot design and its materials characteristics are essential to provide high durability levels over the temperature and flexibility ranges required in service together with sufficient resistance against impact from stones to prevent the material being damaged.

8.9 TORQUE STEER EFFECTS

One of the most critical aspects of interaction between driveshafts and the steering system is also one of the least well understood. Most early front-wheel drive cars performed well enough without problems in this area because they were low powered. Some early FWD designs with high power, such as the 1965 Oldsmobile Toronado and Citroen SM were notably free from torque-steer effects, while most of their contemporaries displayed the problem alarmingly when their power output was increased. Many, if not all, the go-faster conversion kits tested by Autocar magazine in the 1960s for small, high-powered front wheel drive cars darted violently to the right when full engine torque was applied in a low gear, and darted equally violently back to the left when the power was cut.

The primary cause of this phenomenon[4], which stall plagues many FWD cars today, is derived from the drive shafts angularity change at the outboard CV joint (the articulation), which generates a turning moment on the wheel about the kingpin axis. For analytical purposes forces are usually resolved into vectors acting in three (x, y, z) planes and any combination of co-planar forces is similarly resolved into a single force plus a couple (or moment). In the same way, couples can be resolved in two or three dimensions.

In a typical front wheel driveshaft layout, Fig. 8.10, the outboard CV joint is frequently not in line with the wheel spindle because of ride height changes caused by many variable factors, such as vehicle loading, body roll in corners or weight transfer under acceleration or braking. Whenever there is vertical articulation between the driveshaft and the wheel spindle (see Section A2.4 of Appendix 2), a couple is generated about a vertical axis at the hub (the kingpin). Whenever the steering is turned there is also horizontal articulation that causes a similar couple to be generated in the same vertical plane as that of the wheel spindle. The effects about this horizontal axis from the steering angle are usually symmetrical and opposite on each side of the car, cancelling each other out. If not, they are easily absorbed by the suspension. The couple C generated about the

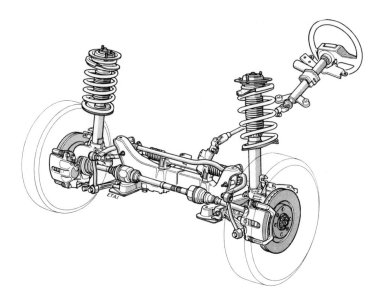

Fig. 8·10 This is a typical front suspension for a modern front-wheel drive car. During body roll or weight transfer the outboard CV joint may not always be in line with the wheel spindle. (*Courtesy Peugeot SA*)

vertical axis is more significant and equal to T tan $\theta/2$, where T is the driving torque and θ the angle of articulation in the CV joint.

As the front wheels move through their full travel range from the maximum bump to rebound position, the direction of the couple changes as the angle θ passes through a value of zero at the horizontal point. As long as the system is symmetrical from left to right, the effects on each side of the car will be equal and opposite, cancelling each other out. If the driveshafts are of unequal length, as is extremely common in FWD cars with transverse engines and offset transmissions, the articulation angles each side will be different and a resultant steering torque generated. The solution is to either arrange for the transmission to incorporate a layshaft and steady bearing for the longer driveshaft, so that it always operates at the same angular articulation as the shorter offset shaft, or to try and design the transmission and wheel centre heights to coincide during acceleration. The former approach will always be more successful than the latter, but the characteristic can never be totally eliminated as the front suspension will always encounter asymmetric conditions at some time or another.

8.10   FRONT WHEEL WOBBLE: 'FLAP'

One of the steering characteristics investigated by suspension engineers over the years is variously described as front wheel wobble, wheel 'flap' or 'veer' vibration. It is due to the interaction of a front end mass connected to the kingpin pivots with lateral flexibility with the results of the caster angle and the caster effect of the front wheels and tyres and depends on the frequency of the wheel inertia about the kingpins against the flexibility inherent in the steering system and the self-aligning torque of the front tyres. In certain conditions, usually at low speed, this type of wheel wobble can be unstable.

The root of the problem is caused by the mass and transverse flexibility of the components between the kingpin pivots. In considering this veer vibration the mass at the rear end of the car is ignored, as also are the small changes in yaw of the car; the wheelbase is considered long enough to make these negligible. The system can then be regarded as that of Fig. 8.11. The wheels pivot about the points p, which are the points where the effective caster applies, i.e. about one sixth of the contact patch behind the wheel centre, which is itself a small distance, the trail, behind the point where the kingpin axis meets the ground. Between these kingpin pivots and the effective mass of the front of the car there exist the spring constraints S. If the wheels are turned to one side and the mass first held, then released, an oscillation will be set up, the mass and the wheels moving in opposite directions. With the car in motion the points p are moved in one direction by the wheel angle. This movement tends to maintain the compression of the left hand spring S in Fig. 8.11 and in so doing puts work or energy into the system. Unless the energy input is removed by damping the oscillation will be self-amplifying.

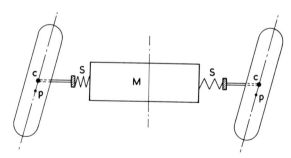

Fig. 8·11   Under certain conditions the steering system becomes excited by 'veer' vibrations

The mass concerned will be significantly smaller than the front end mass of the car and the flexibility may be derived from the presence of insulation rubber in the suspension mounts and steering system, including the rack attachments and even the toeboard structure itself to a small degree. Olley[5] has written of vibrations about an axis passing approximately through the dash and sloping down towards the back of the car. Such a vibration would obviously imply torsional flexibility of the car structure and of the main car mass on its two suspension systems.

This theory agrees with results first observed many years ago by Lanchester[6] and subsequently by Bastow[7] in tests which suggested veer vibrations of this type occurred at higher speeds when the damping of wheel movements about the kingpins was reduced. Two methods of reducing the tendency for this type of wheel wobble are to add friction to the steering system at various points between the column bushes and the kingpin pivots or to tune the steering system mounts to damp rather than excite the characteristic.

8.11 REAR WHEEL STEERING SYSTEMS

Although they only entered general production for the first time on a succession of Japanese models starting in 1986, there is nothing particularly new about rear wheel steering. It is used on dumpers and forklifts for manoeuvrability, on tailskid aircraft and supermarket trolleys. The idea of rear-steer cars, though, has haunted designers for decades, one of the most original concepts being built by Dixon and Rolt into a prototype, appropriately called The Crab, completed in 1946. It was actually a four-wheel steer system that in effect pulled the inside wheels together in a turn at the same time as it pushed the outside wheel apart.

Then in the late 1960s and early 1970s attention turned to rear steer for easier parking. Audi engineers converted one of the first Audi 100 saloons to move almost sideways into a parking meter bay by adding a steering rack to the rear wheels, with the interconnecting link deactivated for normal driving. The same idea was revived by Mazda in 1982 for an advanced research car that first appeared at the Birmingham Motor Show.

Real rear-wheel steering is a much more subtle development than that. It was first designed as an active part of the suspension geometry for the now-famous Porsche Weissach axle used on the Porsche 928 since its launch in 1976 and appeared again under hydraulic control on the 1985 Nissan Bluebird saloon and Nissan Mid-4 experimental coupe. In 1986 it was also launched on the

Honda Prelude and has been extensively investigated by all other major producers.

What is little appreciated, however, is that rear steer has actually featured in the predictable handling of many live-axle cart-sprung systems used before independent rear suspension became so fashionable. Leaf springs wind up under power, which has little effect in a straight line, but causes asymmetric effects that generate rear axle steer when traction is lost at the inside wheel by body roll in a turn.

To understand what rear steering is able to achieve, it is necessary to go back to basic principles and the concept of the Circle of Forces (see Chapter 10) – a fairly accurate theory which states that a tyre footprint, for any given inflation pressure and vertical loading, usually reaches the same limiting friction force regardless of the direction involved. Basically it means that tractive or braking forces decrease the lateral cornering grip, but that the resultant force vector always has the same value. After making due allowance for the dynamic behaviour of the tread pattern, a tyre will skid forwards at the same limiting force as it skids sideways, and at the same resultant force in any direction between the two extremes. It is the main reason why locked wheels cannot be steered.

As already explained, the slip angles in a turn are generated by distortion of the tyre footprint (contact patch) by the cornering forces which must collectively oppose the centrifugal forces involved for the car to be in equilibrium. Slip angles are designed to be unequal front and rear, to give the car its particular handling balance. An understeering car where the front slip angles are greater than those at the rear is inherently more stable than an oversteering car because the lateral forces are more under the driver's control (it does not require opposite lock to change direction). Typically, at moderate cornering speeds, front slip angles might be 7 degrees while those at the rear are only 6 degrees The limit of adhesion for most tyres takes place at a slip angle between 10 and 14 degrees, after which the cornering force available decreases with slip angle as the tyre starts to slide.

Although simple theory states that friction should be independent of footprint area, that is not a true statement for a rolling tyre tread. Factors which reduce the footprint area, such as inflation pressure, tyre loading and wheel camber also influence this limit of adhesion. Under dynamic conditions of cornering there is lateral weight transfer about the roll axis and under power or braking there is longitudinal weight transfer about the pitch axis. The amount of this weight transfer changes the tyre loading and the suspension geometry in most cases, complicating all the issues considerably.

Before tyre profiles started to reduce from 82–85 per cent aspect ratio (section width/height), camber angle changes were not very critical (about 5 degrees positive camber caused only a 10 per cent loss of cornering power). So wishbone systems, or parallel trailing arms which kept the wheels at the same angle as the body during roll were satisfactory, although not as good as rigid beam axles, where the wheels are nearly always vertical to the road surface (the exception being compression of the outside tyre wall under lateral weight transfer and, eventually, inside wheel lift).

More importantly, however, 80-series tyres provided enough ride comfort for the suspension bushes to be fairly stiff in compliance; the tyre sidewalls absorbed the worst of the high frequency vibration and harshness from the road surface. And there was enough flexibility in 80-series tyres to keep most of the footprint in contact with the road during camber changes with suspension movement.

Swing axles, where the wheel is always at right angles to the driveshaft, have the big advantage of moving into negative wheel camber with spring compression, and the equally big disadvantage of moving into positive camber on rebound. When weight is transferred forwards from a rear swing axle in a corner by the driver lifting off or braking, the highly loaded outside wheel can jack up from negative to positive camber, losing cornering power in the process, as described in Section 6.5.

The natural compromise between a swing axle and parallel or trailing links almost universally adopted now for independent rear driven suspension is the semi-trailing arm. It can be arranged to induce slight negative camber to the outside wheel in cornering without the tricky lift-off oversteer of a swing axle. With 80-series and 70-series tyres it works extremely well.

But when tyre profiles are reduced to 60 or 50-series, the pivots must be made softer for acceptable insulation from road shocks by adding compliance to the rubber bushes. This characteristic is shown in Fig. 8.12 (a). Over-run or braking forces generate a horizontal couple that turns each wheel outwards by flexing the inboard and outboard bushes, inducing a slight amount of toe-out, which used to be insignificant but has now reached levels of half a degree or 1.5 mm of toe-out at each wheel rim. And although that presents no problems when running straight ahead (it is a symmetrical effect), it increases the slip angle in a turn where the outside tyre is more heavily loaded, and cuts cornering power much like the behaviour of a swing axle, but not so severely.

With pure transverse wishbones (90 degrees trail angle), the bushes can be made very stiff in the lateral direction and soft only in the longitudinal direction of the bump-induced harshness. But the

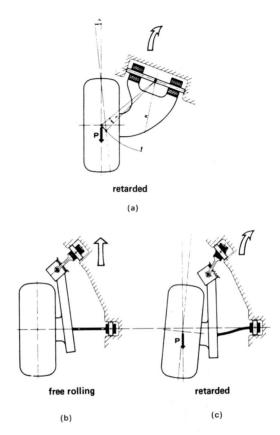

Fig. 8·12 (a) Conventional semi-trailing rear links have enough bush compliance to turn out under braking forces P, causing the more loaded wheel on the outside of a turn to induce oversteer; (b) and (c) On the Porsche 928 design retarding forces have more effect on the forward pivot so that the rear wheel turns in, improving stability when braking in a bend (*Courtesy Dr. Ing. h.c. F. Porsche AG*)

flexibility of the wheel under deceleration or braking increases as the trail angle reduces.

When trail angles were around 25 degrees, all these characteristics could be reasonably controlled to give safe, predictable handling under all kinds of transient conditions. But trail angle also sets the position of the effective centre of the suspension arm and thus the height of the rear roll centre, so in search of improved handling there has been a trend towards reducing it. It started in 1977 with the Opel Senator (which nearly halved conventional trail angles at that time to only 14 degrees), followed by Ford (who first went to 22 degrees with the Ford Granada S-Pack suspension in 1980 and then at around 18 degrees on the Ford Sierra and Granada/Scorpio).

To prevent these toe changes at the rear, Porsche invented what they call the Weissach axle (after the location of their R & D department) first introduced on the Porsche 928 in 1977. Its behaviour is shown in Fig. 8.12 (b) and (c). It cleverly uses a stiffly articulated trailing link to prevent the deceleration loads reaching the front bush. Instead of the drag forces pulling the semi-trailing arm round to toe-out, they effectively lengthen a spring-loaded joint at one end of the trailing link, keeping the toe changes very small.

Nissan's system[8] went one better. Called HICAS (High Capacity Active Control Suspension), it was operated hydraulically above 20 mph by two sets of rams, as shown in Fig. 8.13. On the Nissan Bluebird the rams simply 'drive' the rear subframe round on its rubber bushes, but on the Nissan Mid-4 coupe there are proper

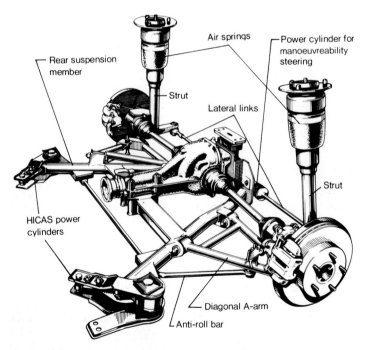

Fig. 8·13   Elements of the Nissan HICAS rear-steer system are shown here. They include a power cylinder for large-angle parking manoeuvres and small hydraulic rams to control the sub-frame pivots in high-speed driving

steering arms and knuckles rather like front hubs. When the conventional front power steering system senses high cornering forces HICAS is activated under microprocessor control to feed in up to ± 0.5 degrees each side. That means there is a full degree of slip angle change available at the rear through the rear wheel steering.

Judged on its own, one degree sounds very little (it is equivalent to about a 3 mm toe change), but it is enough to counteract all the bush compliance and as a slip angle change becomes a significant amount. The cornering power, for example, (defined as the cornering force divided by the slip angle generating it) changes by about 15 per cent per slip angle degree change at normal cornering speeds, which is more than enough to eliminate completely any trace of lift-off instability.

With a typical rear tyre carrying about 300 kg of total static and dynamic load under power, a one degree decrease in slip angle, from 7 to 6 degrees for example, reduces the cornering force from about 180 kg to 160 kg, which in some conditions could well reduce it from the threshold of letting go. Conversely, an increase of one degree caused by lift-off toe-out could initiate rear-end breakaway.

If the same tyre is unloaded by 30 kg to 270 kg by dynamic weight transfer forward under deceleration, the rear cornering power drops and the rear slip angle will rise to over 7 degrees. If the front tyres were running at 7 degrees before the throttle was cut (7 degrees front and 6 degrees rear gives stable understeer remember), the weight transfer would increase their cornering power by a similar amount, and reduce their slip angle to around 6 degrees. So the balance is completely reversed, from 7 front/6 rear to 6 front/7 rear, which throws the car from understeer to oversteer causing noticeable instability.

With the HICAS system the behaviour is completely different. At the critically unstable moment the power steering hydraulics sense the extra front end cornering power from the reduced steering effort and the microcomputer opens the valves to the rear rams so that the rear slip angle is reduced by one degree. This will cancel out the rear toe change and also raise the rear cornering power in step with the increase at the front, which keeps the car in balance.

Like all good ideas, HICAS is simple in its effect. But it is complex and costly in its engineering and critical in its calibration. Nevertheless, as tyre sections come down even further, from 60 to 50 and then 45 per cent, rear steer is going to be essential for stability with the suspension geometry wide tyres require and the harshness insulation they demand in their suspension bushes.

8.12   ACTIVE REAR WHEEL STEERING

Toward the end of 1991 BMW launched a new computer-controlled rear-wheel steer option for the 850i coupe, called active rear axle kinematics (ARK). As can be seen in Figs. 8.14 and 8.15, it is similar to the Nissan HICAS system, steering the rear wheels hydraulically up to 1.5 degrees each way in the same sense as the front wheels according to road speed and the steering input.

The hydraulic elements of the ARK system consist of a reservoir, an engine-driven pump, a pressurised accumulator, an actuator ram and a triple-feed supply network (duplicated pipes to the actuator and a single pipe to the accumulator). The actuator ram is mounted transversely to the centre of the rear sub-frame and drives the inboard pivots for the lower suspension links, which hang from short articulated shackles, left or right across the car. Actuator valves are controlled by a dedicated on-board computer programmed with algorithms dependent upon signals received from the vehicle speedometer, each front wheel (via the ABS system) and an additional steering wheel angle sensor.

Dynamically the system is an intelligently active version of the Porsche Weissach axle, later used on the Opel/Vauxhall Omega/

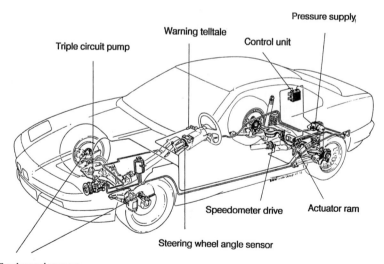

Fig. 8·14   The BMW active rear axle shown here operates under computer control to reduce rear slip angles according to road speed and steering input algorithms

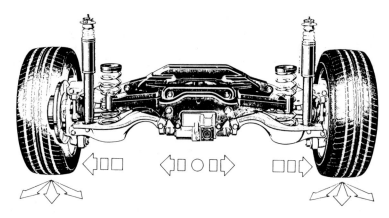

Fig. 8·15   Hydraulic rams mounted in the centre of the rear axle sub-frame force the suspension arms to left or right as required

Carlton and Senator saloons. Those suspensions improve stability during lift-off by using the deceleration forces to articulate the rear suspension arms by means of asymmetrical bush stiffnesses (the front bush of each rear suspension arm is softer than the rear bush, so it can 'steer' the arm very slightly). BMW and Nissan active rear steer systems drive the rear wheels against cornering forces to prevent side loads building up during high speed manoeuvres whenever the computer senses there is a need (such as when making an emergency swerve to avoid a critical hazard).

According to BMW, accident analysis shows that 4 per cent of all road fatalities are due to cars swerving out of control off the road following a sudden manoeuvre. With a conventional steering system the rear axle only participates passively in the steering process. After the driver turns the front wheels, lateral forces are initiated at the front before gradually moving back along the longitudinal axis of the car to affect the rear wheels, which then follow round. Conventional rear axles are developed to provide quick, smooth responses to steering inputs, although in some cases this can make the car feel 'nervous' and become unstable under rapid transient conditions, especially if the driver moves the steering wheel too quickly. This tendency is damped out in production cars but accentuated in rally cars to make directional changes more immediate.

Following extensive research and track testing, BMW decided it was better to vary the relationship between front and rear steered angles as a function of the lateral forces generated, rather than provide a fixed steering ratio balance (as Honda does on the geared Prelude system). Rear steering is only beneficial under relatively high lateral g forces. They also found that too much rear steer induced understeer at the front, which slowed down the steering response. The ARK system therefore calculates lateral g from the road speed, the difference between left and right front wheel speeds, the steering wheel angle and the rate of steering input. It introduces a carefully determined time phase delay between the driver's input and the rear steer reaction so that the response occurs at exactly the same moment as the steering forces from the front start to reach the rear wheels.

Because all steering components are safety critical, BMW has gone to considerable pains to provide reliability in all parts of the operating system. Apart from the triple-feed hydraulic system, the controller is equipped with redundant microprocessors and special hydro-mechanical arrestors lock the rear actuator ram in its neutral position if there is any kind of hydraulic, electrical or total computer failure. The system then reverts to its normal elasto-kinematic behaviour and a warning tell-tale illuminates. Non-volatile memory chips in the computer store all diagnostic data for subsequent interrogation in the workshop.

BMW test drivers in Munich provided a convincing demonstration of the ARK system in action in pouring rain on a teeming wet test track at the launch of the new system. At speeds of first 120 km/h (75 mph) and then 160 km/h (100 mph), an 850i coupe equipped with a switchable system was subjected to a violent lane-change manoeuvre to simulate an emergency swerve. With ARK switched off the rear end swung out and the car rocked back and forth two or three times before it settled back to normal. With the system activated the car stayed flat on the road and immediately locked on to its new position without the delayed lateral swing exhibited before.

8.13 POWER ASSISTANCE

A variety of causes has combined to make static steering torques greater: low profile tyres, the radial tyre, the tendency to front wheel drive and consequent greater concentration of weight at the front of the car. The American manufacturers were the first to apply power assistance to car steering in quantity production. Most of the early examples of power assistance failed to take advantage of it to reduce the number of turns from lock to lock and so improve emergency steering ability. The primary safety advantage of doing this has however now been generally realised and some power steering schemes have less than two turns of the wheel from lock to lock— an extreme example–but figures of $2\frac{1}{2}$ to 3 are more common.

Citroen, with the DS model, realised the advantages of combining power assistance with the rack and pinion steering gear and their example has since been followed by others. In any case the vast majority of power assistance schemes incorporate the hydraulic assistance cylinders in the steering 'box'.

In their first flush of enthusiasm for the use of power assistance the American car manufacturers tended to go for the maximum effect. It has since been realised that the retention of steering wheel feel is important: being able to feel when the self-aligning torque starts to diminish with increasing sideways acceleration on a corner is a useful guide as to when the limit of adhesion is being approach and is therefore a worthwhile safety factor.

With the occasional exception, practice has tended to crystallise into a system where the proportion of power assistance depends upon the steering wheel torque. One means of sensing this torque is a small-diameter shaft (with stops to limit the maximum twist and ensure connection between steering and road wheels even if the assistance pump fails). There are various means of using the relative twist of the shaft to operate the valve. Another means of torque sensing, with a rack and pinion steering, is to allow the pinion housing limited freedom of movement along the rack housing, against a spring constraint. This relative movement operates the valve.

To minimise the piston area required to provide the assistance high pressures are necessary. It is undesirable to have a pump, of sufficient capacity to provide rapid enough wheel movements, to operate against full pressure continuously. It would be consuming unnecessary power and would be causing excessive temperature rise in the steering system oil. The general method of providing free flow except when assistance is required is a piston or rotary valve which has passages for the oil on its way to both sides of the assistance piston and also on its way back to the reservoir. As steering torque is applied and moves the valve it tends to close the passage to one side of the piston and from the other side. Figure 8.16 shows the total pressure drop in relation to the reduction in area of the restriction orifices and increase in area of the corresponding opposite openings. The final limitation to assistance is the setting of the relief valve on the pump delivery which will impose an upper limit to the pressure. Towards the final stages of the restriction the shape of the approaching edges of the valve and passage will also

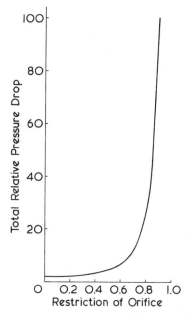

Fig. 8·16   The calculated relative pressure drop obtained from a typical torque sensitive power assisted steering valve implies that most assistance is obtained at the higher torques

control the shape of the curve. Figure 8.17 shows two actual curves of assisting pressure against steering wheel torque; the first for a car, the second for a heavier vehicle.

The designer therefore has a good deal of choice in determining the assistance given at the normal driving steering wheel torques as compared with the final maximum for the stationary car, where feel is obviously relatively unimportant.

With power assistance particularly the maximum torque of the road wheels about the kingpins could greatly exceed the static torque due to the tyres if one wheel were against a kerb. The only limitation which can be imposed on this is the setting of the pressure relief valve on the steering circuit. The stressing of steering system parts can therefore be based on this when power assisted steering is fitted.

Power assistance acts to reduce the effect of road-excited impulses at the steering wheel. As the torque on the steering wheel builds up an opposing pressure is generated. Power assistance may become unavailable either from pump failure or more probably from loss of

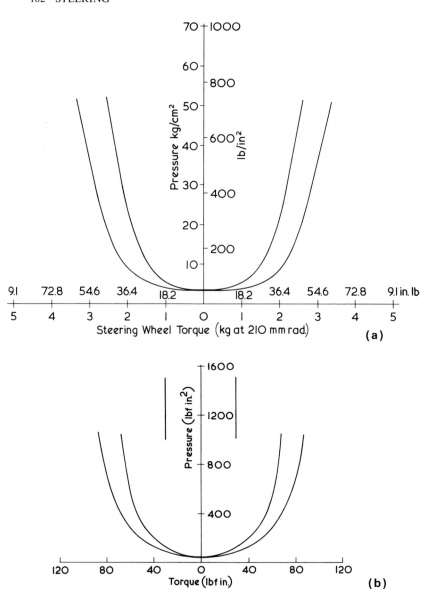

Fig. 8·17   (a) The graphs of steering input torque against steering assistance pressure can be compared with Fig. 8.16. The relief valve setting depends on the application and may be up to 7 MN/m². (b) This corresponding diagram relates to a commercial vehicle. This system is designed to be used up to 14 MN/m². (*Courtesy Burman & Sons Ltd.*)

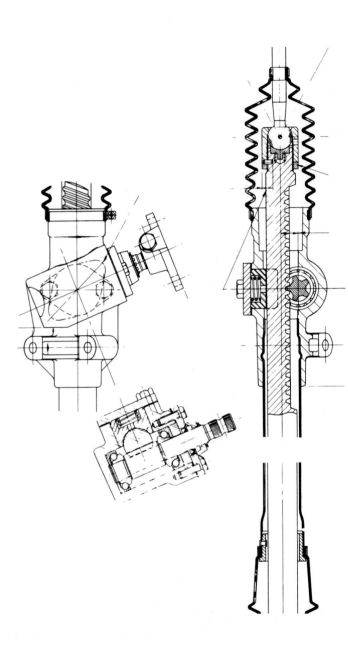

Fig. 8·18 This rack and pinion steering gear has a pinion shaft at $22\frac{1}{2}°$ to the perpendicular to the rack, a five tooth pinion and $42\frac{1}{2}°$ pinion tooth angle. The rack support thimble has a Gothic arch groove form to restrict support to two small areas. There is very small clearance under this thimble. (*Courtesy Burman & Sons Ltd.*)

fluid because of a leak. The steering ratio must leave it possible for a driver to steer the car without assistance even if some restriction in sideways acceleration has to be accepted.

Figures 8.19 and 8.20 show two different ways of applying power assistance to rack and pinion steering gears. Figure 8.21 is a recirculating ball worm and nut steering gear. Figure 8.22 is a larger version of this with power assistance. Figure 8.23 is an example of a valve for a steering box with power assistance, showing the flows for different conditions.

8.14   POWER ASSISTANCE PUMPS

The main problem with the engine driven pump which provides the power assistance is that the maximum assistance is generally required in manoeuvring, as in parking, when engine speed is low, and very little assistance when engine speeds are high; there is an engine speed ratio of perhaps six to one between an idle of 800 to 1000 rpm and a maximum power speed which may rise to 6000 rpm and in some cases even more.

As we have seen, the control valve whose movement is responsive to steering input torque depends upon relatively small movements and as a consequence its passages are restricted. Passing through these passages a flow of six times that required for the parking performance (the latter perhaps 0.15 litre/s) would imply quite unnecessary pressure drops, power losses and heating of the oil. To meet this problem as fully as possible the pump can incorporate a flow control valve (Martin[9]) producing the results shown in Fig. 8.24. This is a development of an earlier type of valve which is not responsive to outlet (system) pressure. The outlet pressure response characteristic is desirable because of the greater reduction in flow through the control valve which it gives when no assistance is required. In this way it minimises power losses and oil heating in the conditions which apply for the greater part of the time. Most manufacturers have not felt this refinement to be necessary and fit the earlier type of flow control valve without this feature. The dumped flow is recirculated to the pump inlet, with precautions to minimise turbulence and shock as it merges with the fresh oil intake from the reservoir.

Various types of pump[10] are used to provide the pressure; one of the largest suppliers to the British motor industry is Hobourn–Eaton. One of their pumps is the rotor-roller type shown in Fig. 8.26; this is a pressure-balanced design with an approximately elliptical cam ring giving two cycles per revolution. A pressurised

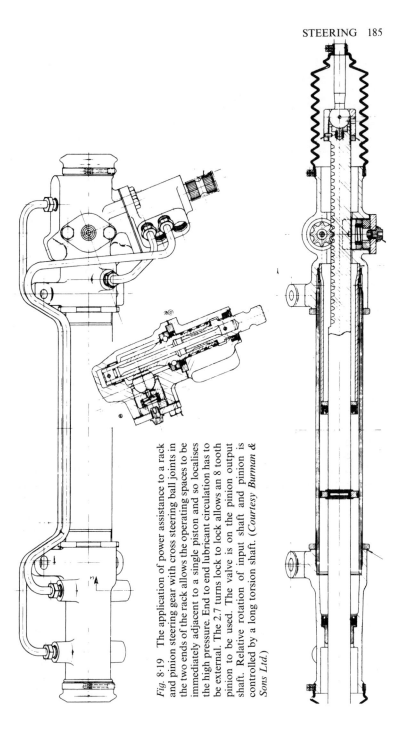

Fig. 8·19   The application of power assistance to a rack and pinion steering gear with cross steering ball joints in the two ends of the rack allows the operating spaces to be immediately adjacent to a single piston and so localises the high pressure. End to end lubricant circulation has to be external. The 2.7 turns lock to lock allows an 8 tooth pinion to be used. The valve is on the pinion output shaft. Relative rotation of input shaft and pinion is controlled by a long torsion shaft. (*Courtesy Burman & Sons Ltd.*)

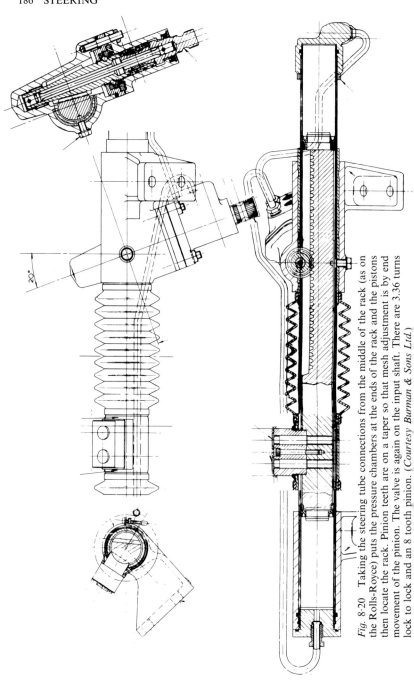

Fig. 8·20 Taking the steering tube connections from the middle of the rack (as on the Rolls-Royce) puts the pressure chambers at the ends of the rack and the pistons then locate the rack. Pinion teeth are on a taper so that mesh adjustment is by end movement of the pinion. The valve is again on the input shaft. There are 3.36 turns lock to lock and an 8 tooth pinion. (*Courtesy Burman & Sons Ltd.*)

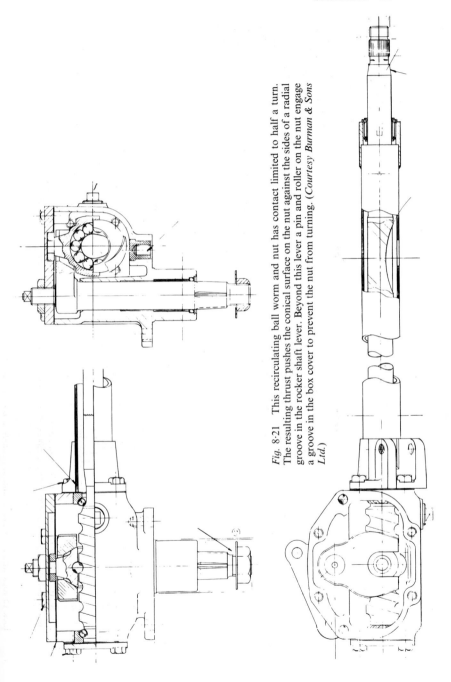

Fig. 8·21   This recirculating ball worm and nut has contact limited to half a turn. The resulting thrust pushes the conical surface on the nut against the sides of a radial groove in the rocker shaft lever. Beyond this lever a pin and roller on the nut engage a groove in the box cover to prevent the nut from turning. (*Courtesy Burman & Sons Ltd.*)

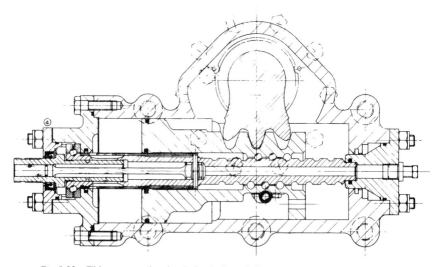

Fig. 8·22   This worm and recirculating ball nut is for a commercial vehicle. The valve on the input shaft is in the middle of one operating space and external piping is avoided by bringing the pump delivery up the middle of the worm. Rack teeth on the nut engage pinion teeth on the rocker shaft. The pinion teeth are tapered to provide a mesh adjustment. (*Courtesy Burman & Sons Ltd.*)

end plate reduces leakage across the ends of the rotor teeth; the rotor pressure balancing allows plain bearings to be used, even at the drive end. Internal and external gear-type pumps are also used, and some vane type. Pressures currently used are tending to increase from the 6.9 MN/m^2 which was at one time generally used to perhaps 10 or even 14 MN/m^2.

Noise is a problem with any car installation; the root of the problem with power assistance systems is that all the types of pump in use produce pressure pulsations and these and their effects have to be minimised. A pulse filter is the first requirement, a length of highly expansible flexible hose at the beginning of the flexible hose from pump to control valve. The second requirement is as much isolation as possible from the steering gear to the car structure. A flexible coupling between the steering box input and the steering wheel is desirable. A rack and pinion gear can be flexibly mounted; a gear with rocker shaft presents more difficulties.

An oil reservoir incorporated with the pump avoids unnecessary external connections and the possibility of further noise transmis-

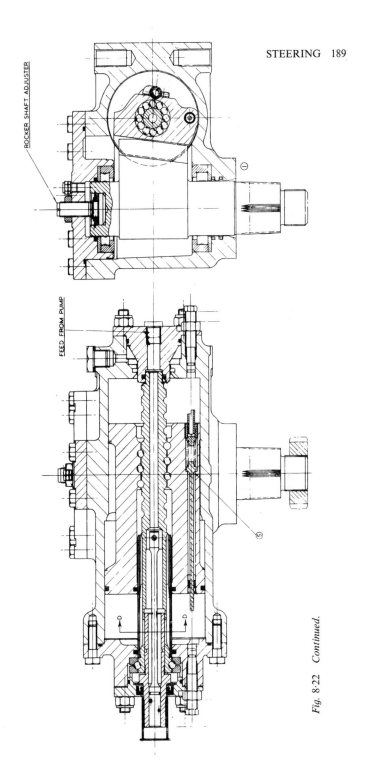

ROCKER SHAFT ADJUSTER

FEED FROM PUMP

Fig. 8·22 *Continued.*

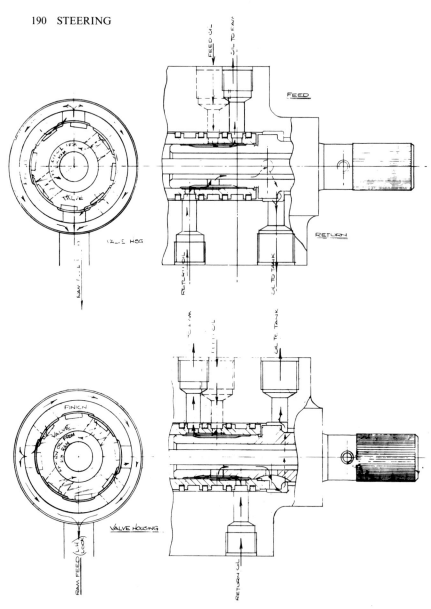

Fig. 8·23 The outside of the pinion extension inside the housing sleeve has four seal rings to produce three grooves sealed from each other. The pump delivery is taken to the centre groove; each outside groove is connected to a ram. Holes connecting the inside of the sleeve to each groove are so placed in relation to longitudinal grooves in sleeve and valve centre that twist in one direction progressively opens up the feed to one ram and closes its outlet to the tank at the same time as the feed o the other ram is closed off and its outlet opened to the tank outlet. (*Courtesy Burman & Sons Ltd.*)

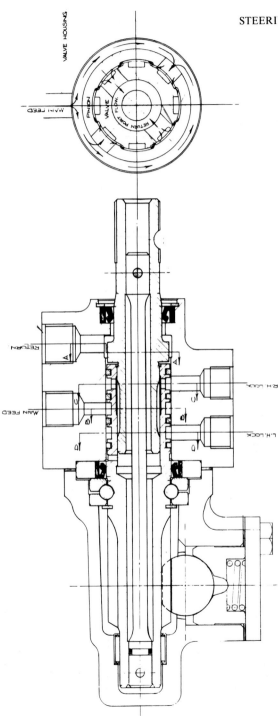

Fig. 8·23 *Continued.*

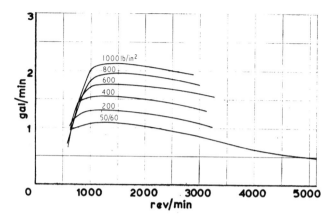

Fig. 8·24   Tying the flow rate to the pressure has not been found generally necessary but the equipment is available[8]. (*Courtesy Institution of Mechanical Engineers*)

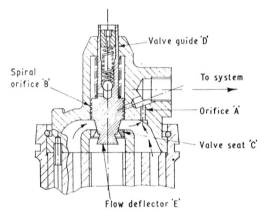

Fig. 8·25   This is the combined flow control and relief valve which gives the characteristics of Fig. 8.24. (*Courtesy Institution of Mechanical Engineers*)

sion. The only connections then necessary are a pressure lead from pump to control valve and a return pipe from valve to reservoir.

REFERENCES

1.   Heacock, F. H., and Jeffrey, H., 'The Application of Power Assistance to the Steering of Wheeled Vehicles', *Proc. Auto. Div. I. Mech. E.*, No.4 (1953-54)
2.   Unkoo, L. and Byeongeui, A., 'A Method to Analyse 'The Imaginary Kingpin Axis' in Multi-Link Type Suspension Systems', *SAE Technical Paper No. 930262* (March 1993)
3.   Curtis, A., and Howard, G., 'Smooth Transfer', *Car Design & Technology*, December (1991)

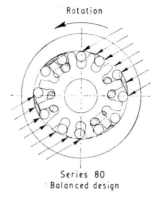

Rotation

Series 80
Balanced design

Pressurized annulus

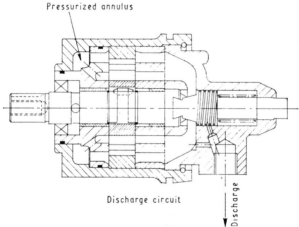

Discharge circuit

Discharge

Fig. 8·26 The balanced pressure pump incorporating the valve of Fig. 8.25. (*Courtesy Institution of Mechanical Engineers*)

4. Bulmer, C., 'Argumentative Torque', *Car Design & Technology* (November 1991).
5. Olley, M., 'Road Manners of the Modern Car', *Proc. Inst. Auto. Engrs.*, Vol. XLI (1946–47).
6. Lanchester, Dr. F. W., 'Automobile Steering Gear Problems and Mechanisms', *Proc. Inst. Auto Engrs.*, Vol. XXII (1927–28).
7. Bastow, D., 'Steering Problems and Layout', *Proc. Inst. Auto. Engrs.*, Vol. XXXII, (1937–38).
8. Nissan Motor Co., 'High Capacity Actively-Controlled Suspension', August (1985).
9. Martin, K. C., 'Power Assistance Pumps for Steering', *Proc. I. Mech. E.*, Vol. 184, PL3A (1969–70).
10. Mochizuki, T., 'Development of the Variable Displacement Vane Pump for the Automotive Power Steering System', *SAE Technical Paper No. 930261* (March 1993)

9
Active, reactive and adaptive systems

9.1 RIDE AND HANDLING LIMITATIONS

It has always been extremely difficult for the suspension engineer to maintain simultaneously a high standard of ride, handling and body attitude control under all driving conditions. The problems stem from the wide operating range created by the many possible combinations of road surface, speed and vehicle load. As the relative unsprung masses increase with reduced vehicle size, the problem becomes increasingly acute on smaller cars.

Conventional suspension systems must always be designed as a compromise. Even with the aid of self-levelling and interconnections between the wheels, any system that is soft enough to provide a comfortable ride cannot also provide a sufficiently stable location of the vehicle body to ensure the best possible handling. Right at the heart of the issue is the often overlooked and fundamental fact that ride is a measure of the ability of the suspension to handle mostly vertical forces applied at ground level, whilst handling and attitude control are influenced much more by horizontal forces acting on the centre of gravity and by ground level couples or moments.

The dynamic performance of suspension systems has progressively improved over the years, as the science of wheel control has developed hand in glove with more advanced analysis techniques and refinement of basic kinematics. The multi-faceted design of wheel geometry, springing media, locating members, damping elements, insulating bushes and tyre characteristics can today achieve standards that are way beyond those even envisaged through complicated hydraulic systems 10 or 15 years ago.

The fundamental difference between an active and a passive suspension is that active systems provide independent treatment of the road induced forces from the body inertia forces. By separating the functional elements of the suspension's task, active systems have the ability to eliminate the traditional compromise between ride and handling characteristics completely.

Strictly speaking an active suspension is reckoned to be one which uses a fast-acting, closed-loop control system like those employed for engine management on today's hi-tech engines. But an active suspension can also be defined more simply as a system which is able to change its characteristics under outside influences to enhance its dynamic performance. In the modern sense, active, or adaptive suspensions are driven by sensors and control systems which react, process and then operate a variety of fast-acting devices.

In every case the objective is to reduce or, if possible, eliminate some of the compromises forced on the designer by a conventional passive system. In general these relate to the limitations imposed on the designer by load, wheel travel and relatively constant spring rates. In dynamic terms, the most restricting of all is the fixed relationship between pitch and bounce frequencies. A low bounce frequency for maximum ride comfort always leads to a disturbingly low pitch frequency and usually excessive body roll.

9.2   REACTIVE SUSPENSION SYSTEMS

As well as being system-driven, it can be argued that some of the less active suspensions can also be reactive or road-driven, and there are several examples where the performance of active systems is simulated quite well by internal processing of the direct road inputs. Two examples are the Citroen 2CV with its interconnected mechanical springs illustrated in Fig. 9.1 and the Morris 1100 which was the first car to use Moulton's Hydrolastic suspension, as shown in Fig. 9.2.

Within this definition of reactive road-driven systems, Hydrolastic was one of the neatest active suspensions conceived. It was first patented by Alex Moulton in 1955 and launched commercially in 1962 as a key feature of the innovative front-drive Morris 1100. Although it worked very well in its original form, it suffered from long-term durability problems in service and never made the transition to the smaller Mini and larger Morris 1800 hatchback and Austin 3-litre saloon models successfully. It was later developed into a Hydrogas system using the same principles, but without the rubber springs, on the 1973 Austin Allegro. For the Mini Metro in 1980, the Hydragas units were separated from each other to act as individual springs.

Dynamically Hydrolastic was road-driven by the load inputs from the wheels and totally controlled from within the system itself.

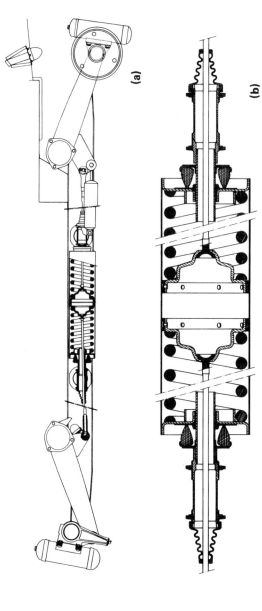

Fig. 9·1 The top drawing shows a general layout for the Citroen 2CV coupled suspension. Rubber buffers act as springs between the canister ends and the frame brackets which provide attitude control. The use of arms at the front implies castor angle change with load (from 14 degrees to a maximum of 22 degrees). The lower drawing shows a detail of the end location buffer. (*Courtesy of Citroen SA*)

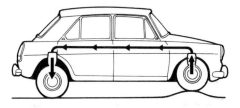

Fig. 9·2 Front and rear suspensions of the Morris 1100 were interconnected by hydraulic pipes so that the springs each side acted in parallel during roll and in series over bumps, giving a soft ride with good roll resistance

It had some very clever features that effectively simulated an active system, developed by a unique cooperation between Dunlop, (who were responsible for the rubber cone springs), Alex Moulton (who conceived the original concept) and Alec Issigonis (who fathered the total project).

In geometric terms the Morris 1100 suspension was fairly conventional: double unequal-length front wishbones and simple fabricated rear trailing arms. As on the Mini, the rear springs were laid down to a near horizontal position and operated by lever arms.

Orthodox steel springs and hydraulic dampers were replaced, however, by the integrated Hydrolastic system which did four specific things: It absorbed vertical shock forces, it damped the subsequent rebound motion without fade (being water-based the working fluid had a constant viscosity), it dissipated the energy of the induced motion and it fed front inputs to the rear in proportion to the vertical wheel velocity. The result was a system that provided both variable rate springs and variable pitch reaction. Pitching moments depend upon the pitch stiffness and the wheelbase dimension, which sets the leverage effect of front and rear inputs about the centre of gravity. A short wheelbase car is very stiff in pitch because the lengths of the lever arms are short.

On the Citroen 2CV and Morris 1100 the wheels were positioned 'at the corners', for handling stability, which increased the wheelbase (the Citroen's was 2.40 m. and the 1100's 2.37 m, each about 65 per cent of the overall length at a time when most small cars had wheelbases of only 55 per cent). To reduce the pitching moment induced by bump reactions on the relatively long wheelbase, front and rear suspensions were interconnected.

In a sense, interconnection between front and rear systems is the simplest possible form of active suspension. If the same spring is shared each side between front and rear suspensions (as on the first 1936 conception of Citroen's 'people's car'), any pitching moment caused by deflection of the front suspension is immediately countered by an equal and opposite moment at the rear, cancelling out the disturbance.

The problems start because the centre of gravity is never on the line joining front and rear suspension pivots so it causes additional moments usually described as dynamic mass transfer. These are totally unresisted by freely-mounted linked springs so the interconnection must be compromised to reduce the excessive squat and dive that would otherwise cause the car to hit its bump stops at the rear when moving off and at the front under braking. The Citroen did this by enclosing the main springs in a floating cylinder mounted between two auxiliary springs reacting against the body at each end.

The Citroen 2CV when it was introduced in 1948 had a suspension which differed from that shown in Fig. 9.1 in one principal detail: the anti-pitch rate was provided by volute springs between the ends of the spring canister and the frame brackets rather than by the ring rubber buffers. In both cases therefore, the original form and that shown here, the anti-pitch rate is dependent upon two things: the rising rate characteristics of the suspension due to the bell crank arm dispositions, which by inspection is more pronounced at the back; and the rate and initial clearances, if any, between the pitch control springs or buffers and the frame brackets, in conjunction with the same suspension leverage characteristics. Because the spring reaction on the tension rods is the same front and rear the leverages of the front and rear suspension bell cranks have to be chosen to be appropriate to the sprung masses front and rear.

The difference between the front-rear sprung mass ratio, driver only and fully laden, has to be catered for in part by the rising rate characteristic at the back and in part by the anti-pitch spring characteristic there. Because of this and the very soft springing there is a noticeable change in attitude with loading. To avoid embarrassment from this at night there is a vertical aiming control on the headlamps.

The Hydrolastic system, Fig. 9.3, approached the pitch problem the other way round by using hollow rubber springs operated by a working fluid that was allowed to flow between front and rear units under certain conditions. This displacement of fluid distorted the shape of the rubber springs and therefore changed their stiffness in proportion.

In this system the two springs each side worked in series over

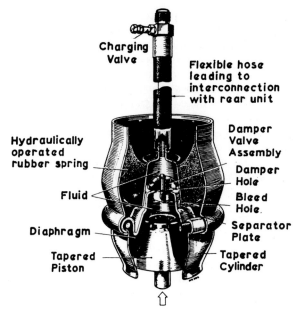

Fig. 9·3   The 'Hydrolastic' spring unit of the Morris 1100 used an hydraulically operated rubber spring coupled between front and suspensions each side of the car

bumps and in parallel under cornering roll, giving a very novel kind of dual rate springs. Although the small bore interconnecting pipes modulated the flow and prevented a simple 2:1 ratio between roll and bump stiffness, the differences were still a considerable advantage. The design of the internal damping valves which controlled the fluid flow as well also responded to the velocity of the input, giving variable damping.

As well as being very susceptible to mass transfer, front/rear interconnection also reacts very unfavourably to unequal static loads which cause excessive tail sag when rear seats are filled with passengers or luggage is carried in the boot. For tuning the pitch frequency to avoid unpleasant resonances the 1100 had twin steel torsion bars inside its rear subframe, and there was also a conventional rear anti-roll bar to reduce the natural understeer of its front-wheel drive.

The second-generation system, known as Hydragas, launched on later BL cars, took the advantages a stage further. The common feature of Hydrolastic and Hydragas coupled suspensions is a nylon-reinforced rubber diaphragm pushed into a liquid (basically water with anti-freeze and anti-corrosion additives) by a conical displacer connected by pushrod to the most convenient suspension lever. The conical displacer provides an increasing piston area with bump movement. In the Hydrolastic the liquid displaced by the diaphragm goes through the damper valve in a steel dividing plate, above which there is a rubber spring enclosing the upper part of the space from which goes the connection to the corresponding unit at the other end of the car. The pitching movement is damped by fluid movement through the damper valves at both ends of the car and by passing through the connecting pipe.

The rubber comprises inner and outer, frusto-conical steel members, approximately parallel to each other, with a thick rubber washer bonded between them. Liquid pressure under the unit forces up the inner cone and the intervening rubber is compressed and sheared to provide the spring movement.

The rising rate characteristic of both suspensions provides the anti-pitch rate. The total suspension rate results from: (1) the increasing diaphragm area, (2) the load-deflection curve of the rubber spring, (3) the leverage characteristics of the suspension linkage, and (4) the torsional rate of the rubber bushes at various places in the linkage.

The later Hydragas system (Fig. 9.5) uses an enclosed volume of inert (nitrogen) gas to replace the rubber spring of the 'Hydrolastic'; the other main difference is that the coupling connection is made to the space between the diaphragm and the damper valve, so that pitch damping is due to the fluid resistance in the connecting pipe, whose diameter therefore becomes much more important.

The coupled suspension is obviously far more sensitive to accelerating and braking forces as a source of attitude changes; it is therefore necessary to incorporate as much anti-dive and anti-squat as possible without detriment. The trailing arm rear suspensions employed from the beginning by Issigonis and Moulton have looked after the back end of the car. The front suspension in the latest 'Hydragas' designs also incorporates a measure of this feature.

As explained earlier, Sections 2.6 and 2.7, the human body is most

---

Fig. 9·4   Moulton 'Hydrolastic' and 'Hydrogas' coupled suspension systems used a fluid to transfer loads between front and rear units and provide damping. In bounce the displaced fluid passes through the damper valve to either deflect the rubber spring or compress the gas. In pitch the resistance depends upon (1) the leverage variation between wheel and diaphragm, (2) the variation of diaphragm area with deflection and (3) the parasitic rate of the front and rear suspension caused by rubber bushes and hysteresis. In the 'Hydrolastic' system pitch movement is damped by the damper valve; in the 'Hydrogas' system pitch is damped by flow resistance through the coupling pipes

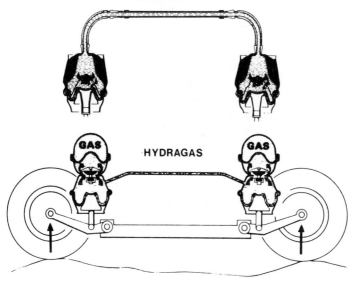

BOUNCE

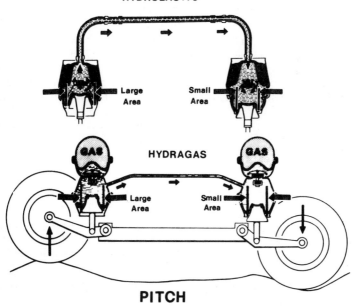

PITCH

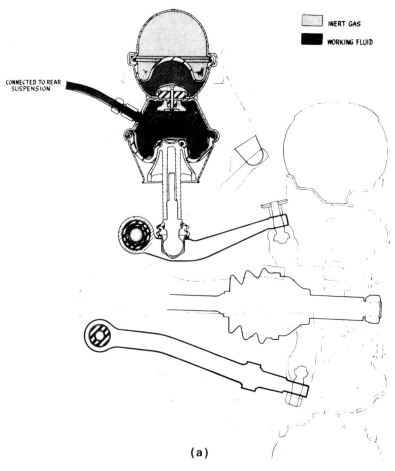

INERT GAS

WORKING FLUID

CONNECTED TO REAR
SUSPENSION

(a)

Fig. 9·5   Moulton 'Hydragas' units were mounted on top of the upper wishbone and combined an inert gas spring with a working fluid

sensitive to transverse accelerations, next to fore and aft accelerations and least sensitive to vertical accelerations. The philosophy of the Moulton coupled suspensions is that reduced pitch excitation and lower pitch frequency allow a higher bounce frequency. This higher bounce frequency implies a high enough anti-roll rate, in total, to ensure a reasonable roll angle in cornering. Adjustment of front/rear mass transference is obtained by the front end roll centre height and the use of a very limited swing axle effect in front to get

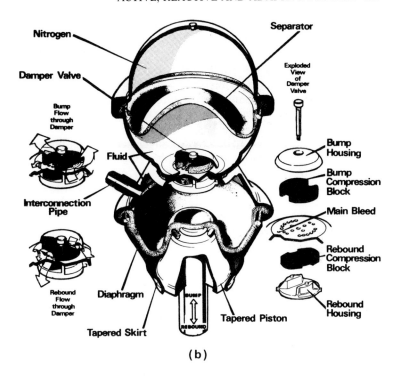

(b)

some reduction of outward camber thrust. This avoids the front anti-roll rod necessary with the uncoupled suspensions to keep the roll angle reasonable and get sufficient front mass transference to give good handling.

All the advantages of interconnection endowed the Morris 1100 with outstanding ride and handling balance for a 1962 car in its class.

At Citroen their adventurous hydropneumatic suspension first introduced in 1953 on the rear of the Citroen Big Six Traction Avante was carried over to the front and rear of the new Citroen DS19 in 1955. It did not use interconnection other than to provide self-levelling under load, however, and was only adaptive in static terms under the influence of pressurised hydraulic controls which changed the spring rates and damping to provide a near-constant ride frequency.

It probably stimulated Moulton into filing his Hydrolastic patent and led directly to many other hydropneumatic systems, notably from Mercedes-Benz for the Mercedes-Benz 600 in 1964 and later Mercedes-Benz S-Class models and a German component supplier called Langen AG of Dusseldorf in 1965.

Non adaptive but self-levelling air suspension dates back even further to Firestone experiments in the 1930s which eventually resulted in air springs being fitted to Greyhound buses in 1952. Air suspension was also adopted by Cadillac in 1957 but dropped only three years later.

The system used by Citroen (and Langen) employed spheroidal shaped steel containers in which a rubber bag filled with nitrogen under pressure is compressed by the action of the working fluid (mineral oil). Various valves in the system control the flow and pressure of the fluid to provide a constant static ride height regardless of load, damping of the wheel movements and a variable rate for the springs caused by changes to the effective area of the convoluted rubber diaphragm separating the fluid from the gas.

But the Citroen system is actually prevented from responding to rapid changes in wheel position and cannot really be considered as an active system in the same way as Hydrolastic can. The Langen system on the other hand extended Citroen principles much further towards an active system by interconnecting the hydraulic lines front to rear. Unlike Hydrolastic, the connections were made diagonally and both front and rear spring units were mounted at the rear.

The advantage of this approach was that although the stiffness of the springs in roll was less than in a non-diagonal connection, the diagonal pitching moments were resisted better. Langen spent several years developing their system for production and fitted prototype units to several cars, including a Morris 1100, a Ford Taunus 12M, a Citroen DS19 and a Mercedes-Benz 220S, but it was never adopted as original equipment.

9.3   COUPLED FRONT AND REAR SUSPENSION EFFECTS

As already mentioned, coupled suspension first appeared on the Citroen 2CV. Fully coupled suspensions, without a supplementary anchorage of some kind from one or both suspensions, would imply a car without fore and aft attitude stability.

The effect of coupling can be understood from Figure 9.6. For the sake of simplicity we assume equal spring rates S at each end of the car, Fig. 9.6 (a), and equal loads on each axle. An obstruction of unit height passed over by the front wheels, with no time for body movement, will imply a total upward force S on the sprung part of

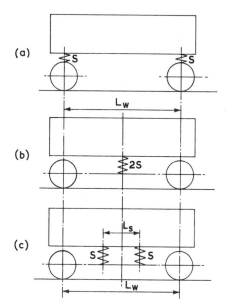

Fig. 9·6 (a) An uncoupled suspension in simplified schematic form (b) A coupled suspension with no attitude stability (c) A coupled suspension with attitude stability depending on a reduced front and rear spring separation as compared with the wheelbase

the car and a pitching moment about the car centre of gravity of $S(L_w)/2$.

With coupled suspensions, Fig. 9.6 (b), and no anchorage the upward force on the sprung part of the car is $1/2(2S) = S$, again but there is no pitching moment about the centre of gravity.

We must have some inherent attitude stability of the sprung part of the car so we decide to use our original two springs of rate S and to mount them on the equaliser bar at a distance apart L_s, Fig. 9.6 (c). The total upward force on the sprung part of the car for our unit deflection of the front wheels is:

$$\left\{\frac{(L_w + L_s)/2}{L_w}\right\}S + \left\{\frac{(L_w - L_s)/2}{L_w}\right\}S = \frac{S}{L_w}\left(L_w + L_s 2 + \frac{L_w - L_s}{2}\right) = S$$

The pitching moment about the car centre of gravity is:

$$\left\{(L_w + L_s) \quad 2L_w \quad \left\{\frac{SL_s}{2}\right. - \left\{\frac{(L_w - L_s)}{2L_w}\right\}\frac{SL_s}{2} = \frac{SL_s^2}{2L_w}\right.$$

The pitching moment is therefore reduced in the ratio of $\{L_s/L_w\}^2$.

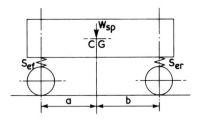

Fig. 9·7 The quantities and dimensions necessary to arrive at an anti-pitch rate

We see therefore that the difference between any wheel or pair of wheels passing over a bump is not in the total upward force produced on the sprung mass but in the pitching moment applied to it. An indication of this reduction is the ratio of pitch to bounce frequencies. For $k^2/ab = 1$ this is in the ratio L_s/L_w, for the simplified assumptions of Fig. 9.6. More generally, for the still simplified layout of Fig. 9.7, the moment of inertia is $(W_{sp})k^2$, the anti-pitch rate about the centre of gravity is $(S_{ef})a^2 + (S_{er})b^2$ Nm/rad, S_{ef} and S_{er} being the effective spring rates at front and rear suspensions respectively, and the pitch frequency is:

$$f_p = \frac{1}{2\pi}\left(\frac{S_{ef}a^2 + S_{er}b^2}{W_{sp}k^2}\right)^{1/2} \tag{9.1}$$

If we have an arrangement of coupled suspensions for which the anti-pitch rate about the centre of gravity is M_{ap} Nm/rad, the pitch frequency will be:

$$f_{pc} = \frac{1}{2\pi}\left(\frac{M_{ap}}{W_{sp}k^2}\right)^{1/2} \tag{9.2}$$

so that the ratio of frequencies, coupled to uncoupled, is

$$\left(\frac{M_{ap}}{S_{ef}a^2 + S_{er}b^2}\right)^{1/2} \tag{9.3}$$

As shown, in Appendix 3, Table A3.4, for uncomfortable disturbances, the ratio of accelerations bearable, bounce to pitch, is of the order of 1.7 in the neighbourhood of the probable frequencies. This relationship implies equal frequencies: if we are reducing the pitch frequency by coupling suspensions we will be able to stand

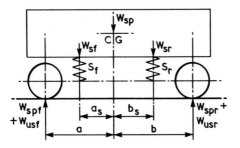

Fig. 9·8   A more comprehensive picture of the effect of coupling, with some anti-pitch rate as required to maintain the desired attitude

higher fore and aft accelerations at the head than we would with uncoupled suspensions. This makes any attempt at calculating the optimum ratio of pitch to bounce frequency a complicated exercise, which would in any case require to be finally tested against a sufficient number and variety of subjective impressions.

There are a number of factors involved. Moulton and Best point out some of them and others are implied. For instance, in a car without coupling of the suspensions it is normal and correct practice to give the front suspension a greater static deflection or lower frequency than the rear, to minimise pitch. In a car with coupled suspensions there are two inducements to lower the rate of the front suspension: it should reduce the pitch excitation; and a higher rate at the back will be less affected by the extra mass of passengers and luggage, most of which comes on the back.

Figure 9.6(c) is an idealised diagram of a car with coupled suspensions: equal masses front and rear, equal distances of the springs between equalising bar and sprung mass fore and aft of the centre of gravity. A more general picture is given in Fig. 9.8. Front and rear wheels are at distances a and b respectively from the centre of gravity; the springs of rate S_f and S_r, are at distances a_s and b_s from the centre of gravity and have reactions W_{sf} and W_{sr}.

$$W_{sf}a_s = W_{sr}b_s \qquad (9.4)$$

$$W_{spf}a = W_{spr}b \qquad (9.5)$$

and by inference the anti-pitch rate is

$$S_f a_s^2 + S_r b_s^2 \qquad (9.6)$$

This could also be given as

$$S_{pf}a^2 + S_{pr}b^2 \tag{9.7}$$

where S_{pf} and S_{pr} are respectively the front and rear effective spring rates in pitch.

Because $S_{pf}a^2 = S_f a_s^2$,

$$S_{pf} = S_f\left(\frac{a_s}{a}\right)^2 \tag{9.8}$$

and correspondingly at the rear.

Moulton and Best[1] have suggested that a good relationship is that

$$\frac{S_{pf}a}{S_{pr}b} = 0.6 \tag{9.9}$$

9.4   ADAPTIVE SUSPENSION DAMPING

As the dynamic performance of suspension systems has improved progressively in recent years, the search for ideal damping character-istics from the dampers has intensified. Although conventional velocity-conscious units can deal competently with a wide range of operating requirements, the increased understanding of wheel control has served only to highlight the need for some form of 'intelligence' in the dampers that can discriminate between different damping requirements, even when they occur at the same wheel velocities.

Automotive engineers can now control damper logic through an on-board microprocessor fed with inputs from a variety of sensors and driving adjustable valves built into relatively conventional units[2]. Although alternative damping methods have been extensively explored, none has so far proved to be competitive with the energy density of the hydraulic unit, whose design and development has many years experience behind it.

The most important and ever present operating condition the shock absorber has to deal with is the road profile, which is varied and totally random in its character. Frequency inputs to the suspension from this source appear as either irregular or repetitive waveforms, or even as single sharp disturbances generated by potholes or trench repairs. Many of these conditions present conflicting demands on the suspension damping, whose primary task is to minimise the disturbances felt inside the body while maintaining adhesion between the tyre and the road.

The highest damping forces are required when repetitive road inputs cause a resonance of the sprung mass. Holding down the response amplitudes satisfies both comfort and adhesion requirements. Short single disturbances on the other hand are best controlled with smaller damping forces which then have the benefit of transmitting smaller forces into the body. The effects of adjustable damper valve settings are shown in Fig. 9.9.

Accelerating or braking causes longitudinal mass transfer that can excite forced oscillations of the unsprung masses (wheel tramp or hop) and cause pitching motions that are particularly disturbing to passengers. Damping forces can only affect pitch motions while the attitude of the vehicle is changing, and are completely ineffective as soon as a steady state is reached and the suspension velocity is zero. They can slow down the rate of pitch change, but then the levels are much higher than those necessary for ride control and consequently transmit larger impulses into the body over road disturbances.

Lateral mass transfer caused by handling or cornering manoeuvres, and the associated body roll, can also be modified by the

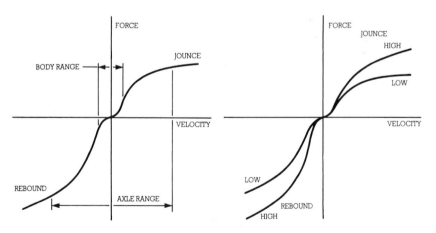

Fig. 9·9 The effect of an adjustable valve on damper performance (right) is compared with a conventional single-setting unit (left). Control over the range of body movement is similar in both cases but the differences during high amplitude suspension movements are significant. (*Courtesy Ford Motor Co.*)

damper settings. But, as with longitudinal mass transfer, damping can only affect the transient motions, not the steady state conditions. Damper settings likely to influence handling responses significantly are generally higher than those required for ride control in straight line running, although small changes can influence stability in high-speed lane-change manoeuvres.

To approach these conflicts with a 'clean sheet' design, Ford research engineers started with a complete list of ideal adaptive damping possibilities. It used the processing power of a modern on-board computer to control damping characteristics in bounce and rebound for different static loading, in response to speed and to changes in the vertical, longitudinal and transverse acceleration of the suspension.

Two such adaptive damping systems have been designed and fitted to a Ford Granada and a Ford Escort[3] for appraisal. In the Granada installation an inductive displacement transducer was mounted between one rear wishbone and the vehicle body. Signals were filtered and fed in digital signals form to a microprocessor, which calculated an average wheel to body height on the move over a 14 second sample of amplitudes and compared this with instantaneous values measured 20 times per second. Control signals were then generated to vary the pressure in a vacuum powered hydraulic cylinder which was connected via hydrostatic lines to progressively adjustable valves in each damper.

Various logic sequences were programmed into the computer for evaluation of the vehicle dynamics on the road and test track. In one typical sequence, damping characteristics were increased for a short fixed interval (2 seconds, for example) whenever the difference between the instantaneous and average ride heights exceeded 15 mm, after which it reverted to the softer settings again provided there were no more inputs beyond this threshold. This design maintained good body control over long wavelength disturbances with a generally soft feel to the ride. As the transducer was fitted on one suspension unit only it also responded to roll, although in contrast to a transverse accelerometer some movement was required before any response could be generated.

In the Escort installation a much simpler approach was used, with two self-levelling air struts fitted at the rear only, to supplement the existing steel springs. Inductive height sensors were built into the dust shields of the dampers, which were fitted with two stage (high/low) electrically operated adjustment valves for bounce and rebound. The on-board microprocessor controlled both levelling and damping functions, through air pressure signals proportional to vehicle loading and interpretation of any larger than normal low frequency body movement.

Soft damper settings are selected for the driver only or single passenger condition, hard settings for four people or equivalent loads. Similar logic to that used on the Granada was programmed in to select the harder settings for short periods when excessive body movement was detected.

Control of sprung and unsprung masses was well maintained at all times, with ride characteristics that were perceived as softer than the standard vehicle on most road surfaces. In some conditions it was hard to detect much difference, however, but the hardware and systems used were only in the first stages of development and operating over quite slow response times.

In more recent times several cars have adopted electronically controlled dampers either adjustable by the driver, as in the case of the Opel system in Fig. 9.10 or under computer control as in the case of the Bilstein system in Fig. 9.11.

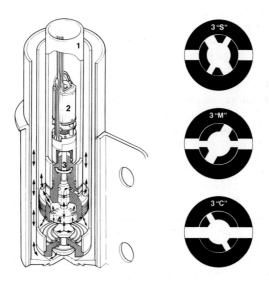

Fig. 9·10 Electronically adjustable dampers operated by a driver's switch have become fairly common in recent years on luxury cars. This system is fitted to the Opel Senator (*Courtesy Adam Opel AG*)

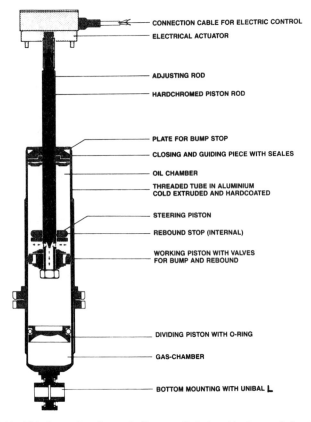

Fig. 9·11   This fast acting electronically controlled ajustable damper is fitted to the Porsche 959. It is largely made from aluminium to reduce the unsprung weight and improve heat dissipation. (*Courtesy Bilstein AG*)

9.5   POTENTIAL GAINS FROM INTERMEDIATE SOLUTIONS

The function of a suspension system is to minimise the movements of the sprung mass which cause discomfort to the occupants of the car. Reduced movements mean reduced accelerations. Chapter 3 has shown that, with due regard to frequency, it is reduced accelerations that improve comfort.

Accelerations are produced by forces. Forces transmitted to the sprung mass must come by way of either the springs or the dampers. Softer springs reduce the extra force developed by a given wheel movement and therefore the energy imparted by the springs to the body. There are, with the basic passive suspension system, two lower limits to spring softness: continuing frequencies below about 0.75 Hz result in sickness; and the variations in the load carried by a car, because they are not equally shared between the four wheels, cause attitude changes which increase with increasing spring softness and can become unacceptable for one or more of three reasons. One is the undesirable redistribution of the total available suspension movement between bump and rebound; the second is the premature contact with bump or rebound buffers which generally provide the increase in spring rate which experience has shown to be desirable as the suspension nears the end of its available travel; the third is the deflection in headlamp beam which is a nuisance to other cars and to the driver himself.

Appendix 1, Figs A1.5, A1.6 and A1.7 show the desirability of increasing damping forces in controlling, which means reducing the amplitude of, movements of any mass which because of spring constraints has a natural frequency of vibration. Appendix 1, Fig. A1.7 reminds us that in a vehicle suspension there are two masses involved, and two separate springs, but only one damper. Damping control of the smaller mass, generally known as the unsprung, can only be obtained by reaction from the larger. The tyre, which provides the spring between the unsprung and the road, is inherently unable to provide any effective damping.

The natural frequency and the critical damping force of a suspension system vary as the square root of the spring stiffness. Softer springs not only reduce the forces transmitted to the sprung mass, for a given disturbance, by the springs themselves, they also reduce the forces provided by the dampers for a given degree of damping control. Figure 9.12 shows how both the damping force and the spring force diminish with the reduction in natural frequency of the sprung mass. The relationship between spring and damper induced transmitted energy remains constant regardless of frequency. This mutual relationship is also independent of the amplitude, though the amounts transmitted will vary as the square of the height of the initiating disturbance. Any effect due to increased amplitude of the sprung mass at or near its natural frequency is ignored in this graph. The intention is merely to demonstrate the potential improvement which might be obtained if either the spring rate or the damping force could be instantaneously varied as the wheel follows the contour of the road disturbance.

The effect of damping force variations on amplitude at and near the natural frequency is shown in Appendix 1, Fig. A1.5. Figure 9.13 shows that increase of damping between the two masses, i.e. in

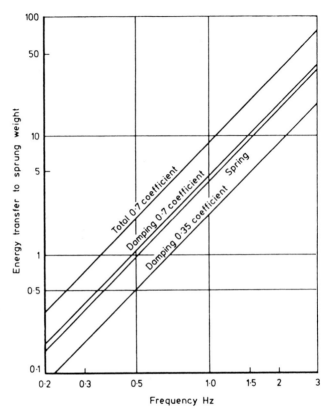

Fig. 9·12   This illustration serves two purposes: it shows how the energy transfer between unsprung and sprung weight is shared between that due to spring rate and that due to damping, with an indication how both vary with spring rate; and its shows how important that spring rate is in reducing the effect of road disturbances on the sprung weight. Considerable reductions in spring rate are only possible in conjunction with height control. Energy transfer varies as the square of the height of the disturbance

parallel with the suspension spring, does reduce the amplitude of the smaller mass enough to reduce the total energy input to the spring mass although the damping then provides a larger share of that energy transfer. A nuisance in this connection is that the high rate of the tyre as a spring implies that the critical damping force for the unsprung is higher than that for the sprung. A given damping force is therefore a higher proportion of critical for the sprung than for the unsprung mass.

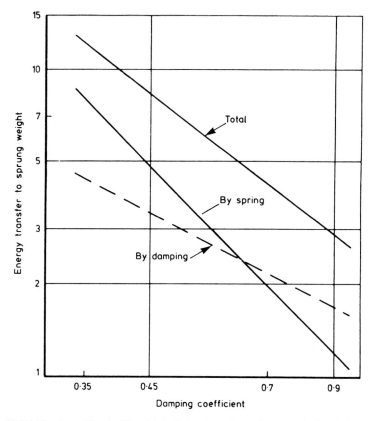

Fig. 9·13   Appendix 1, Fig. A1.5 shows how dynamic magnifier, and hence amplitude, are reduced by increase of damping force. Energy transfers from unsprung to sprung weights vary as the square of the unsprung amplitude. This diagram shows how increased damping reduces energy transmission to the sprung weight by reducing deflections. Even though the proportion of that energy transfer due to damping increases as damping increases, the individual transfers due to damping and spring rate are both reduced by increased damping

Increased damping is beneficial in controlling movements of sprung and unsprung masses subjected to periodic disturbances, but there are adverse effects on an initial or continued disturbance. A general compromise is the practice of having less damping on bump than on rebound movement. There are limits to this differentiation. If the bump damping is too much reduced the control of the amplitude of the unsprung mass near its natural frequency may be impaired and the general effect therefore may be disadvantageous;

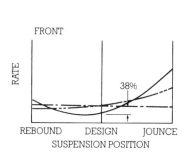
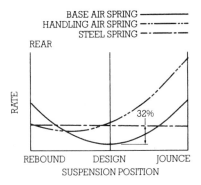

Fig. 9·14 Much softer springs with variable rates up to 38% softer than conventional linear steel springs can be specified using electronic ride height controls

the need to maintain good contact between tyre and road is also a limitation on the amount by which rebound damping can be increased.

Some disadvantages of soft springing are overcome by standing height control. Softer springs, with the advantages to be seen in Fig. 9.14, can then be used. This is the first step towards activity in the suspension system. As now fairly widely applied its speed of operation has been deliberately restricted so as to avoid ill-timed intervention.

Further reductions in energy transfer to the sprung mass can be achieved by active control of damping to reduce it when it is disadvantageous and increase it when it is beneficial; and to provide a fast enough response to use the mechanism of standing height control to limit or prevent roll in cornering or dive and squat movements under fore and aft accelerations.

Electronic devices currently available can provide fast enough responses to make active control of damping possible. Sensors for at least position, velocity and acceleration are available; and small computers can provide data storage and processing capability for a control philosophy, such as that used for instance in engine management for emission control or economy, to respond in any desired way to the signals from the chosen sensors. Component and vehicle manufacturers have shown that mechanical means can react quickly enough to prevent cornering roll, or dip and squat.

Active control of damping, by electrically operated damper valves for instance, requires a small electrical power input; height control by hydro-pneumatic means requires a power input to the oil pressure pump, not much to the usual slow standing height control, more to a system with quicker reactions to avoid roll, dip and squat, most to provide a fully active suspension. Such systems are now available on some versions of the Citroen XM and new Ford Mondeo, as well as several top models from Japan.

An idea of what could be achieved by such control can be obtained from Fig. 9.15, based on Karnopp[4]. Curves (a) and (e), though produced by different methods, are very similar to those shown in Appendix 1, Fig. A1.7(a). A difference is the hump in the unsprung mass curve under the natural frequency hump of the sprung mass. It reflects the reduced damping on the unsprung mass due to the movements of the sprung mass near that frequency. The difference between curves (c) and (d) in Fig. 9.15 confirms the benefits of reduced unsprung mass. Both curves show the improvement on the sprung mass of increased active damping. Thus, Karnopp indicates that the possible gain from active damping is the difference between curves (a) and (b); even a part of this would be valuable.

High damping is beneficial; but it does increase the effect of the initial bump, or rebound, disturbance. Figure 9.16 is interesting because it shows the benefit of reducing the frequency of the sprung mass, in this case from 1 Hz to 0.5 Hz, on the product of the dynamic magnifiers, and hence on the behaviour of the sprung mass under continuing excitation.

The other beneficial effect of reducing the frequency is to reduce the energy input to the sprung mass. As we saw in Fig. 9.1, both spring and damping force energy inputs vary as the square of the sprung mass frequency, so that halving this has reduced the energy put into the sprung mass by a given disturbance to a quarter of its original value. In both cases, at 0.7 critical damping, the damping contributes some 65 per cent of the total energy put into the sprung mass.

The final consideration is that the rate at which the movement from a single impulse dies down is important. The relevant Equation is

$$x = e^{-nt}A(\cos \mu_c t)$$

The first part of this, e^{-nt}, defines the rate of decay; the bracket term defines the number of vibrations in a given time, $n = W/(2F_d)$. For 1 Hz, F_d is twice as much as for 0.5 Hz, for a given proportion of critical damping; for 1 Hz therefore the decay to a given proportion of the original displacement will take twice as long as for 0.5 Hz. In each second of decay time there will be twice as many vibrations.

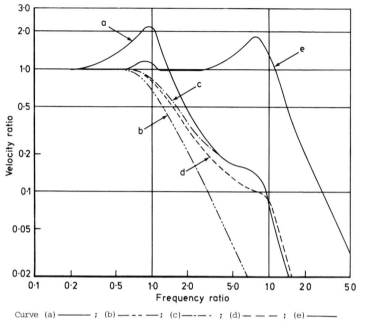

Curve (a) ———— ; (b) — - - — ; (c) —·—·— ; (d) — — — ; (e) ————

Fig. 9·15   Velocity ratios from that imposed by road irregularities, for suspensions with passive and active damping, at different excitation frequencies. Specially prepared from information in Karnopp[1]. Curve (a) Sprung mass, passive damping, 1398 Ns/m, 0.312 critical sprung mass, 0.257 critical unsprung mass. Curve (b) Sprung mass, active damping, one degree of freedom, 'ideal' damping 3168 Ns/m, 0.707 critical. Curve (c) Sprung mass, active damping 3168 Ns/m, 0.707 critical sprung mass, 1398 Ns/m, 0.257 critical unsprung mass. Curve (d) Sprung mass, active damping 3168 Ns/m, 0.707 critical sprung mass, reduced unsprung mass 0.1 of sprung, damping 1196 Ns/m, 0.257 critical. Curve (e) Unsprung mass, passive damping, associated with curve (a), damping 1398 Ns/m, 0.257 critical. General particulars: $W_{sp} = 267$ kb, $W_{us} = 36.6$ kg for curves (a), (c) and (e), $W_{us} = 26.7$ kg for curve (d). $S_s = 18\,700$ N/m, $S_t = 184\,000$ N/m. Resultant frequencies: 1.33 Hz sprung mass; 11.84 Hz unsprung mass for curves (a), (c) and (e), ratio 8.9; for curve (d) 13.87 Hz, ratio 10.4

The decay of the 1 Hz vibration contains four times as many swings as that of the 0.5 Hz.

These considerations apply equally to passive suspensions, but cornering roll, and dip and squat, provide limitations which can be considerably changed by an active form of height control, to be discussed in the next section. Nevertheless, active damping, i.e. any form of damping control which reduces damping when the damping force is acting in the direction of the sprung mass movement, and

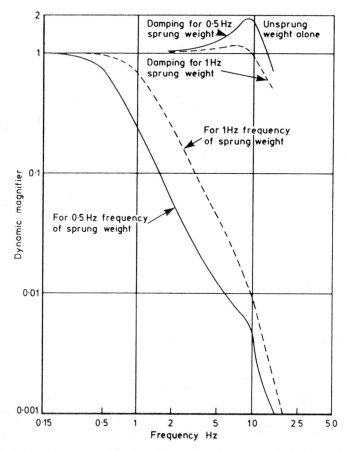

Fig. 9·16   The products of the dynamic magnifiers for sprung and unsprung weights are shown for frequencies of the sprung weight of 1 Hz and 0.5 Hz, with 0.7 critical damping in each case. The lower frequency shows an overall advantage, in spite of the reduced damping of the unsprung weight which is inherent in the reduced frequency

increases it when it opposes that movement, does serve to reduce the initial disturbance and should increase the rate of decay. In any case, the proper starting point for any suspension improvement should be the best one can or could do passively, including adequate wheel movements, and taking advantage of any change in limitations which the degree of activity proposed will allow.

Figure 9.16 shows too that the reduced damping force associated with a lower frequency has the disadvantage of reducing the damping on the unsprung mass.

An early example of one form of adaptive damping control was developed by the Armstrong Patents Co. Ltd. As far as damping is concerned it is based on the idea of two levels of damping, with the usual differentiation between bump and rebound. Switching between the two is achieved electro-mechanically. The dual tube damper, Fig. 9.17, is provided with a third tube to enclose a gas spring, which by suitable initial design can either act on its own or in conjunction with a lower-than-usual rate spring. Height control, using this gas spring, is normal at the rear and optional at the front, where it is less necessary. This has the usual differential between doors open and closed for speed of correction. It works by oil injection and a small pump, which can be driven either from the engine or by electric motor. The control system has sensors for speed, throttle opening, brakes applied and steering movement, as well as from the doors, and for standing height. The dampers normally operate at the low level of damping. When a surface undulation is met which causes suspension movement beyond a pre-fixed limit, the damper valves change to the hard setting. After a single disturbance the dampers return to the soft setting. Repeated inputs cause the hard setting to be retained. The pre-fixed body movement which produces the change to the hard setting reduces as speed increases. The hard setting is also brought in by sudden steering movement, braking and throttle opening. The gas spring is so proportioned that compensation for increased load puts up the spring rate to maintain a substantially constant periodicity. The control function is provided by a microcomputer with the settings tailored to the particular vehicle to which it is fitted. A typical layout of the complete system as applied to a car can be seen in Fig. 9.18.

9.6   ADAPTIVE RIDE HEIGHT CONTROL

The benefits of standing height control have already been stated. There is a tendency to relate damping forces to both sprung mass and the spring stiffness, so that the reduction in damping force energy transmitted to the sprung mass when spring rates are reduced may not be as much as Fig. 9.1 might suggest.

Adaptive height control may be used only to reduce, or preferably eliminate, cornering roll and at least to reduce brake dip and acceleration squat, with the ride as such only profiting by the softer

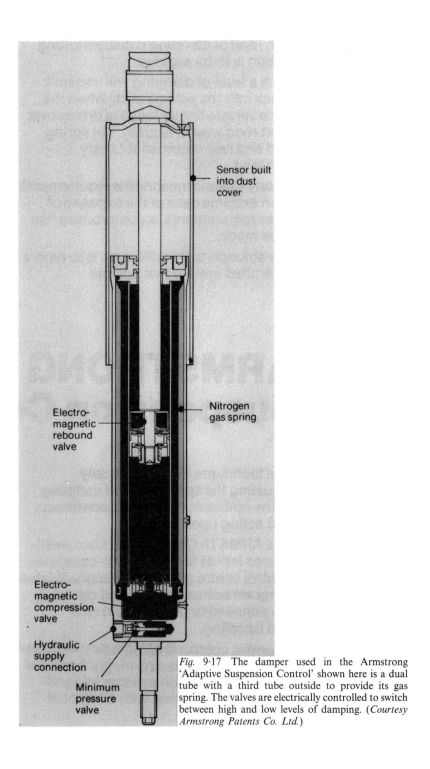

Sensor built into dust cover

Electro-magnetic rebound valve

Nitrogen gas spring

Electro-magnetic compression valve

Hydraulic supply connection

Minimum pressure valve

Fig. 9·17 The damper used in the Armstrong 'Adaptive Suspension Control' shown here is a dual tube with a third tube outside to provide its gas spring. The valves are electrically controlled to switch between high and low levels of damping. (*Courtesy Armstrong Patents Co. Ltd.*)

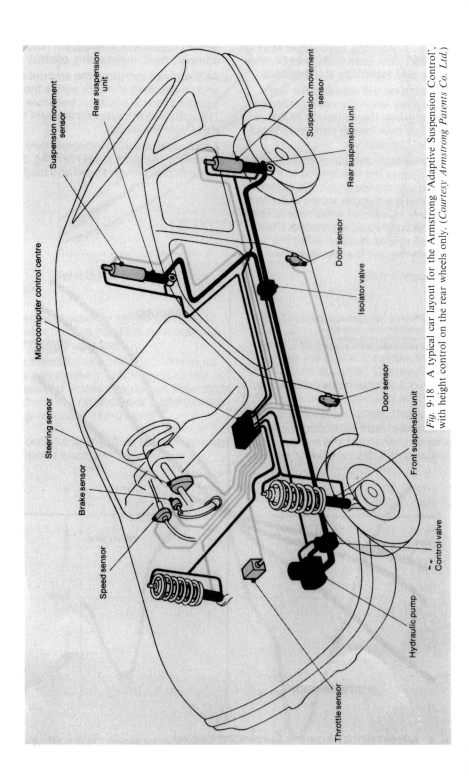

Suspension movement sensor

Rear suspension unit

Suspension movement sensor

Rear suspension unit

Microcomputer control centre

Door sensor

Isolator valve

Door sensor

Steering sensor

Front suspension unit

Brake sensor

Speed sensor

Control valve

Throttle sensor

Hydraulic pump

Fig. 9·18 A typical car layout for the Armstrong 'Adaptive Suspension Control', with height control on the rear wheels only. (*Courtesy Armstrong Patents Co. Ltd.*)

springing; alternatively it may be combined with some form of adaptive damping control.

Where constant piston area control has to deal with very large load variations, as at the back of a front drive car where the fully laden mass may be twice as much as in the one-up condition, the reduction in gas volume by the doubled pressure tends to harden the ride too much; and the doubling of the load also means that it is difficult to get a satisfactory compromise on damping forces. An ideal suspension would avoid these defects.

An example of a mechanically regulated height control suspension[5] which does rather more than eliminate cornering roll and limit dive and squat is shown in Fig. 9.19. The layout of the system includes the usual hydraulic reservoir, pump and hydraulic accumulator, with a fluid displacer, control valve and pneumatic spring for each wheel. The special features in are the use of double acting hydraulic displacers at the rear wheels, the underside of each piston being coupled to the top of the opposite front displacer, and the control valves. The tops of the two rear displacers are connected to a common gas spring and there is a single control valve at the rear, connected to the middle of the axle or otherwise indicating the mean height of the two rear wheels.

The control valves are shown in Fig. 9.20, which shows the effective layout of each front suspension, except for the omission of the connection to the opposite side rear displacer underside. The use of a bell crank lever to convert wheel movement into operation of a piston valve to admit pressure oil to the top of the displacer or release it is normal. The unusual feature of the valve is the addition of the offset mass to the horizontal arm of the bell crank, and the connection from the suspension arm to the bell crank, which incorporates a spring and damper in parallel, bearing the same relationship to the offset mass as the suspension spring and damper bear to the sprung mass of the car. Slow movement of the vehicle on its springs, as in taking off or adding load, will operate the bell crank normally and restore the suspension to its normal position.

The depression of the front end of the car under braking would act in the same way, and the extra pressure in the two front springs would act on the underside of the double-acting pistons at the rear. This, in conjunction with the rear control valve, would restore the rear suspensions too to their normal position. A similar process in reverse would look after acceleration squat. The interconnection front and rear speeds up the reaction and reduces the demands on the pressure system and therefore the pump and motor.

It is in cornering that the reason for the side to side connections front to rear become obvious. Increase of load on the outer front

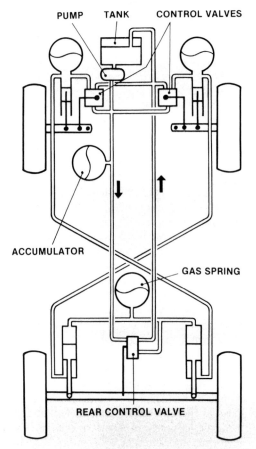

PUMP   TANK   CONTROL VALVES

ACCUMULATOR

GAS SPRING

REAR CONTROL VALVE

Fig. 9·19   The general layout of the Automotive Products 'Active Suspension' can be seen from this diagram. At the front end the arrangement is very similar to that of any vehicle with height control, except for the special control valves and the pipes to the rear actuators. At the rear, the actuators are double acting; their tops are connected to a common gas spring so that there is no ani-roll stiffness from the normal fluid system; there is a single height control valve. The cross connections from the front actuators, each to the opposite side rear actuator lower part, control the rear weight transfer in cornering. The text explains how cornering roll is avoided. (*Courtesy of Automotive Products Co. Ltd.*)

wheel, increasing the pressure above the actuator, will automatically reduce the load on the inner rear wheel, because of the extra pressure on the underside of the piston there. Decrease of load on the inner front wheel, by its reduced pressure above its own piston

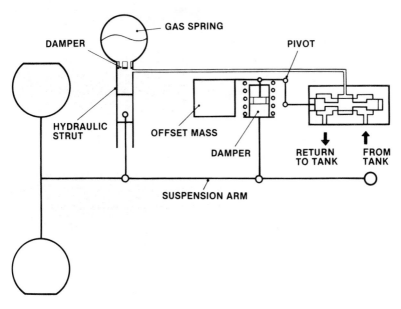

Fig. 9·20   A connection from the suspension arm controls the height control valve via a bell-crank lever. The horizontal arm of this bell-crank has an offset mass, the offset sideways a matter of convenience, the offset downwards below the pivot being responsible for valve movement to avoid cornering roll. The connection itself is special in that it includes a spring and damper in parallel, whose characteristics in relation to the bell-crank mass match those of the suspension spring and damper in relation to the sprung weight. The action is explained in the text. (*Courtesy of Automotive Products Co. Ltd.*)

and under the outside rear wheel piston, increases the load carried by the outer rear wheel. The control valves will provide the volume changes in the front springs to maintain the car level. Putting the centre of gravity of the offset masses below the bell crank pivot, as shown, will provide the extra wheel movements to allow for the tyre deflections.

Upward deflection of the wheels, increasing the spring loads, will accelerate the body upwards. The connecting rod will impart the same acceleration to the offset mass on the bell crank arm, the bell crank will not move and the suspension springs will act normally, without demands on the pressure system.

The two tendencies mentioned earlier, of spring stiffening and reduced effective damping under much increased load, tend to be self-cancelling and only a predominance of one over the other will result in appropriate movement of the bell crank and hence of the

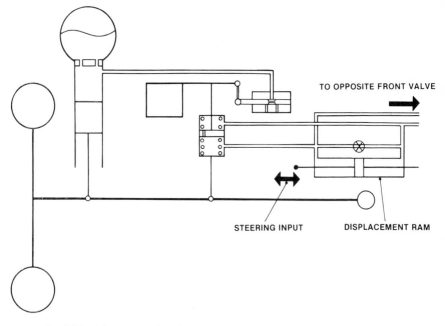

TO OPPOSITE FRONT VALVE

STEERING INPUT   DISPLACEMENT RAM

Fig. 9·21   Advance warning of cornering, to avoid delay in the anti-roll control, is obtained by this connection between the steering system and the operation of the bell-crank on the height control. There is a controlled leak between the two sides so that the effect is temporary, the offset mass on the control valve taking over as sideways acceleration builds up. (*Courtesy of Automotive Products Co. Ltd.*)

valve. To reduce delays in valve operation in cornering, a connection from the steering which will operate the valves in advance of the development of sideways acceleration, can be arranged as shown in Fig. 9.21. Special features in the control valves keep power demands to a minimum. The system was applied experimentally to a variety of vehicles, including private cars, double deck buses, farm and fighting vehicles, including the Ford Granada described in the following Section.

9.7   NO-ROLL SUSPENSION SYSTEMS

The first truly active suspension, stabilised to eliminate pitch and roll, was also developed by Automotive Products in the early 1970s. A prototype Rover 3500 P6 was used for some very convincing demonstrations at the time and a similar system fitted to a Ford Granada research vehicle for assessment in 1974.

The AP system was an extension of the diagonally interconnected Langen principles, used in conjunction with a primary main system, several motion sensors and a very fast acting, high capacity hydraulic pump. Unlike the Citroen hydropneumatic system where time delays are built in to prevent any fast reactions influencing the ride height control, the AP suspension was designed to provide the fastest dynamic responses possible.

Control of the system was by a mechanical pendulum valve designed to match exactly the normal behaviour of the vehicle. Any transient bump signals were therefore filtered out, but any change in the steady state conditions caused fluid to be pumped to whichever strut needed to be jacked or relaxed to control the body motion.

These early AP systems generated self-levelling under inertia loads to provide virtually zero roll and zero pitch characteristics that controlled the wheel camber angles so well that cornering speeds through a test chicane were between 9 and 15 per cent faster than in a similar car without the system. But the system operated by generating a displacement error that was then corrected, all of which took time to respond. And the two-edged sword which killed off the concept before it reached production was that the faster the response time, the more the ride was upset. Another example of a similar concept developed by Volvo is shown in Fig. 9.22.

9.8 ACTIVE SUSPENSION SYSTEMS

Lotus effectively removed all these constraints in their active system by replacing the spring and damper units with irreversible double-acting hydraulic actuators. By measuring instantaneous loads and displacements of each wheel and processing the data to control the actuators, a sophisticated set of microprocessor activated synthetic springs was created.

The original stimulus for the Lotus system[6,7] stemmed from the aerodynamic developments which took place in Formula 1 between 1977 and 1982. Aerodynamic downforce generated by airfoils and skirts increased by a factor of three to a level well in excess of the car's static mass (a car weighing 750 kg, for example, typically generated a purely aerodynamic downforce of around 1200 kg at 150 mph). As the loads were all applied to the chassis and transmitted to the tyres through the suspension, the demands on the springs and dampers were extreme. Instead of merely coping with 750 kg mass, the suspension had to handle close to 2000 kg!

Fig. 9·22   The benefits of zero or anti-roll suspension are clearly illustrated in this comparison between two Volvos. The car at the top has conventional suspension, while the car below has computer controlled suspension designed to resist roll. (*Courtesy Volvo Cars*)

To compound the problem, the adhesion provided by these forces allowed cornering accelerations of over 3.5g. It was all well beyond the limitations of conventional springs and dampers and although skirts were totally banned in 1982, cutting the downforces to peak levels of around 550 kg or only 70 per cent of the car's mass, Lotus went ahead with their research.

The first test car shown in Fig. 9.23 was an Lotus Esprit, followed

Fig. 9·23   Lotus Engineering was one of the first companies to develop an active ride system, as demonstrated here on these two Esprit coupes. The car in the upper picture is conventional, while the one in the lower picture has an active ride system. (*Courtesy Lotus Engineering*)

by a Lotus T92 Formula 1 car. They both used an advanced and sophisticated system of suspension control. It was based on precision signal conditioning units designed by a special group of advanced electronics engineers at the Cranfield Institute of Technology working with Texas Instruments in nearby Bedford and used digital control of analogue inputs to maintain hydraulic pressure, tailor the dynamic attitude of the car at speed and monitor the health of the system at all times. The exceedingly complex systems converted forces, accelerations and displacements to coordinates that were then relayed to the hydraulic servo valves after being compared with actual positions and processed in a fast-acting feedback loop.

The result on the Esprit as the systems were developed was dramatic. Control of body motion over bumps and the complete absence of roll or pitch in transient manoeuvres provided feelings of security and precision which made a quantum leap from even today's high standards at Lotus.

The real value of the Active Suspension cars to Lotus at that time was more of a development tool[8] than a serious project for future production cars. They had the ability to alter stiffness, damping, attitude changes, self-levelling characteristics and all the complex interrelationships between these and other parameters from the cockpit with the car in motion. By totally eliminating the time delay required to change parts or recalibrate suspension settings between subjective tests completely transformed the assessment process. It freed up the development engineers' time to reach better performance compromises and also allowed new investigations to be made into the various possible strategies available for future adaptive systems.

The fundamental difference between an active and conventional suspension is that active systems provide independent treatment for road induced forces and for body inertia forces. They therefore have the ability to eliminate the traditional compromise between ride and handling characteristics completely.

In most of the systems being investigated, road disturbances are treated 'passively' as in a conventional system, but with much softer than normal spring and damper settings. Body forces generated by cornering, braking and accelerating are controlled by the 'active' elements in the system which resist roll and pitch in both the transient and steady state conditions to maintain the vehicle level and the road wheels more upright, for maximum handling and road holding performance.

To achieve this functional independence, conventional coil springs are replaced by hydropneumatic struts and gas springs with damper valves incorporated in the gas spring assembly. A Lotus suspension unit is shown in Fig. 9.24. Although each front strut and gas spring supports a front corner of the vehicle in the usual way, it is also connected to the underside of each diagonally opposite rear strut as well. The upper area of each rear strut is connected to a common rear gas spring to support the rear of the vehicle, with

Fig. 9·24 The Lotus active ride units comprise fast-acting hydraulic rams and gas springs controlled by a highly developed on-board computer. (*Courtesy Lotus Engineering*)

relative piston areas being used to control the roll couple distribution, which is independent of ride frequencies.

Ride height sensors operate self-levelling valves that increase or decrease the hydraulic pressure in the struts to compensate for any load condition, with either electronic or viscous-damped delay mechanisms to allow normal wheel movement on the road. Front strut pressures are also controlled by fast response inertia sensors or valves that can differentiate between bump movements and roll or pitch inputs, and respond individually in an optimised way. The first active ride systems developed by Ford used mechanical controls, but the potential offered by electronic sensors and on-board computers has now resulted in a new generation of equipment.

As a first stage in reaching production with active suspension systems of this type, the Lincoln-Mercury Division of Ford in Dearborn has developed an electronically-controlled air suspension (EAS) that was introduced on the 1984 Lincoln Continental Mark VII models. It is shown in Fig. 9.25. For its day the system was a

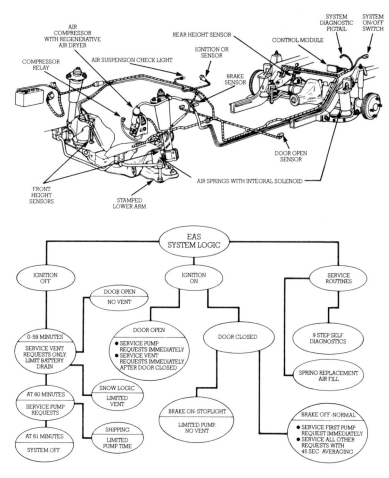

Fig. 9·25   The Lincoln-Mercury electronic air suspension introduced in 1984 employed very sophisticated controls with advanced system logic

very advanced self-levelling installation that provided a constant ride height and consistent handling regardless of load, as would be required for an active system, but without the dynamic controls to restrict roll and pitch. Much of the hardware and control strategy could be applied to an active system.

Because constant suspension travel is always made available through the self-levelling mechanism, spring rates are between 32 and 38 per cent lower than would have been practical for the same

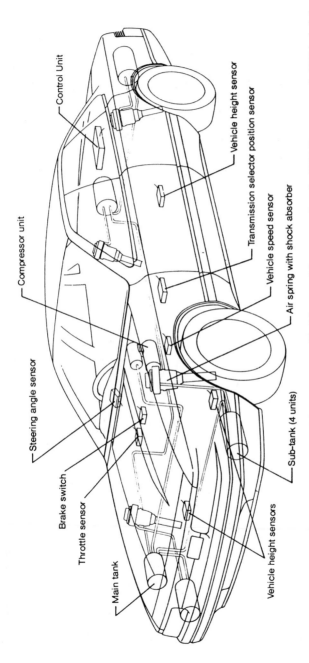

Fig. 9·26 The electronically-controlled suspension system proposed by Nissan and demonstrated on the CUE-X concept car in 1986 included steering input sensors to provide a total 'driving envelope' that optimises the suspension for all driving conditions

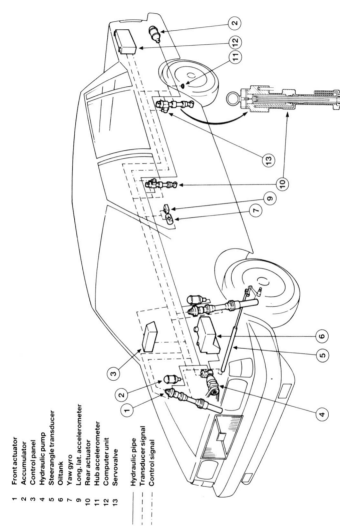

1 Front actuator
2 Accumulator
3 Control panel
4 Hydraulic pump
5 Steerangle transducer
6 Oiltank
7 Yaw gyro
9 Long. lat. accelerometer
10 Rear actuator
11 Hub accelerometer
12 Computer unit
13 Servovalve

――― Hydraulic pipe
――― Transducer signal
―‐‐― Control signal

Fig. 9-27 The layout of the experimental Volvo computerised suspension is similar to that proposed by Nissan

car with conventional steel springs. Earlier experimental work on an active control system for a European Ford Granada operated effectively with spring rates that were 20 per cent lower than standard at the front and 45 per cent lower at the rear, which illustrates the degree of potential ride improvement offered by advanced systems of this type.

On the Lincoln system there are four air springs supplied by an electric air compressor, a single-chip microcomputer control module and three electronic Hall-effect height sensors mounted at each front corner and over the rear axle. Their linear signal is processed along with dynamic signals that measure the suspension frequency as it rides, by counting the up and down motions over a time base of 45 s. Included in the computer logic are certain fundamental assumptions, like not to make any height adjustments when the brakes are applied, to start making height corrections immediately after a door or the boot lid has been opened – but never downwards in case the door jams on the kerb. Output from the computer activates either an electric pump for the air springs, or vent valves, as required.

Apart from some very meticulous suppression of unwanted electrical inputs, the Lincoln system also has a novel 'watchdog' circuit to protect its functions and the vehicle battery during long parked periods. To prevent the computer getting confused by the ignition being switched on and off several times (as with a difficult cold start or fuel flooding for whatever reason), its power supply is arranged to remain active for one hour after the ignition has been switched off, after which time the microprocessor interrupts itself until the ignition is switched on again.

Several other manufacturers have proposed active or semi-active suspension systems for cars of the future and adaptive damping systems are already in production for models like the Citroen XM and Ford Mondeo. Typical examples of system layouts are shown in Figs. 9.26 and 9.27. For most drivers most of the time the optimisation of conventional suspension systems using the latest computer aids as development tools provides totally acceptable ride and handling characteristics.

REFERENCES

1. Moulton, A. E. and Best, A., 'From Hydrolastic to Hydrogas', *Proc. Auto. Div. I. Mech. E.* (1978–79)
2. Mizuguchi, M., Chikamori, S., Suda, T., and Kobayashi, K., 'Electronically-Controlled Suspension (ECS)', *Proc. FISITA Congress XX, SAE Technical Paper* No. 845051 (1984)
3. Richardson, R. M., 'Adaptive Suspension Damping', *Proc. FISITA Congress XX, SAE Technical Paper* No. 845053 (1984)

4. Karnopp, D., 'Active Damping in Road Vehicle Suspension Systems', *Vehicle Systems Dynamics*, Vol. 12, No.6 (1983)
5. Pitcher, R. H., 'Technology Showcase: Active Ride Control System', *J. Terramechanics*, Vol. 22, No.4 (1986)
6. Wright, P. G. and Williams, D. A., 'Application of Active Suspension to High Performance Road Vehicles', *Proc. I. Mech. E.*, C239/84 (1984)
7. Wright, P. G. and Williams, D. A., 'The Case for an Irreversible Active Suspension System', *SAE Technical Paper* No. 890081 (1989)
8. Hurdwell, R., and Pilling, J., 'Active Suspension and Rear Wheel Steering Make Powerful Research and Development Tools', *SAE Technical Paper No. 930266* (March 1993)

10
Drive layout and its effects

10.1 BACKGROUND TO FRONT WHEEL DRIVE

There have been different ways of driving a car since the beginnings of motoring when the engine was squeezed in wherever there was a convenient space. The natural instinct at that time, however, was to replace the horse with an engine which pulled from the front in the same kind of way. It was the complication of driving the steered wheels with the technology available which forced the adoption of rear wheel drive almost universally.

It is interesting to note in this context that one of the first steam carriages in Europe, built by Jacques Cugnot in 1766, operated by driving the front wheels, but it was not successful. Most of the real pioneering front wheel drive systems before 1950 came from the USA and were founded on the design of the Miller Indianapolis racing cars which first appeared in 1925.

The first recorded front-drive car of any note was revealed at the 1904 New York Auto Show by J. Walter Christie. It used a transverse V4 engine in unit with the final drive and independent sliding pillar front suspension. Christie's designs proved very successful in racing and at one time held the unofficial lap record on the banked Indianapolis brick-surfaced race track.

Ben Gregory of Kansas built a series of front-drive prototypes in 1919 and some of his ideas were adopted by Harry Miller for his racing cars which totally dominated American racing from 1925 until the World War 2.

Only a year later Alvis in the UK built a racing car with a supercharged straight-eight engine in a front-drive chassis for the then current Grand Prix formula, which was followed by a production sports car with the same drive system. And at the same time in France, J.A. Gregoire built the first front-drive Tracta.

Independent front suspension, when it arrived, only compounded the drive shaft problems and demanded something considerably better than the universal joints available at that time, which were large, heavy, limited in their angles of operation and prone to break up if abused. Some adventurous pioneers fought back against convention because they were convinced of front wheel drive logic, but in the main they had little way of understanding the dynamic characteristics of what they were doing, with the result that most early front wheel drive cars were poorly executed.

Dreams of easy-to-drive high performance front-drive production cars did not die in conflict with the engineering problems involved, however. While the Americans followed Miller's lead with sports cars like the 1929 Cord, European design took off in a distinctly different direction. In 1931 DKW introduced two front-drive mini cars and a year later Adler launched the 1.5-litre front-drive Trumpf, Audi came out with two front-drive models and André Citröen produced his first traction avante.

And so the balance between front and rear wheel drive looked set to stay, with the bulk of the post-war car industry steering well clear of front wheel drive and all the reliability problems it introduced. There were many prototypes, of course, but no design approval for a new front-drive system until Issigonis caused something of a design revolution with the 1959 Mini.

There were lots of reasons at the time why front wheel drive was right for the Mini and would have been wrong for the Ford 105 Anglia, launched the same year with rear wheel drive. There were certainly no Mini influences at all in the first Ford front wheel drive car, the Cardinal project, designed in the USA for production there and in Germany and launched only in Germany as the 1962 Taunus 12M. It was not until Fiat had shown what front wheel drive could really do for a small car with the 127 that the Fiesta concept was given the approval it needed to go ahead.

Between the Mini and the Fiesta there were Renaults, Panhards and DKWs, Saabs and Lancias, all with various front-drive systems, although by 1972 less than 5 per cent of the cars available on the British market were front wheel drive. By 1982 more than 70 per cent of the cars sold in Britain used front wheel drive and by 1984 practically the whole of the US industry had switched to front drive designs, as had the bulk of Japanese production.

10.2 FRONT VS. REAR DRIVE ARGUMENTS

Every new car launched from then on, with one or two notable exceptions like the BMW range, the Ford Sierra and Mercedes 190, featured not just front wheel drive but a total system that proved very effectively how good front wheel drive engineering had suddenly become. And in the market, more and more buyers seemed to understand and appreciate the well-publicised advantages of extra interior space and greater stability in slippery conditions.

Yet there were several major discrepancies in philosophy between models designed to compete in precisely the same market segment which still makes the whole question worthy of detailed investigation. Why, it was asked, have BMW and Mercedes declared a permanent dedication to rear drive cars? And why, when the Ascona and Cavalier became so much more successful in new front wheel drive form, did Ford stay with rear wheel drive for their new Sierra but 10 years later change to front wheel drive for the new Mondeo?

There are some very good reasons why there is a significant and widespread shift to front wheel drive now more than in the past, which go well beyond the dynamic aspects of front and rear drive concepts. And some of the conclusions are not the expected ones.

10.3   MODERN DESIGN PRIORITIES

Most car designers believe that the drive layout of any new car should be the best available solution to the total design requirement. To act responsibly in today's energy-conscious environment, this means designing the most efficient vehicle in each market segment, as defined by the product planning analysts. Priorities for large cars are therefore different from those of small cars and as the packaging gets 'tighter', Fig. 10.1 shows the advantages that are gained from changing a rear-drive design to front wheel drive. The attractions of front against rear wheel drive, however, change to produce a cross-over effect from one system to the other, as shown in Table 10.1. This view would appear to be supported by BL Cars (now the Rover Group), which after a long history of rear drive models and a mixed range for many years now builds nothing but front wheel drive. Within the industry there is no sign of unanimity about basic concepts or the specific point at which the cross-over, if any, occurs.

With some notable exceptions like Audi and Citroen, which both have a very long history of front wheel drive, and Rover, which has been radically influenced by its co-operative technical liaison with Honda, there is little dispute among the various engineers that for the best design solutions with the technology of today, small cars up to about 120–150 bhp should be front wheel drive and large luxury

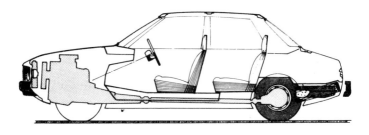

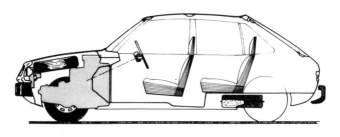

Fig. 10·1   The differences in package efficiency and overall length that result from changing from rear to front wheel drive are shown clearly in this transverse comparison of two alternative layouts. (*Courtesy Renault SA*)

cars should be rear wheel drive. BMW believe that, for what they call 'driving quality', the steering must be independent of drive influences regardless, which produces some nicely positive and finely balanced steering systems. Volkswagen and Audi, like Saab, have proved that it is quite feasible to produce excellent high-powered front wheel drive designs, although for the ultimate high performance Audi coupe and their V8 limousine, they have resorted to something other than front wheel drive. Fig. 10.2 shows the four different drive arrangements possible in a front wheel drive design.

The way the design requirements cause a shift of emphasis between front and rear wheel drive according to the car type is an analysis fully supported by a study of power against weight for about 80 typical middle-of-each-range European cars, Table 10.1. Each of the considerations which go into the design process of reaching a concept decision is worth examining in detail according to categories related to their effects on the final car.

Table 10·1   DESIGN REQUIREMENTS IN DIFFERENT MARKET SECTORS

Minicar	Small car	Family car	Luxury car	Performance saloon	Sports car/Coupé	Rally or track car
Versatile accommodation	Versatile accommodation	Versatile accommodation	Distinctive style	Fast appearance	Sleek styling	Priority to function
Small frontal area	Small frontal area	Low C_d and reasonable area	Low C_d	Low C_d	Low C_d	Ground effect and low C_d
Small engine	Small engine	Choice of engines with diesel option	Wide choice of engines, optional diesel, possibly with turbo	Large engine with fuel injection and/or turbo	Large engine with fuel injection and/or turbo	Maximum power output
Good performance	Good performance	Good performance	Smooth performance	Fun to drive	Fun to drive	Quick responses; ultimate handling
Maximum fuel economy	Good fuel economy	Good fuel economy	Good fuel economy for class	Good fuel economy for class	Performance first	Performance first
Low cost	Low cost	Low cost	Value for money	Value for money	Cost secondary	Cost no object
Ride secondary	Adequate ride	Good ride	Good ride	Good handling	Good handling	Maximum roadholding
Easy to service and repair	Easy to service and repair	Easy to service and repair				Fast repairs at pit or service stops
Minimum weight	Minimum weight	Minimum weight	Controlled weight	Good power-to-weight ratio	Good power-to-weight ratio	Low weight
Maximum package for size	Maximum package for size	Maximum package for size	Maximum package for size	Reasonable luggage room	Reasonable luggage room	To carry long-range fuel tank and large-section spare tyre
Some noise acceptable	Reasonable noise	Low noise	Very quiet interior	Quiet at high speed	Quiet at high speed	Noise not important
4 seats	4 seats	5 seats	5 seats	'2 + 2'	'2 + 2'	2 seats only
← FWD →			← FWD or RWD →			← RWD →

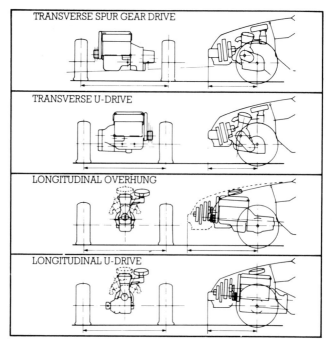

Fig. 10·2 There are basically four possible drive arangements for front wheel drive as shown here. Each results in a different front-end package with significant effects on styling and aerodynamics. (*Courtesy Ford Motor Co.*)

10.4 WEIGHT AND MASS DISTRIBUTION

At first glance and particularly for small cars, there might appear to be other significant weight benefits with front wheel drive. According to studies carried out by BMW[1], on a typical 900 kg car, elimination of the prop shaft and its universal joints saves about 9 kg, while the shorter body described above saves a further 11–14 kg.

But the extra proportion of front-end weight affects the steering effort and the braking balance to the point where even for medium-sized cars power steering, brake servo and a load-sensitive brake apportioning valve may be required. And to maintain a luxury ride quality on certain models, some kind of levelling device at the rear may also be essential. The weight of these additional components could easily cancel out the weight saving achieved.

The regrouping of components at the front in an front wheel drive design increases the proportion of sprung mass at this end from about 52 per cent in the driver-only condition to about 62 per cent, which adds 20 per cent to the steering effort. Providing adequate wheel travel for a smooth ride with under all laden conditions also becomes more difficult as the ratio of fully laden to unladen axle loading at the rear also goes up, from 1.6-to-1 with rear wheel drive to 1.8-to-1 or worse with front wheel drive.

On level ground with the driver only on board, the extra static weight with front wheel drive over the driving wheels helps traction. Uneven torque and wheelspin can be countered easily before the car twitches out of line, unlike rear wheel drive where there is bound to be some fishtailing. This is the main reason why many drivers prefer front wheel drive in slippery conditions.

While front-drive cars have a better static weight distribution for traction, the dynamic weight transfer rearwards which occurs as soon as torque is applied reduces the tractive effort available at the front wheels. Adding extra passengers or trying to tow a caravan or trailer similarly reduces the static traction advantage and compounds the dynamic effects considerably.

With a coefficient of friction below 0.6, which is typical of any wet or icy road, the relative traction available between front wheel drive and rear wheel drive depends entirely on the load being carried; front wheel drive provides better traction only when carrying a light load. In soft snow there is the additional advantage that the front wheels with front wheel drive may be able to 'cog' in as they drive, while with rear wheel drive they must be pushed against the snow from behind and more easily build up wedges under their leading edges.

10.5   DYNAMIC CHARACTERISTICS

When the weight transfer effects are related to the friction required to generate cornering forces in the tyres, the strong power-on understeer inherent in all powerful front-drive cars results. In extreme conditions there is also a marked secondary influence on stability as well.

As understeer is generated, the natural inclination of the driver is to apply more lock, to maintain his chosen line through a bend. Should the driving torque suddenly be reduced, for example if he needs to lift off for a hazard, there will be a sudden increase in cornering power which creates the classic front-end tuck-in characteristic so common in front wheel drive cars. With rear wheel drive the dynamic decrease in rear axle loading in the same situation can cause a loss of tyre grip and oversteer, although the latest generation of independent rear suspension systems now seem able to eliminate this characteristic completely.

A fully-laden front wheel drive car shows a greater difference in behaviour from its unladen condition and is more difficult to control than a similar rear wheel drive car, because the changes in axle loadings are greater with front wheel drive. Tyre loadings are similarly more unbalanced with front wheel drive giving rise to uneven wear rates front to rear, sometimes by as much as 3 to 1, as shown in Table 10.2.

BMW studies also show that front wheel drive cars as a group have a stability advantage in cross winds, especially if the driver holds the wheel tightly, as he is prone to do in these conditions. But the variations between cars in each group are greater than the differences between the two systems, which confirms that stability has to be built into the basic design by development of the aerodynamic lift and suspension characteristics. Although it is probably easier to make front wheel drive cars more consistently stable in the unladen condition, they become much more difficult when fully laden or towing.

Equally challenging from the design standpoint is the need with front wheel drive to absorb all the driving forces of the wheels through the engine/transmission mountings. To suppress engine and drive line vibrations, soft mounts are required, while hard mounts are needed to prevent drive wind-up. In a rear wheel drive layout, these two requirements are well separated and can be designed for individually. The problems with front wheel drive are compounded in the transverse installation at least by the often restricted room for engine movement on the mounts. Many manufacturers of front wheel drive cars have been forced to add hydraulic dampers or tie bars (which provide unwanted acoustic paths to the structure in

Table 10·2 COMPARISON OF TYRE LOADINGS WITH FRONT AND REAR WHEEL DRIVE

Wheels	Tyre Usage	FWD	RWD
Front	Braking	20%	17%
	Steering	24%	24%
	Traction	24%	0%
	Cornering	17%	15%
		85%	56%
Rear	Braking	5%	8%
	Traction	0%	24%
	Cornering	10%	12%
		15%	44%
Total		100%	100%

themselves) to engine mounts in attempts to strike an effective balance between these conflicting requirements.

An often related problem with a transverse front wheel drive design is that engine movement introduces bending moments into the exhaust system which can shorten its life and make it difficult to arrange on properly insulated hangers. With a conventional longitudinal design, engine rocking produces only small torsional forces in the exhaust system, low amplitude vertical shake being the only source of bending.

Unbalanced front-end mass with front wheel drive is aggravated by weight transfer during braking, especially when unladen. Front brakes must therefore have a much greater capacity than the rears and in most cases a proportioning valve to prevent rear wheel lock in extreme conditions is essential. The availability of cheap ventilated front discs combined with modern pad materials seldom makes front braking performance a problem, but the legal requirement for the system to operate with reasonable efficiency in the event of a partial failure has led to the introduction of diagonal split systems on most front wheel drive cars, which slightly adds to the cost.

When it comes to really high performance, the mid-engined rear wheel drive car has a distinct advantage on the track and the road, hence its total domination in racing. In rallying on loose stages, the responses of the car required by the driver are totally different and success with front wheel drive has only been achieved in spite of its concept, not because of it. In this kind of event the driver needs a car which is 'nervous' in the extreme, not to the point of being unstable, but able to change direction in a flash at any time, even when sliding, and that is one thing front wheel drive cars cannot do at all well.

All these apparent limitations of front-drive design can be solved, of course, by conventional engineering methods, as the abundance of safe, effective and quite powerful front-drive cars available today demonstrate. At the smaller end of the market they have total domination and prove beyond doubt that the concept is effective and efficient.

At the upper end of the market, where carrying capacity and consistent comfort quality are more important, rear wheel drive is generally the only way to go. In between, it is the effectiveness of the design and particularly its execution which decides how good or otherwise each concept turns out to be in practice. But whatever arguments are raised for either system, there seems to be something fundamentally wrong in unbalancing the car with one pair of wheels doing more than half the work. It is to the credit of their designers that this fact is totally obscured in many of the latest front wheel drive cars, and even some of the better developed earlier ones.

10.6   FOUR-WHEEL DRIVE

Basically there are two types of four-wheel drive, designed for two distinctly different purposes. Part-time off-road systems have been developed in many various forms from the concept of the American army wartime Jeep. Permanent all-weather on-road and rally car systems have mostly been spawned from the various successes of the Range Rover and Audi Quattro.

The first main thrust in four wheel drive development came at the end of 1918 when various US government departments tried to lay down a specification for a 'go anywhere' kind of lightweight military vehicle. Many different types of prototype were built, from stripped down Ford Model Ts to special tracked machines. The winning design used a 1932 Austin Seven saloon as the starting point that eventually turned into the specification for the now famous World War II Jeep.

After the war a team of British engineers proposed a more sophisticated agricultural version of the Jeep that was developed into the Land Rover. By 1985 there were over 60 four-wheel drive cars on the European market.

In practical terms there are only two reasons why two-wheel drive

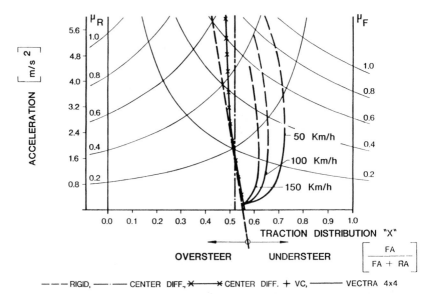

Fig. 10·3   Traction distribution between front and rear axles for three different four-wheel drive systems varies with the acceleration. A viscous drive to the rear axle gives the most consistent understeering behaviour. (*Courtesy Adam Opel AG*)

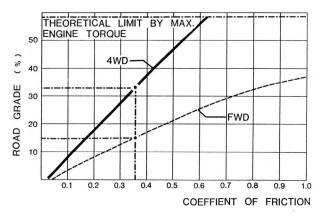

Fig. 10·4   Gradeability is a primary advantage of four-wheel drive as shown here. As the gradient of a hill gets steeper, so the benefits increase. (*Courtesy Adam Opel AG*)

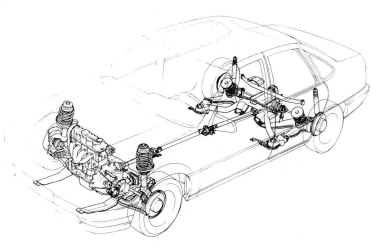

Fig. 10·5   The Opel Vectra. used a hang-on transmission unit to transmit drive from the front-wheel drive gearbox to the rear axle. (*Courtesy Adam Opel AG*)

may not be sufficient. One is the problem of driving in low friction conditions such as mud, ice or packed snow, when the tractive effort needed to move off may be too much for one axle to transmit with or without a self-locking differential. The other is the difficulty of getting high power down on the road safely in an ultrafast car.

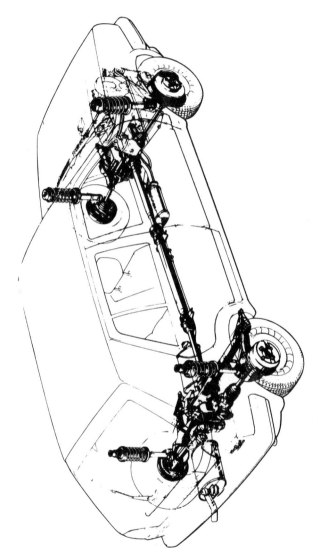

Fig. 10·6 The Volkswagen Golf Synchro is another clever adaptation of a front wheel drive layout. (*Courtesy Volkswagen AG*)

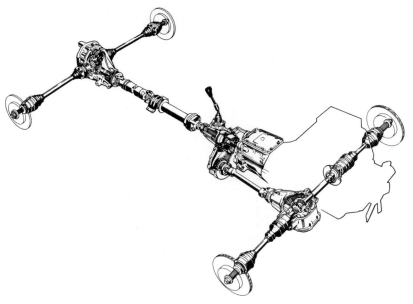

Fig. 10·7   The Ford Sierra 4x4 system is based on a rear drive design with chain drive from the in-line gearbox and a forward running transfer shaft[2]. (*Courtesy Ford Motor Co.*)

When there are deficiencies in a 4x2 system, the cross-over between the first and the second parameters starts to show up in everyday driving.

Opel studies in the late 1980s clearly demonstrated the different driving behaviour of three different four-wheel drive systems in terms of the available traction, Fig. 10.3. With vehicle acceleration plotted against friction coefficients of the front and rear axles show the traction distribution X as a percentage. For total front wheel drive, $X = 1$ and for total rear wheel drive $X = 0$. The data was measured with the vehicle loaded with one passenger at a speed of 50 km/h. A driveline concept with the rear axle driven by a viscous coupling resulted in understeer at any speed, as indicated by the solid lines for 50, 100 and 150 km/h.

The gradeability advantages of four-wheel drive are one of the primary customer motivations. Fig. 10.4 shows just how significant the advantages can be. On a 30 per cent hill with a friction coefficient of 0.35 the maximum climbing ability for the four-wheel drive vehicle is over twice that of the front-drive alternative.

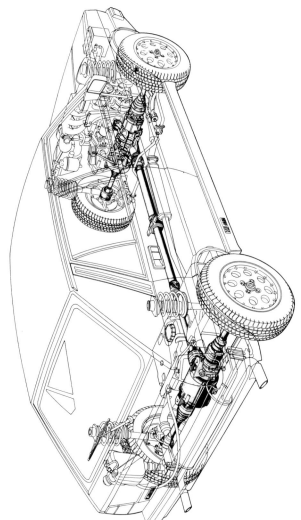

Fig. 10·8   The highly successful Lancia Delta Integrale was derived from a compact front drive system. (*Courtesy Lancia SpA*)

Four different layouts of four-wheel drive drivetrains are shown in Figs. 10.6, 10.7. 10.8 and 10.9.

REFERENCES

1. Howard, G., 'Front or Rear Wheel Drive?', *Motor* (September 1982)
2. Mansfield, R., Design development and testing of the Sierra XR4x4, *Proc. Auto Div. I. Mech. E.*, C11/86 (1986)

11

Computer aids and design techniques

11.1 COMPUTER USE IN SUSPENSION DESIGN

Although the first use of computers in suspension design and development dates back over 25 years, rapid and recent advances in graphic displays, measurement techniques and processing time are putting a new emphasis and value on the results of interactive studies. Today the visual display unit linked to a powerful high-speed computer running advanced dynamic suspension and vehicle models are the basic tools of the suspension design trade.

Computer aids in suspension design eliminate much of the guesswork, empirical measurement and practically all the tedious calculations that were previously required to determine safe stress levels and acceptable durability standards as the preliminary stages to a new system design. Carefully developed programmes[1] now allow not only the thousands of simultaneous equations of dynamic movement to be solved rapidly by the high-capacity, high-speed computer systems accessible through local workstation terminals that now form a familiar part of every large design department.

Advanced computer graphics of the type shown in Figs. 11.1, 11.2 and 11.3 are regularly used to simulate actual parts in action under strain, often showing differences in stress levels by keyed colour graduations, like a thermal image picture of heat radiation. Three-dimensional representations also act as valuable visual aid to the experienced eye of a component engineer working on a new design, with light source angle of view and magnification all under keyboard control.

This kind of computer-aided design (CAD) is currently being integrated with computer-aided manufacture (CAM) into a new operating science known as computer integrated engineering (CIE)[2]. It is having dramatic effects on the whole process of creating new vehicles and components, and updating existing models.

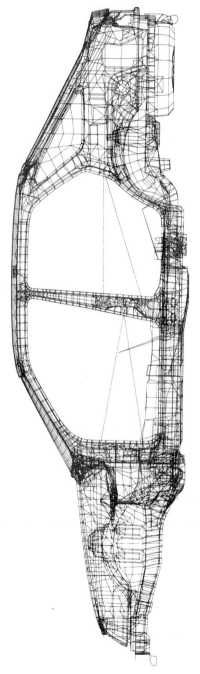

Fig. 11-1   Representations of a vehicle structure by a mesh of several thousand integrated struts and panels allows the stresses in the body and chassis components to be analysed and optimised. (*Courtesy Ford Motor Co.*)

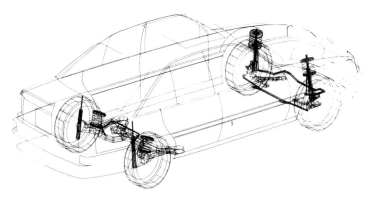

Fig. 11·2   Computer programmes are now commonly used to study the behaviour of front and rear suspension systems in great detail. (*Courtesy Adam Opel AG*)

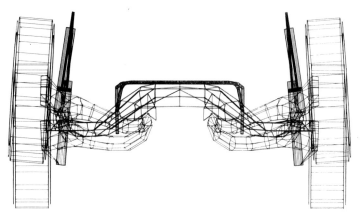

Fig. 11·3   This typical rear suspension can be examined frame by frame to determine its precise kinematic characteristics under all kinds of operating conditions. (*Courtesy Adam Opel AG*)

11.2   FINITE ELEMENT ANALYSIS

Stress analysis for both the supporting elements of the integral body/chassis unit and each component part of the suspension system is performed with impressive accuracy by a mesh of Finite Elements (FE) built up into a framework of several thousand finely detailed interlinked struts built up into triangles, squares and rectangles[3]. From the first applications of FE programmes used to handle only discrete parts of a full system, new tools have been developed that can now simulate the considerably more complex models required to represent authentic dynamic behaviour.

Early FE work was limited originally to stress and strain calculations by the inability of the computer systems to handle the non-linear events and relatively large displacements typical of vehicle suspensions under dynamic loads. Setting up representative mathematical equations of motion for the inter-related parts was too complex and time-consuming for the skills and abilities available within engineering department staffs. But with new generation computers came automated and user-friendly programming interfaces that eliminated the tedium and lowered the threshold of acceptance by traditional mechanical engineers.

As already mentioned, FE methods of structural analysis represent a complex component or assembly as a multiplicity of regions or elements within which simple stress (and strain) assumptions are taken to apply. Each element interacts with those adjacent to it and these inter-relationships are expressed as a system of linear simultaneous equations containing many different unknown variables. Without the considerable processing power of modern computers, the equations would be impossible to solve. From the initially impressive ability to solve hundreds of equations rapidly, today's supercomputers can handle hundreds of thousands simultaneously in even less time.

The method was first used by the aircraft industry and has now been adopted by shipbuilders, civil engineers and the automotive industry. It has allowed the science of stress analysis to be extended way beyond the first two-dimensional studies into the realms of three dimensions where the computer can solve equations for each given load input to satisfy the conditions of equilibrium at common points on each element's boundaries to give a set of displacements as the answers. From these solutions and the elemental stiffnesses the programme works back to obtain stress levels and if required further processing to derive the vibration characteristics.

FE methods are such a powerful computer tool that their analytical capabilities now outstrip stress engineers' knowledge of loadings and material properties in a component such as a suspension member. Using techniques known as comparative stressing, new designs can be developed for optimum shape, weight and strength from a database of previous test results.

11.3 COMPUTER DATABASES AND HOW THEY ARE USED

By analysing new proposals for their section moduli (relative strength in bending), moments of inertia (relative stiffness) and cross-sectional area (relative weight) direct comparisons can be made with existing or historical designs to derive performance predictions. Instead of laboriously building co-ordinate inputs to a computer programme from manual readings of shape and section thickness, digitising tablets are now used to save time and increase accuracy.

Data and specifications derived in the development processes are stored in memory devices, transferred to component suppliers on magnetic tapes and often used directly to make parts on Numerical Control production machines. Where drawings (called 'hard copies' in computer parlance) are required they are usually generated automatically at extraordinarily high speed in computer controlled drafting machines. In many cases data transfer between terminals is achieved by telephone or fibre-optic land-lines, satellite tele-communications links or microwave transmissions.

11.4   CASE STUDY: FORD'S COMPUTER SYSTEMS

To appreciate the perspective of computer applications in engineering design, it is worth looking at Ford's European operations as an interesting case study. There are now over 5,000 desktop computer terminals in use by Ford in Europe and several hundred portable lap-top machines used in vehicles to operate development programmes and record experimental data while vehicles are being tested.

Computers are also used extensively for the automation of test procedures through the introduction and maintenance of advanced component rigs and sophisticated data collection vehicles. Hardware is built into an integrated European computer network of IBM compatible mainframes ranging from IBM 4331 through Amdahl 580 to an IBM 3081K, a CDC 730 and several DEC VAX computers with links to Europe and the USA. There are also some small UNIVAC and Boroughs systems with mini-computers from DEC, Prime, Datapoint, Computervision, General Automation and Wang, as well as many IBM compatible stand-alone personal computer systems.

11.5   COMPUTER SOFTWARE USED IN SUSPENSION RESEARCH AND DEVELOPMENT

All the large car manufacturers and suppliers, and even some of the smaller specialist consultants, also have a considerable number of advanced computer programmes well developed for use in the

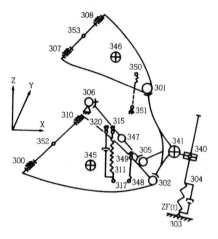

Fig. 11·4 Many computer simulations like this mathematical model of a single wheel system are used in the early stages of suspension design

design and analysis of ride and handling issues. They range from a single-wheel model, Figs. 11.4 and 11.5, used to predict the non-linear effects of suspension movement on vehicle ride to a sophisticated simulation of the total vehicle, Figs. 11.6 and 11.7, that can include steering, brake and drive torque, bush performance and side forces if required.

The primary advantages of all these programmes is that they allow the first prototypes to be built closer to the optimum, which can shorten the lead time for new models and release more time for the refining and development of the production systems. Although originally developed for use on large mainframe computer systems, like those housed in the vast Ford computer complex at Dearborn and accessible to European engineers through transatlantic communications links and the latest Cray supercomputers used by Ford, General Motors and the Volkswagen-Audi group, some have been rewritten for use on the latest generation of relatively small high-speed minicomputers locally available throughout the industry.

Some of these programmes have been developed by the technology-based computer software and engineering analysis industry for sale to design departments across the world. Others have been developed by the car makers in-house to suit their own needs and systems. One of the primary dynamic programmes, developed and copyrighted by Mechanical Dynamics Inc. of Ann Arbor, Michigan, and in widespread general use all over the world is called ADAMS (Automatic Dynamic Analysis of Mechanical Systems). The

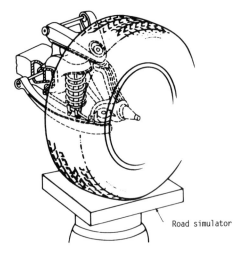

Fig. 11·5   Much of the computer data used in simulations is gathered from instrumented vehicles and laboratory rigs like this. The road simulator is driven by the data collected at the proving ground

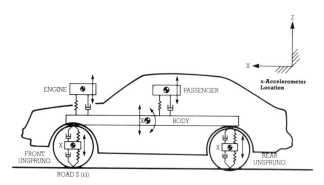

Fig. 11·6   This typical computer model of a car and suspension system has six degrees of freedom with simulations of the engine and body masses, the passengers in their seats and each unsprung tyre and wheel assembly. (*Courtesy Ford Motor Co.*)

ADAMS programme is able to perform ride, handling and durability analysis both for advanced research and product development. It can take account all the compliance steer effects of front and rear suspensions and the characteristics of tyre flexibility. Its main advantage is that it allows designs to be developed closer to their optimum before hardware has been built.

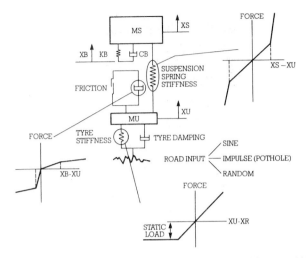

Fig. 11·7   Complex wheel and spring systems can be represented by several idealised elements with simplified but representative relationships

The origins of the ADAMS programme go back about 25 years, but it has been of most value since it has been possible to incorporate adequate tyre data. It is based on a three-dimensional multi-degree of freedom rigid-body system which performs large amplitude displacements to predict velocities, accelerations and forces. Total vehicle handling simulations are constructed to duplicate actual vehicle kinematics, statics and dynamics, including non-linear load/deflection and force/velocity characteristics as well as time-dependent steering inputs, brake and drive torques and external forces like side-wind gusts.

Outputs available include time response plots of displacement velocities and accelerations of any modelled part, forces between two parts and detailed animated graphics that can be viewed statically or frame-by-frame through a storage terminal. Simple 'stick and circle' representations on the computer screen accurately of the type shown in Fig. 11.8, depict vehicle behaviour under a wide variety of driving conditions including U-turns and 360-degree circle tests at speeds up to the overturning limit and slalom or lane change manoeuvres up to spin-out.

Another suspension modelling programme designed to simulate the handling characteristics of a complete vehicle has been developed by Ford and is known by the acronym of FRESH (Ford Research Handling) simulation. This system was primarily developed to capture the vehicle behaviour necessary to study questions

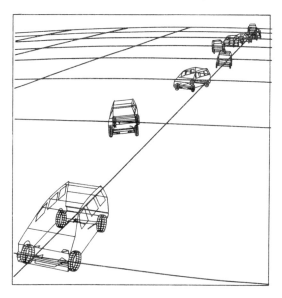

Fig. 11·8 Computer models can display responses to steering inputs in three-dimensional representations of vehicle behaviour like this slalom test of a small front wheel drive hatchback. (*Courtesy Adam Opel AG*)

of dynamic response and the often intangible qualities described as 'driving feel'. Of particular interest were the characteristics of front-wheel drive vehicles, rough road handling, aerodynamic effects and the behaviour at the limit of tyre adhesion. Issues of vibration, noise and structural loads were not considered initially, to simplify the procedures and calculations.

The structural elements of the body are therefore represented as a rigid system, with the suspension modelled as a set of kinematic relationships that govern both the position and orientation of the wheels relative to the body. Tyre forces and moments are resolved into components at the centre of each wheel and quantified by reference to co-ordinate points fixed on the body. Both independent and solid axle systems can be modelled for all aspects of their dynamic behaviour.

Although conventional terminology is used to describe movement about the three normal axes – pitch, roll and yaw – some aspects have been developed into more complex and realistic relationships. Simple fixed roll centre height, for example, is replaced by a variable suspension formula which more accurately represents rear-end 'jacking' in extreme manoeuvres. The processing power of the computer also allows complete dynamic equations to be used, including the higher order terms often ignored in previous analyses.

To complete the authenticity of the model and represent the behaviour of the vehicle in transitional conditions like braking or accelerating in a turn, the rotational motion of the wheels has also been included. Special attention was also paid to modelling the steering system in order to represent torque-steer phenomenon and free-control response (hands-off stability). Details of driving torque and drive-shaft angles are also included for front-drive vehicles.

The resulting mathematical model has 17 degrees of freedom including six modes for the sprung mass, four describing wheel motion relative to the sprung mass, four describing wheelspin conditions and three describing the steering system. It is defined by 30 coupled first order differential equations, increased to 38 by including the forward and lateral accelerations of the wheels. Although some simplification of the tyre behaviour has been made, using previously determined values for the forces generated by the slip angles, the programme still occupies about 7,000 lines, most of which are documentation, input/output and plotting routines and general overhead and management procedures.

FRESH simulations are capable of reproducing a wide range of operating conditions and control situations. They have been used to predict performance of different suspension systems on a particular vehicle, to study rough road handling, to predict cross-wind stability of different aerodynamic configurations and to investigate torque-steer effects in front-drive designs. Flat road directional response is a particular study where FRESH has proved useful. By specifying a steering input which increases slowly until the limit of capability is reached, a pseudo steady state cornering curve of lateral acceleration against steering wheel angle can be generated for any chosen speed. Another typical analysis predicts the rate of yaw generated by a transient 'step steer' input (a favourite road appraisal test of jerking the wheel suddenly in a swerve manoeuvre). Different suspension characteristics including system inertia produce markedly different transient responses which can be illustrated on a plot of yaw change rate against time.

Other applications of the FRESH programme can be used to generate response time histories for random steering inputs and to investigate the effects of different body shapes or suspension designs on aerodynamic stability. By running models with alternative configurations through a simulated 25 mph (40 km/h) 90 degrees side gust, wind tunnel findings can be related more closely to actual driving performance. Overall the FRESH handling simulation programme is proving to be an accurate and efficient tool for predicting the dynamic behaviour of vehicles. Careful development of the structure and frequency content has reduced the computer effort while retaining the solution accuracy.

Another example of a suspension computer aid is the DRICOM (Drive/Compose) optimisation mechanism used to establish initial suspension geometry so that wheel envelopes can be developed for the package engineering of a new model or system to proceed. It runs on large mainframe computers like the Honeywell Multics or the Control Data 176, but can be adapted to any of the latest engineering systems like the Cray[4].

The DRICOM programme primarily predicts static movement and clearances required to accommodate different ride heights, steering and drive-line angles and the effects of component changes in the early stages of vehicle design. The front suspension element in the combined programme is known as COMPOSE (Computer Oriented Mechanism Programmed for Optimum Suspension Effect), while the rear suspension element is known as DRIVE (Driveline/Rear Suspension Interaction and Vehicle Effects).

COMPOSE is a computer simulation of the complete front suspension and steering mechanism of an independently-sprung FWD vehicle. It locates all pertinent points of a fully symmetrical suspension in three-dimensional vector space and analyses the relationship between these points as the system moves from full bump travel (jounce) to full rebound and from extreme left turn to extreme right turn. It was specifically developed to analyse front suspension with front-wheel drive, where there is complex inter-action between the suspension and steering which completely controls the universal-joint angles. As a new suspension layout is designed from basic parameters and assumptions, a single database is developed from which all vehicle and component engineers can work and which can be reproduced through computer graphics as a 'stick' model. The clearance envelopes required to interface with engine compartment layout, toe board position and all the other package considerations are therefore fixed at a very early stage.

Within these constraints the programme can then be used to development a feasible suspension in detail and generate viable alternatives. It can accept both wishbone and strut location systems to a wide variety of designs with either front or rear wheel drive. It responds to all standard angles and relationships of kingpin inclination, toe, track dimensions, caster, camber and Ackermann effect, as well as anti-lift, anti-dive and roll centre geometry in printed and graphic form. It rejects configurations which violate the specified constraints and can analyse up to almost 60,000 variations of a given suspension.

DRIVE can be used for a wide range of suspension configurations from link-located solid axles to fully independent systems. It investigates the noise, vibration and harshness (NVH) effects of drive shaft angles as well as clearances for a variety of powertrain alternatives. Through DRIVE it is possible to optimise joint angles better to reduce torsional excitations and improve interior comfort levels. Test vehicle built following analysis with DRIVE have shown exceptionally good NVH characteristics.

11.6   SUSPENSION DESIGN TECHNIQUES

The design process for suspension components begins with an exchange of ideas between the management office controlling the total programme and the engineering department involved, to determine the concept and to establish the functional, weight and cost objectives. These will be influenced by many factors such as customer demand, the engineering and manufacturing capability of the company and its suppliers, the package and cost constraints and the overall timing plan. During development potential failure modes and effects are forecast and any concerns eliminated by established methods of modification. Stress analysis is studied using the latest CAD systems and data generated for automatic drafting and CAM techniques. From this data, materials and parts are procured to the specification required.

Prototypes are then built for exhaustive testing on special accelerated durability rigs and on vehicles driven over extended distances at both security screened company proving grounds and in worldwide locations, including Alpine passes and hot and cold climates. During this period many special tests are devised to prove out the parts under development in association with the component suppliers. These often involve techniques such as computer-controlled vehicle simulation durability rigs and vibration tests using stress mapping and cumulative damage analysis of results.

Coincidental with these activities, manufacturing and purchasing feasibility are sought together with visits to suppliers to monitor progress and resolve any concerns which may arise. From then on the engineering responsibilities are extended to include any aspects involving the production coordination of the finished parts, including supervision of the functional build and launch phases on the assembly lines and any service concerns during the model life in question.

11.7   CAD/CAM INTEGRATION

At first glance the logic and desirability of providing uninterrupted data flow from CAD workstation to the finished working parts might seem a simple task to achieve. When the penetration of CAD systems was relatively low there were considerable difficulties in applying the computer benefits across the board. It took a radical change in working methods and often totally new concepts in manufacture using higher levels of automation and robotics to reach worthwhile levels of integration.

The completion of the process, known as computer integrated manufacturing (CIM), now allows designers to respond much more quickly to market changes with greater flexibility. Current methods demand high levels of experience and expertise, especially is such complex subjects as suspension design. CIM spreads the knowledge base much further (almost to every computer terminal) and eventually will be integrated with commercial data processing, marketing, stock control and finance. In 1986 European manufacturing companies spent about $12 billion on equipment and systems for applying CIM methods across the board, from terminals to robots. By 1990 the annual figure had more than doubled, something that is likely to be repeated before 1995

REFERENCES

1. Christos, J. P., 'A Simplified Method for the Measurement of Composite Suspension Parameters', *SAE Technical Paper* No. 910232 (February 1991)
2. Thatcher, R., 'Using an ALIAS', *Automotive Visions*, Issue 1, Vol. 2 (October 1992)
3. Scarlett, M., 'Elementary, Dear Designer', *Car Design & Technology*, Issue 1 (June/July 1991)
4. Various authors, 'Automotive Applications of Supercomputers', *SAE Publications* (1988)

Appendix 1: Suspension calculations and worked examples

A1.1 BASIC SUSPENSION SYSTEM

The suspension system at each wheel, or of the complete vehicle, can be regarded as being that shown in Fig. A1.1. The unsprung mass W_{us} associated with the wheel has between itself and the road a spring of rate S_t, the tyre, and between itself and the spring mass W_{sp} a spring of rate S_s, the suspension spring, in parallel with which is the damper. The combined rate of the two springs in series is S_c where

$$\frac{1}{S_c} = \frac{1}{S_s} + \frac{1}{S_t} \tag{A1.1}$$

A1.2 VIBRATIONS OF BASIC SYSTEM: APPROXIMATE FREQUENCIES

There are two modes of vibration of this system: that in which sprung and unsprung masses are in phase; and that in which they are opposed. It is general practice to take the approximate frequency f_s of the sprung mass W_{sp} kg on a spring of rate S_s N/m. Assuming the vibration is simple harmonic produced by an angular velocity ω, then

$$\omega = \left(\frac{S_s}{W_{sp}}\right)^{1/2} \quad \text{and} \quad f_s = \frac{1}{2\pi}\left(\frac{S_s}{W_{sp}}\right)^{1/2} \tag{A1.2}$$

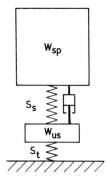

Fig. A1·1   Simplified vehicle suspension system

The corresponding frequency f_{us} of the unsprung mass W_{us} kg on a spring rate of $(S_s + S_t)$ N/m is

$$f_{us} = \frac{1}{2\pi}\left(\frac{S_s + S_t}{W_{us}}\right)^{1/2} \tag{A1.3}$$

A closer approximation of the natural frequency of the sprung mass is:

$$f_s = \frac{1}{2\pi}\left(\frac{S_c}{W_{sp}}\right)^{1/2} \text{Hz} \tag{A1.4}$$

A1.3   TRUE FREQUENCY, SPRUNG MASS

To obtain the true frequencies for the two conditions we have effectively to split up the system. Figure A1.2 shows how we must do this for the in-phase movement of the two masses to get the true frequency of the sprung mass. Here we consider the unsprung mass W_{us} separately mounted on a part of the type 'spring'; the part in question has a rate of $S_t x$, the remainder a rate of $S_t(1 - x)$. x has to satisfy the condition that

$$f_s = \frac{1}{2\pi}\left(\frac{S_{ci}}{W_{sp}}\right)^{1/2} = \frac{1}{2\pi}\left(\frac{S_t x}{W_{us}}\right)^{1/2} \tag{A1.5}$$

where S_{ci} is derived from

$$\frac{1}{S_{ci}} = \frac{1}{S_s} + \frac{1}{S_t(1 - x)}$$

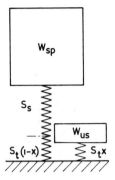

Fig. A1·2   Equivalent system to obtain true frequency of sprung weight

To find the true frequency therefore we have to satisfy the condition

$$\frac{\{S_s S_t(1 - x)\}/\{S_s + S_t(1 - x)\}}{W_{sp}} = \frac{S_t x}{W_{us}} \qquad (A1.6)$$

which may be more conveniently expressed as

$$S_t \cdot x = \frac{W_{us}}{W_{sp}} \left\{ \frac{S_s S_t(1 - x)}{S_s + S_t(1 - x)} \right\} \qquad (A1.7)$$

With

$$\left\{ \frac{S_s S_t(1 - x)}{S_s + S_t(1 - x)} \right\}$$

relatively insensitive to x. x can be found by successive approximations.

The amplitude of the movement of the unsprung weights is easily found if required.

A1.4   TRUE FREQUENCY, UNSPRUNG MASS

Figure A1.3 shows how we must split up the system to find the true frequency of the unsprung weight. The line OO represents the nodal point of the suspension spring.

$$f_{us} = \frac{1}{2\pi} \left\{ \frac{S_s/x}{W_{sp}} \right\}^{1/2} = \frac{1}{2\pi} \left\{ \frac{S_t + S_s/(1 - x)}{W_{us}} \right\}^{1/2} \qquad (A1.8)$$

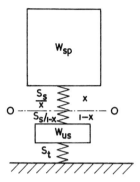

Fig. A1·3   Equivalent system to obtain true frequency of unsprung weight

Proceeding as before we have to solve the equation

$$\frac{S_s}{x} = \frac{W_{sp}}{W_{us}}\left\{S_t + \frac{S_s}{(1 - x)}\right\}$$ (A1.9)

Here also, with $(S_t + S_s/(1 - x))$ relatively insensitive to x we can easily find x by successive approximations.

It will be seen from the examples in this Appendix that Equations A1.3 and A1.4 give results close enough to the true frequencies to make the more elaborate calculations needed for those true frequencies generally unnecessary.

A1.5   SPRING/MASS SYSTEMS: WORKED EXAMPLES

Example 1.1

Sprung weight, simple expression.

$$f_s = \frac{1}{2\pi}\left(\frac{S_s}{W_{sp}}\right)^{1/2} \text{ (Equation A1.2)}$$

$$S_s = 20 \text{ kN/m}, \quad W_{sp} = 500 \text{ kg}$$

$$f_s = \frac{1}{2\pi}\left(\frac{20 \times 10^3}{500}\right)^{1/2} = 1.0066 \text{ Hz}$$

Example 1.2

Sprung weight, closer approximation.

$$f_s = \frac{1}{2\pi}\left(\frac{S_c}{W_{sp}}\right)^{1/2} \text{ (Equation A1.4)}$$

$$S_t = 266.7 \text{ kN/m}, \quad S_s = 20 \text{ kN/m}$$

$$\frac{1}{S_c} = \frac{1}{20 \times 10^3} + \frac{1}{266.7 \times 10^3}$$

$$S_c = 18\,604.8 \text{ N/m}$$

$$f_s = \frac{1}{2\pi}\left(\frac{18\,604.8}{500}\right)^{1/2} = 0.9708 \text{ Hz}$$

Example 1.3

Sprung weight, exact expression. The full calculation of f_s from Equation 1.5 gives the value 0.9706 Hz.

Example 1.4

Sprung weight, exact expression, doubled unsprung weight. Increasing W_{us} from 50 kg to 100 kg reduces the frequency to 0.97036 Hz.

Example 1.5

Unsprung weight, approximate expression.

$$f_s = \frac{1}{2\pi}\left(\frac{S_s + S_t}{W_{us}}\right)^{1/2} \text{ (Equation A1.3)}$$

$$W_{us} = 50 \text{ kg}$$

$$f_{us} = \frac{1}{2\pi}\left(\frac{20\,000 + 266\,700}{50}\right)^{1/2} = 12 \cdot 052 \text{ Hz}$$

Example 1.6

Unsprung weight, exact expression. By the full calculation, Equation A1.8, $f_{us} = 12.05496$ Hz

Example 1.7

Unsprung weight, doubled unsprung weight, approximate expression. Increasing W_{us} from 50 kg to 100 kg reduces the frequency (from 12.052 Hz, Example 1.5) to $f_{us} = 8.5218$ Hz

Example 1.8

Double unsprung weight, exact expression. $f_{us} = 8.52605$ Hz

Example 1.9

Sprung weight, doubled unsprung weight, exact calculation. From Equation A1.4, f_s would still be 0.9708 Hz. By the exact method it is 0.97036 Hz

A1.6 EFFECT OF VISCOUS DAMPING ON NATURAL FREQUENCY: CRITICAL DAMPING

One interest we have in the viscous damping is whether it has any considerable effect on the natural frequency of the suspension system. Timoshenko[1] provides the necessary formulae to find out what effect damping does have on frequency. It is convenient to relate the damping to critical damping, i.e. that at which the motion of the weight, once disturbed, just ceases to be oscillatory. It merely returns to its static position after disturbance.

This condition is met[2] when the damping force required for critical damping

$$F_{dc} = 2W\omega_c \qquad (A1.10)$$

Because $\omega_c = (S/W)^{1/2}$ this can also be expressed as

$$F_{dc} = 2(WS)^{1/2} \qquad (A1.11)$$

The dynamic magnifier at resonance

$$D_c = \frac{W\omega_c}{F_d} \qquad (A1.12)$$

F_d being the particular damping force existing.

From Equations A1.10 and A1.12, for critical damping, i.e. when $F_d = F_{dc}$,

$$D_c = \frac{W\omega_c}{2W\omega_c} = 0.5$$

Ker Wilson[2] suggests that in engineering, generally, damping is unlikely to be greater than that giving $D_c = 3.5$, which implies damping of $0.5/3.5 = 0.14$ critical. Collected information is that damping may range from 0.25 critical for a suspension with a good deal of inherent friction to 0.35 or even 0.38 critical for a suspension free of friction. The higher figures are also liable to be for more softly sprung cars. Because, Equation A1.11, the damping force for critical damping varies as the square root of the spring rate (Equation A1.11) there could be a tendency to arrive at the same damping force for a given spring weight regardless of the static deflection of the suspension, but taking account of the inherent friction. In suspension damping the automobile engineer has clearly found it desirable to exceed the general engineering maximum figure.

If we take $x = F_d/F_{dc}$ the periodic time of a vibration as compared with an undamped one is increased in the ratio

$$\frac{t_1}{t} = 1 + \frac{x^2}{2} \tag{A1.13}$$

where t_1 is the periodic time of the damped vibration. We see the convenience of expressing damping as the proportion of critical damping as this is the value of x in this equation. For our extreme figure of 0.38 the maximum probable ratio of increase in periodic time is therefore likely to be $1 + 0.38^2/2 = 1.07$.

A1.7 EFFECT OF DAMPING ON FORCED VIBRATION AMPLITUDES

The second interest we have in viscous damping is its effect on the amplitude of forced vibrations. Vibrations of the unsprung mass can be excited either by periodic irregularities in the road surface over which the vehicle moves or by out-of-balance of the road wheel. The vibrating system is effectively that of Fig. A1.4. The sprung mass is regarded as the anchor; the spring rate S, Equation A1.3, is $S_s + S_t$; a damping force F_d acts in parallel. The relative amplitudes of the disturbance and the mass are represented by a dynamic magnifier D.

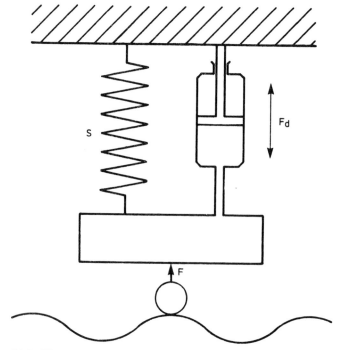

Fig. A1·4   Vibrating system for Figs. 1.5 and 1.6

For road irregularities

$$D = \cfrac{1}{\left[\{1 - (\omega/\omega_c)^2\}^2 + \cfrac{(\omega/\omega_c)^2}{D_c^2} \right]^{1/2}} \qquad (A1.14)$$

in which ω/ω_c is the ratio between the frequencies of the applied forces and the natural frequency of the system. As defined by Equation A1.12, $D_c = W\omega_c/F_d$.

For the undamped vibrations D_c is therefore infinite and the expression simplifies to

$$D = \frac{1}{1 - (\omega/\omega_c)^2} \qquad (A1.15)$$

This becomes infinite at $\omega = \omega_c$ and negative above this frequency. Because the latter does not apply to the results of Equation A1.14,

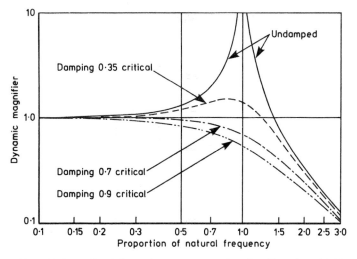

Fig. A1·5   Undamped and damped response curves based on Equations A1.15 and A1.14 are shown here. They are for constant excitation over frequencies close to resonance and for damping levels of 0.35, 0.7 and 0.9 critical

for easy comparison the undamped curve is plotted ignoring this negative sign, Fig. A1.5. The dotted lines on this graph represent the effects of damping at various proportions of critical, at speeds close to resonance.

For excitation due to road wheel out-of-balance the relationship is

$$D = \frac{(\omega/\omega_c)^2}{\left[\{1 - (\omega/\omega_c)^2\}^2 + \dfrac{(\omega/\omega_c)^2}{D_c^2} \right]^{1/2}} \qquad (A1.16)$$

In this case for zero damping this simplifies to

$$D = \frac{(\omega/\omega_c)^2}{1 - (\omega/\omega_c)^2} \qquad (A1.17)$$

Here ω is the rotational speed of the wheel.

Figure A1.6 shows both the undamped and damped values, for frequencies close to resonance. If we take the road wheel circumference as about 2.3 m, the road speed corresponding to a sprung mass frequency of about 1Hz is 2.3 m/s or 8.3 km/hr. It is unlikely that any probable out-of-balance of the road wheel at this speed will

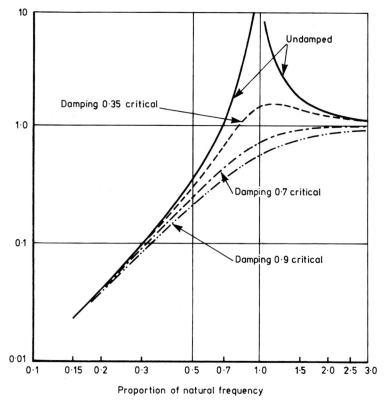

Fig. A1·6   Undamped and damped response curves for exciting forces varying as the square of the speed are shown here. They are based on Equations 2.17 and 2.16 and are at damping levels of 0.35, 0.7 and 0.9 of critical

seriously excite vibrations of the sprung mass. At the probable frequencies of the unsprung mass the speeds at which resonance is likely to occur are from 65 to 100 km/hr (40 to 62 mph).

For an out-of-balance of x kg m, because the centripetal acceleration is $r\omega^2$

$$\text{Out-of-balance force} = x\omega^2 \text{ N} \qquad (A1.18)$$

ω being the wheel speed. Example 1.10 indicates the amplitudes that might be generated at the resonant speed for the two unsprung weights considered. The out-of-balance considered in the examples, 0.0144 kg m, corresponds to about 20 in oz. For once the lighter unsprung is at a disadvantage: the higher frequency increases the out-of-balance force, it is acting on a smaller weight and produces larger amplitudes.

For excitation of the sprung mass, at say 1 to 1.5 Hz, the road disturbance spacing required will vary between 1.9 and 2.8 m at 10 km/hr and progressively more at higher speeds.

The conventional suspension system of Fig. A1.1 can be regarded as a system in which road irregularities will excite the unsprung mass, which will then pass on modified disturbances to the spring mass. The probable result on the latter should therefore be the product of the two dynamic magnifiers.

Figure A1.7 shows the results of such calculations, for damping levels, of 0.35 and 0.7 of critical of the sprung mass and for unsprung masses of 0.1 and 0.2 of the sprung mass. S_t/S_s is taken as 13.34. The resulting values of ω_c for the unsprung masses are 8.8 and 12.4 times that of the sprung mass, for $W_{us} = 0.2W_{sp}$ and $W_{us} = 0.1W_{sp}$ respectively.

Damping levels of 0.35 and 0.7 critical for the sprung mass become 0.28 and 0.57 critical for $W_{us} = 0.1W_{sp}$ and 0.2 and 0.4 critical for $W_{us} = 0.2W_{sp}$. The lighter unsprung therefore scores on two counts in its effect on the sprung mass: the frequency ratio is greater; and it is more effectively damped.

The response curves for $W_{us} = 0.2W_{sp}$ appear in Fig. A1.7(a); those for $W_{us} = 0.1W_{sp}$ are in Fig. A1.7(b). The sprung mass curves are common to both.

The method is approximate in that it assumes that damping of the unsprung is that from an unmoving sprung mass. Chapter 9 has results from a more exact method.

A1.8   CRITICAL DAMPING: WORKED EXAMPLES

Example 1.10

Critical damping force for the sprung weight; amplitudes of movement of the unsprung weight and probable maximum damping (sections 1.5 to 1.7).

Assumptions: $W_{sp} = 500$ kg, $S_c = 18\,600$ N/m, $\omega_c = 6.1$ rad/s (Frequency $= 6.1/2\pi = 0.9708$ Hz. The value of S_c is derived from $S_s = 20\,000$ N/m, $S_t = 266\,000$ N/m.)

(1)   For the sprung weight, the critical damping force F_{dc} at its natural frequency is given by (Equation A1.10):

$$F_{dc} = 2W_{sp}\omega_c$$
$$= 2 \times 500 \times 6.1 = 6100 \text{ Ns/m}$$

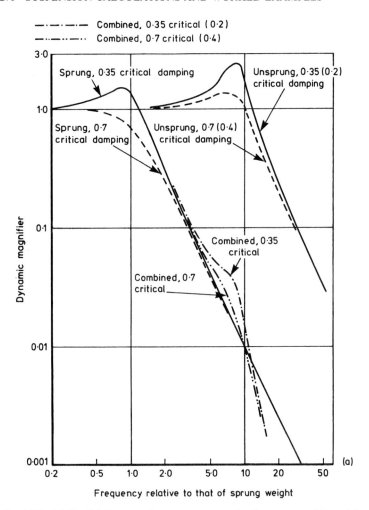

Fig. A1·7 (a) The full lines are the response curves for the sprung weight and the unsprung of 0.2 of the sprung weight at 0.35 critical damping of the sprung weight. The associated dotted curves are for 0.7 critical damping. The remaining two curves are the products of the dynamic magnifiers for sprung and unsprung weights at 0.35 and 0.7 critical damping. As pointed out in the text, the associated damping levels for the unsprung weight are 0.2 and 0.4 critical

The damping force is 6100 N at a speed of 1 m/s; the units therefore are Newtons/metres per second which reduces to Ns/m as given above.

(2) For the following cases the damping is assumed to be 0.35 critical, i.e. 0.35 × 6100 = 2135 Ns/m.

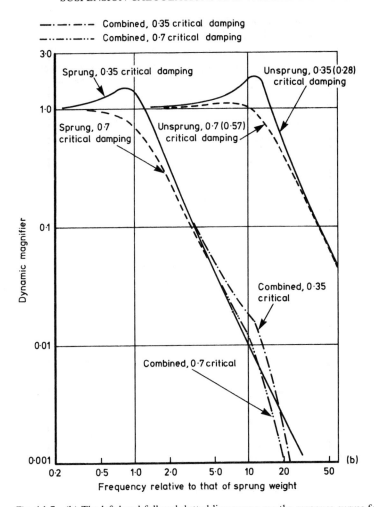

Fig. A1·7 (b) The left hand full and dotted line curves are the response curves for the sprung weight at 0.35 and 0.7 critical damping. The corresponding curves on the right are for the unsprung weight of 0.1 of the sprung, at the same damping loads which correspond to 0.28 and 0.57 critical for the unsprung. The higher effective damping level of this lighter unsprung reduces its maximum values and the greater difference in frequencies tends to reduce the impact of the unsprung

(a)   Original unsprung weight W_{us} = 50 kg

$$\text{Natural frequency} = \frac{1}{2\pi}\left\{\frac{286\,000}{50}\right\}^{1/2} = \frac{75.63}{2\pi} = 12.037 \text{ Hz}$$

Critical damping for this unsprung weight at this frequency, $F_{dc} = 2 \times 50 \times 75.63 = 7563$ Ns/m. It will be noticed that this is more than that for the sprung weight.

The dynamic magnifier at resonance, D_c, is given by Equation A1.12,

$$D_c = \frac{50 \times 75.63}{2135} = 1.771.$$

(b)   For the doubled unsprung weight of 100 kg the natural frequency is

$$\frac{1}{2\pi}\left\{\frac{286\,000}{100}\right\}^{1/2} = \frac{53.479}{2\pi} = 8.511 \text{ Hz}$$

and $F_{dc} = 2 \times 100 \times 53.479 = 10\,696$ Ns/m.

By a different method, following from $0.5/D_c$ = proportion of critical

$$D_c = \frac{0.5 \times 10\,696}{2135} = 2.505$$

(c)   An assumed road wheel out-of-balance of 0.0144 kgm produces at the resonant speed of the lighter unsprung weight $(W_{us} = 50 \text{ kg})$ a force due to centripetal acceleration $0.0144 \times 75.63^2 = 82.37$ N. The deflection due to this force is $82.37/286\,000 = 0.000288$ m. The amplitude at resonance is therefore

$$0.000288 \times 1.771 = 0.00051 \text{ m}$$

(d)   For the heavier unsprung mass $(W_{us} = 100 \text{ kg})$ the deflection due to the out-of-balance force is

$$\frac{0.0144 \times 53.479^2}{286\,000} = 0.000144 \text{ m}$$

The amplitude at resonance is $0.000144 \times 2.505 = 0.000361$ m. This result is to be expected; the heavier unsprung weight is less affected by a given amount of out-of-balance. The situation is different for a road-excited vibration of approximately fixed amplitude (the 'approximate' qualification springs from the effect of the unsprung weight variation on tyre deflections).

Example 1.11

Variation of dynamic magnifier with frequency and proportion of critical damping (Section A1.7).
Assume: $W_{sp} = 500$ kg, $S_c = 18\,600$ N/m, $\omega_c = 6.1$ rad/s
(a) $F_d = 2000$, (b) $F_d = 6000$
From Equation A1.10

$$F_{dc} = 2W_{sp}\omega_c = 2 \times 500 \times 6.1 = 6100 \text{ Ns/m}$$

So (a) 2000/6100 = 0.33 critical, (b) 6000/6100 = 0.98 critical
(a) From Equation A1.12, at resonance

$$D_c = \frac{W_{sp}\omega_c}{F_d}$$

$$= \frac{500 \times 6.1}{2000} = 1.525$$

From Equation A1.16,

$$D = \frac{1}{\left[\{1 - (\omega/\omega_c)^2\}^2 + \dfrac{(\omega/\omega_c)^2}{D_c^2} \right]^{1/2}}$$

At $\omega/\omega_c = 0.7$,

$$D = \frac{1}{\left[(1 - 0.7)^2 + \dfrac{0.7^2}{1.525^2} \right]^{1/2}} = 1.457$$

At $\omega/\omega_c = 1.0$,

$$D = \frac{1}{\left\{ 0 + \dfrac{1}{1.525^2} \right\}^{1/2}} = 1.525$$

At $\omega/\omega_c = 1.4$,

$$D = \frac{1}{\left\{ (1 - 1.96)^2 + \dfrac{1.4^2}{1.525^2} \right\}^{1/2}} = 0.7528$$

(b)   At resonance,

$$D_c = \frac{500 \times 6.1}{6000} = 0.508$$

At $\omega/\omega_c = 0.7$,

$$D = \frac{1}{\left\{0.2601 + \dfrac{0.7^2}{0.508^2}\right\}^{1/2}} = 0.681$$

At $\omega/\omega_c = 1.0$,

$$D = \frac{1}{\left\{0 + \dfrac{1}{0.508^2}\right\}^{1/2}} = 0.508$$

At $\omega/\omega_c = 1.4$,

$$D = \frac{1}{\left\{0.9216 + \dfrac{1.4^2}{0.508^2}\right\}^{1/2}} = 0.343$$

A1.9   RELATIVE PITCH AND BOUNCE FREQUENCIES: k^2/ab RATIO

The curves of pitch for Figs. 3.13(b) and (c) assume that the frequency of oscillation is unaffected by pitching as opposed to bouncing movement of the car. This is generally nearly true. To be true the front and rear end masses would have to be effectively concentrated in front and real 'axle' vertical planes across the car. If this condition is met then the moment of inertia I of the car about a transverse axis through the centre of gravity, Fig. A1.8(a) is:

$$I = W_f a^2 + W_r b^2 \tag{A1.19}$$

Because a and b are the distance of the centre of gravity from the front and rear wheels, $W_f a = W_r b$. Substituting in the second term of Equation (A1.19) we get:

$$I = W_f a(a + b) \tag{A1.20}$$

Now $W_f = Wb/L$, so

$$I = \frac{Wab(a + b)}{L} = Wab \tag{A1.21}$$

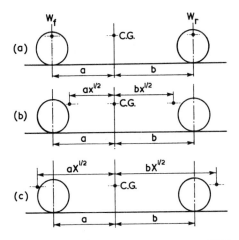

Fig. A1·8   (a) Mass diagram, $k^2/ab=1$, (b) mass diagram, $k^2/ab < 1$ and (c) mass diagram, $k^2/ab > 1$

The usual expression for the inertia I of a body is Wk^2 where k is the radius of gyration. It follows therefore that the ratio k^2/ab is an indication of how far the car departs from the characteristic of equal pitch and bounce frequencies. A typical value for k^2/ab could be 0.9.

A1.10   EFFECT OF k^2/ab RATIO ON PITCHING TENDENCY

The fact that k^2/ab is generally less than 1 has two effects:

(1)   The pitch frequency is higher and therefore for given amplitudes the accelerations will be greater.
(2)   Because the resistance to pitching is less a given exciting force will produce a greater amplitude of pitch. Looking at a vehicle suspension with tyre acting as a spring, the less the resistance of the sprung mass to the pitching action resulting from a given road ridge as a disturbance the less the type deflection and therefore the greater the deflection of the vehicle suspension and therefore the greater the initial pitch amplitude of the spring mass on its suspension.

Olley[3] says: 'The most disagreeable ride motion is 'pitching', i.e. the oscillation in which one end goes down as the other comes up, as distinct from 'bouncing' in which both ends move up and down together.' Olley was writing of a period when, as far as Great Britain was concerned, front axles were still generally fitted, front end suspension frequencies were still higher than those at the rear and k^2/ab ratios were generally lower than today (perhaps 0.6), so that pitch frequencies were higher and pitch was more likely to be excited. The reason for the lower k^2/ab ratio was that engines generally were still much further back in relation to the front wheels and car overhangs at front and rear were less.

Today we tend to take relative freedom from pitch for granted. But this freedom from the phenomenon exists only as long as we continue to provide the correct relationships of front and rear suspension frequencies and minimise the pitch excitation.

A1.11 k^2/ab RATIO AND PITCH FREQUENCY

The effect of k^2/ab ratios less than unity and therefore pitch frequencies higher than bounce frequencies (the effect referred to in (1) in Section A1.10) needs to be discussed further. Passing over the disturbance in the first place feeds into the vehicle suspensions a given amount of energy, which the damping in those systems immediately starts to reduce. With $k^2/ab = 1$, pitch and bounce frequencies equal, the sprung mass effectively can be replaced by masses W_f and W_r on the front and rear wheel centre planes in side elevation, Fig. A1.8(a). It does not matter whether the car is pitching or bouncing, the amplitudes of the front and rear suspensions will be those we have calculated and shown in Figs. 3.13(a), (b) and (c).

Consider now the state of affairs of Fig. A1.8(b). $k^2/ab = x < 1$. We can replace the system by two masses W_f and W_r, not as in the case above but at distances $x^{1/2}a$ and $x^{1/2}b$ from the centre of gravity. The moment of inertia, from Equation A1.21, will be

$$W(x^{1/2}a)(x^{1/2}b) = Wabx = Wk^2$$

If we assume equal static deflections of the front and rear springs we can show that the pitch rate of the car on its suspensions is $S_c ab$. The moment of inertia of the sprung weight about its centre of gravity is $W_{sp}k^2$. The pitch frequency is therefore

$$\frac{1}{2\pi}\left\{\frac{S_c ab}{W_{sp}k^2}\right\}^{1/2}$$

If we take $k^2 = abx$ we can rewrite this as:

$$\text{Pitch frequency} = \frac{1}{2\pi}\left\{\frac{S_c}{W_{sp}}\right\}^{1/2}\left\{\frac{ab}{abx}\right\}^{1/2}$$

$$= \frac{1}{2\pi}\left\{\frac{S_c}{W_{sp}}\right\}^{1/2}\frac{1}{x^{1/2}}$$

As the bounce frequency $= 1/2\pi\{S_c/W_{sp}\}^{1/2}$

$$\text{Pitch frequency} = \text{Bounce frequency} \times \frac{1}{x^{1/2}}$$

For a given pitch frequency and corresponding angular velocity ω_c the maximum velocity of W_f will be $x^{1/2}a\omega_c$. The angular velocity has a linear relationship with the frequency for a given angular amplitude so that for a maximum pitch angle α the velocity will vary as $x^{1/2}a$ because of its radius and $1/x^{1/2}$ because of its frequency, as compared with the front wheels for a ratio $k^2/ab = 1$. The maximum velocity is therefore the ratio of $(x^{1/2}a/x^{1/2})1/a = 1.0$ to that of the front wheels with k^2/ab equal to unity. There will therefore be no increase in angular amplitude as a result of k^2/ab being less than 1, merely an increase in frequency; the stored energy will be the same in each case for a given maximum angular displacement. The effect of changes in the k^2/ab ratio is therefore confined to changes in pitch frequency. It will not result in changes in angular displacement, i.e. in effective front and rear wheel movements. It is interesting and ironic that the change to independent front suspension, which made possible the lower front end suspension frequencies required to minimise pitching tendencies, was accompanied by an increase in the k^2/ab ratio which reduced the frequency changes between pitch and bounce.

A1.12 k^2/ab RATIO ABOUT VERTICAL AXIS, EFFECT ON TRANSIENT BEHAVIOUR

Olley refers to the 'ideal' case of $k^2/ab = 1$. We have to think not only of k^2/ab in relation to the transverse axis through the centre of gravity but also of that for a vertical axis through the same centre of gravity. It is probable that the k^2 figures for the two cases will not be very different. What difference there is makes the plan view k larger than the elevation one. A car is wider than its height, the wheels are included at each corner rather than a part of the unsprung weight. This greater value of k is undesirable.

Before we show why this is so we must get a preliminary understanding of what happens to the tyre when the sideways forces between it and the road, which are necessary for cornering, are developed. This is considered in more detail later and the reader can if he so desires refer to Sections 7.9 to 7.11 for the full explanation.

The tyre has sideways flexibility. If a sideways force is applied to a stationary tyre supporting a load on a flat surface there will be a movement of the tyre rim in relation to the road in the direction of the force applied to the tyre via the rim. Effectively all the tread elements in contact with the road will be deflected sideways in relation to the rim.

When a tyre is rolling the tread as it touches the road at the front of the contact patch is effectively undeflected sideways. To produce the required sideways force the average deflection of all the tread elements in contact with the ground has to be the same as the sideways deflection of the stationary tyre. A tread element can only acquire sideways deflection by the tyre rolling with a sideways drift such that the rearmost tread element before it lifts off will have a sideways deflection about twice that of the static tyre under the same sideways force. The drift angle is therefore approximately that whose tangent is the sideways deflection of the static tyre divided by half the length of the contact patch.

To develop a steady sideways force and drift angle a tyre has to roll forwards at least by the length of the contact patch. In practice a greater length is required.

Let us now consider the three possibilities:

(1) $k^2/ab = 1$
(2) $k^2/ab < 1$
(3) $k^2/ab > 1$

(1) As we have seen, $k^2/ab = 1$ corresponds in effect to front and rear end masses being concentrated in the front and rear axle planes, Fig. A1.9(a). Any steering force applied to the front wheels by applying a steering angle will have no immediate effect on the rear wheels. These will only begin to generate sideways force, to take the back end of the car around the corner, as the car begins to move in a radius and a centripetal acceleration has to be produced at the back end of the car.

(2) With $k^2/ab < 1$, the disposition of the equivalent masses is shown in Fig. A1.9(b). With the moment of inertia, $Wk^2 = Wabx$, and the 'percussion' centre at which the sideways

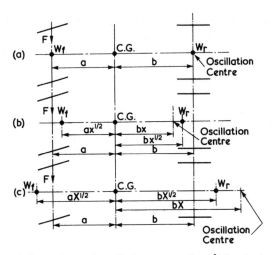

Fig. A1·9   (a) Percussion and oscillation centres for $k^2/ab = 1$. Application of cornering force has no immediate eɛect on rear end. (b) Percussion and oscillation centres for $k^2/ab = x < 1$. Application of cornering force F moves the back end outwards and so starts to generate cornering force there. (c) Percussion and oscillation centres for $k^2/ab = X > 1$. Application of cornering force F moves rear end of car inwards and so generates cornering force in opposite direction to final force. Feeling of rear end float results

force is applied at a distance a forward of the centre of gravity the oscillation centre about which the vehicle will tend to pivot is at a distance y behind the centre of gravity, where $ay = k^2 = abx$. It follows that $y = bx$. As soon as the sideways force is applied to the front some front drift angle will be impressed on the rear tyres, in the same direction as the final one to provide the centripetal acceleration. The transition period is thereby shortened.

(3)   With $k^2/ab > 1$, the disposition of the equivalent masses is shown in Fig. A1.9(c). Here $Wk^2 = WabX$ where $X > 1$. On the same percussion centre theory the oscillation point for the vehicle will be at a distance Y behind the centre of gravity where $Y = Xb$. Application of a steering force at the front wheels produces effective rotation about this point $(XB - b)$ behind the rear wheels and so induces an initial drift angle on the rear wheels which is in the opposite direction to the final one. This lengthens the transition period and produces a sensation of 'floating' at the back end of the car.

One reason why rear end steering is not to be recommended is to be found here. Steering at the rear implies that the initial force to start the car into a corner, applied at the rear, is in the opposite direction to the force finally required in steady state cornering and precision of control would be difficult to obtain, especially in the necessarily protracted transition period. This reversal of the direction of the force on the rear tyres while initiating a turn will also reverse the self-aligning torque. The message conveyed by this self-aligning torque to the driver will therefore be confusing. The final self-aligning torque direction is such as to tend to increase the steering angle applied and so to increase the initial steering angle to more than the driver intended.

Another reason for disliking rear end steering would be that with it the rear end of the car, even without any tyre drift on corners, would run wider than the front wheels; apart from making things more difficult for the driver, it seems preferable to arrange to hit a kerb rather than a vehicle travelling in the opposite direction, if misjudgement is to produce an impact at all. Perhaps the main reason against rear steering is given by Olley[4] and attributed to Schilling. This is that if the car has rear steering and is close to the limit of adhesion on the rear tyres the driver can only attempt to ease the situation by straightening the rear wheels. This increases the drift angle on the rear tyres. It is liable therefore to take the tyres from drifting to actual sliding. The driver's attempt to improve matters is liable to precipitate the disaster he has tried to avert.

A1.13 k^2/ab RATIO ABOUT VERTICAL AXIS – DESIRABLE VALUE

The value of k^2/ab about the vertical axis through the centre of gravity of a car obviously affects its speed of response to disturbances producing rotation avout that axis. The lower the ratio, the higher the accelerations produced by given disturbances and the less time the driver has to make his correction before it is too late. Conversely, however, the less the force which is required to stop a spin once it has started.

Ignoring the question of specialised vehicles which are likely to be driven by those with faster than average reactions, there seems much to be said for aiming at a value of k^2/ab close enough to 1.0 to avoid rear end float but not so much below as to make spins happen too fast for the average driver to be able to catch up with them.

A1.14 PITCH EXCITATION: COUPLED SUSPENSIONS

With conflicting requirements for ride and handling it is tempting to see whether the requirements for ride can be met without sacrificing on the handling characteristics. The answer is that they can.

Even with all wheels independently sprung the track laying armoured fighting vehicle has effectively a very short wheelbase in relation to its length. Some calculations made during World War II suggested that the k^2/ab ratio was effectively between 2.5 and 3.0 for a cruiser tank. Even with static deflections between 5in and 6in (0.127 m and 0.152 m, implying 1.4 and 1.28 Hz respectively) it was noticed that the road ride was very soft-seeming and that pitch excitation was low, though the resistance to pitch when fore and aft accelerations were produced was well below the normal for a car; attitude changes were in any case increased by track tension effects.

The use of tracks and the steering arrangements associated with them masked with tanks any steering problems due to the k^2/ab ratio. The desire to combine a low pitch excitation and reasonable stability against attitude changes due to accelerations led naturally to the idea of coupled suspensions, front and rear, with an independent means of determining the anti-pitch rate. Different ideas for achieving this are discussed in Chapter 9.

A1.15   ATTITUDE CHANGES DUE TO BRAKING

Figure A1.10 makes it clear that when a car is decelerated by a force F there is inevitably a transference of weight from the rear to the front of

$$\frac{FH}{L} \qquad (A1.22)$$

Similarly when the car is accelerating or climbing, and a force F is required for this, the corresponding weight transference from front to rear must be FH/L. If the car has soft springing, or coupled front and rear suspensions with a low effective anti-pitch rate, and the

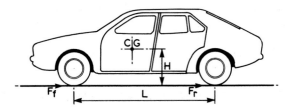

Fig. A1·10   The weight transference from rear wheels to front during braking is FH/L where $F = F_f + F_r$

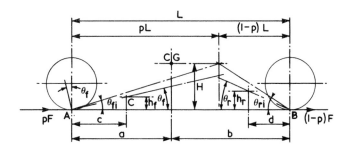

Fig. A1·11 Retarding forces acting on a car with outboard brakes and drive; this diagram relates mainly to braking with front brake proportion p, but with appropriate diﬀerences can be used to arrive at what happens with single and double axle drive

suspensions are not designed to be responsible for some of the transfer by the position, direction and magnitude of the forces fed into the sprung part of the vehicle, these weight transfers can result in embarrassingly large attitude changes. It is useful therefore to see what can be done in the suspensions to minimise or eliminate these attitude changes.

Consider first the case of a front suspension which has an effective pivot point C, Fig. A1.11. A force F is applied at the contact point of the tyre and road, A. Applying the force here means that we are considering either an axle or an independent suspension with outboard brakes. The horizontal force F can be taken as really or effectively being transferred to the sprung part of the vehicle at C. Because C is at a height h_f above the ground and the applied force F, therefore, has a moment Fh_f about it, there must be a vertical force also applied to the sprung part of the vehicle at C. This force is Fh_f/c.

The existence of an effective or real centre C means that the up and down movement of the wheel contact point in relation to the vehicle must lie instantaneously on the perpendicular to AC through A. This instantaneous movement therefore must be at an angle θ_f to the perpendicular to the ground from A, where $\theta_f = \tan^{-1} h_f/c$. If the linkage is such that the movement lies in a straight line at this angle θ_f to the vertical, there will be no point C except at infinity. The line AC at θ_f to the horizontal remains important. Wherever on this line the pivot point may lie, the horizontal and vertical forces remain F and $F \tan \theta_f$.

What we are immediately concerned about, however, is the remaining moment trying to tilt the car forward. This is the result of the horizontal and vertical forces fed into the sprung part of the vehicle at C. The centre of gravity of the sprung part of the vehicle is at a height H and distance a behind the front wheels. Then the moment producing the forward tilt on the springs due to the force F and the front suspension is

$$F(H - h_f) - \frac{Fh_f}{c}(a - c)$$

which can be simplified to

$$\text{Tilting moment} = F\left(H - \frac{h_f a}{c}\right) \qquad (A1.23)$$

This we recognise at the moment due only to the horizontal force if the pivot point were taken as being on the perpendicular to the ground passing through the centre of gravity; the vertical force then would of course have no moment about the centre of gravity.

Consider next the situation where a complete car is braked, with front and rear suspensions either using axles or having outboard brakes. Brakes are arranged to give a determined ratio between front and rear wheels. This may be fixed, or fixed for any particular retardation. For any total retarding force F the ratio will be fixed. Let us assume that this ratio gives the front end retarding force pF and the rear $(1 - p)F$, for the sprung weight. The total tilting moment, Fig. A1.11, is

$$pF(H - a \tan \theta_f) + (1 - p)F(H - b \tan \theta_r)$$

if we refer the forces to the vertical through the centre of gravity. This results in a weight transfer affecting the springs of

$$\frac{F}{L}[H - pa \tan \theta_f - (1 - p)b \tan \theta_r] \qquad (A1.24)$$

If the combined front and rear suspension rates are respectively S_{cf} and S_{cr} the attitude change produced is:

$$\frac{F}{L}[H - pa \tan \theta_f - (1 - p)b \tan \theta_r]\left(\frac{1}{S_{cf}} + \frac{1}{S_{cr}}\right)\frac{360}{2\pi L}$$

which can be rationalised to

$$\frac{57.3F}{L^2}[H - pa \tan \theta_f - (1 - p)b \tan \theta_r]\left(\frac{1}{S_{cf}} + \frac{1}{S_{cr}}\right) \qquad (A1.25)$$

There will almost certainly also be a total vertical reaction because vertical forces from front and rear suspensions will not cancel out. This vertical reaction is

$$pF \tan \theta_f - (1 - p)F \tan \theta_r$$

which will produce a vertical movement of the car on its suspension of

$$\frac{pF \tan \theta_f - (1 - p)F \tan \theta_r}{S_{cf} + S_{cr}} \tag{A1.26}$$

For this to be zero $p \tan \theta_f = (1 - p) \tan \theta_r$, which implies that the lines AC and BD produced must meet on the vertical which divides the wheelbase in the ratio $p: 1 - p$. To satisfy the requirement of no attitude change due to braking and no lift or drop the lines AC and BC produced (Fig. A1.11) must intersect on this vertical line dividing the wheelbase in the ratio $p: 1 - p$ at a height H equal to that of the centre of gravity (Bastow[5]). This implies that

$$\tan \theta_{fi} = \frac{H}{pL} \tag{A1.27(a)}$$

and

$$\tan \theta_{ri} = \frac{H}{(1 - p)L} \tag{A1.27(b)}$$

the suffix i implying ideal.

It is unlikely this requirement will be met. On the front wheels increase in the angle θ_f implies contact point movement which tends towards the perpendicular to disturbing forces from road bumps. If the brakes are not applied such disturbing forces will pass close to the wheel centre (through it but for wheel rotational inertia effects) and originate from in front of the wheel centre.

A1.16 ATTITUDE CHANGES DUE TO TRACTION

The same theory applies to tractive efforts when live axles are used. It is highly improbable that a four wheel drive vehicle will have two axles and the same torque ratio front to rear as the brakes. One can say, therefore, that any solution which avoids attitude change and lift or drop on braking will undoubtedly have attitude or car height change, or both, when driving. Thus a compromise between braking and driving will become necessary.

Let us first look at the case of a single rear driving axle. We can decide to aim for one of two extremes: (1) no deflection of the rear suspension but deflection of the front suspension due to the weight transference FH/L, or (2) no attitude change except that due to a vertical reaction at the centre of gravity. Because the front and rear suspensions have, ideally at least, different static deflections, such a vertical reaction will produce a slight attitude change.

To satisfy condition (1) consider the case we have just examined. Make $p = 0$ and reverse the direction of the force. $(1 - p)L = L$. Therefore

$$\tan \theta_r = \frac{H}{L} \qquad (A1.28)$$

The attitude change is

$$\frac{57.3\,FH}{L^2 S_{cf}} \qquad (A1.29)$$

To satisfy the condition (2) let us consider first making $\tan\theta_r = H/b$. The horizontal force F is transferred to the sprung weight at the hgieht of the centre of gravity. As far as the rear linkage is concerned this is moved towards rebound by its share of the vertical reaction at the centre of gravity, FHa/bL The front suspension had a corresponding force moving towards rebound, $Fhb/bL = FH/L$. In addition, because there is no force F on the front suspension, there is the weight transference there of FH/L. To counteract the latter we need to aim the reaction from the ground contact point above the centre of gravity to oppose a moment FHa/L. The total moment to be opposed is therefore FHb/L from the rear and $2FHa/L$ from the front. The moment arm about the ground required for this is

$$\frac{FH}{L}(b + 2a) = FH\left(\frac{L + a}{L}\right)$$

and

$$\tan \theta_{ri} = \frac{H}{b}\left(\frac{L + a}{L}\right) \qquad (A1.30(a))$$

With drive from a front axle only we have a corresponding condition that the attitude change is confined to that due to the generally slight effects of the difference in effective static deflections of the front and rear suspensions if

$$\tan \theta_{fi} = \frac{H}{A}\left(\frac{L+b}{L}\right) \qquad (A1.30(b))$$

A1.17 ATTITUDE CHANGES: INBOARD BRAKES AND INDEPENDENT SUSPENSION AT DRIVE END

We must now consider the case of inboard brakes, and associated with this drive through independent suspensions without hub reduction gears. As far as the suspension is concerned, the retarding force F is applied at the hub centre, Fig. A1.10; the torque Fr implied by this is carried to the sprung part of the car by the drive shaft. Let us consider the braking condition, with forces pF and $(1 - pF)$ applied to front and rear hubs. To counteract the force F at the hub we need an angle θ of the line, starting from the wheel centre, whose tangent is $(H - r)/a$. We have however from the horizontal force pF on the front wheels a torque pFr through the drive shaft and $pF(H - r)$ from the force itself about the centre of gravity. This implies a total of

$$pF(H - r + r) = pFH$$

By analogy with the first case therefore we need the same type of diagram as we had for axles or outboard braking but starting at the wheel centres and not at the ground. For zero attitude and height changes therefore we still need (Equations A1.27(a) and (b))

$$\tan \theta_{fi} = H/pL$$

and

$$\tan \theta_{ri} = H/(1 - p)L$$

Fig. A1.12.

From drive from a single end, rear or front, Equations A1.28, A1.29 and A1.30 continue to apply with θ_r and θ_f being measured from the wheel centres.

A1.18 PERCENTAGE ANTI-DIVE AND ANTI-SQUAT: CALCULATION REQUIREMENTS

Reference is sometimes made to the percentage of anti-dive or anti-squat of a particular suspension or car. If we are thinking in terms

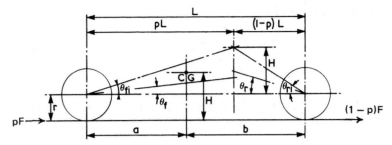

Fig. A1·12   This diagram corresponds to Fig. A1.9 but relates to inboard braking and drive

of braking we can only consider it in relation to the complete car and refer it to the proportion of the complete elimination of attitude change which has been achieved. This proportion is

$$\frac{pa \tan \theta_f + (1 - p)b \tan \theta_r}{H} \tag{A1.31}$$

and the percentage correction is 100 times this.

If we are interested in how that correction is subdivided between front and rear we have to compare θ_f and θ_r with the ideal angles θ_{fi} and θ_{ri} which as we have seen are $\theta_{fi} = \tan^{-1} H/pL$ and $\theta_{ri} = \tan^{-1} H/(1-p)L$

The percentage correction of the front is therefore

$$100\frac{(\tan \theta_f)}{(\tan \theta_{fi})} \tag{A1.32(a)}$$

and of the rear

$$100\frac{(\tan \theta_r)}{(\tan \theta_{ri})} \tag{A1.32(b)}$$

We can do a corresponding exercise for four-wheel drive by substituting p_d, the front torque proportion in driving, for p, the front braking proportion, if there is a fixed torque ratio between front and rear drives. Because p_d is never likely to be the same as p the proportion of anti-squat will differ from the proportion of anti-brake-dive.

Total avoidance of attitude change is highly improbable because of the bad effect of such an angle θ_f on the front suspension reaction to road bumps. We must therefore expect a vertical reaction at the centre of gravity as well as an attitude change. The vertical reaction at the centre of gravity will be shared out between front and rear suspensions in the proportion of their sprung weights. Because, as we have already said, there are ideally differences between front and rear suspension effective static deflections such a vertical reaction at the centre of gravity will result in a very slight attitude change. This attitude change has been ignored; it is considered likely to be small compared with the other attitude changes to be expected. It is easily calculated if we know S_{cf} and S_{cr}. To include this effect in the formulae would be an unnecessary complication likely to cloud our recognition of the fundamentally important requirements.

If the drive is confined to one end of the car the major attitude change can be avoided if $\tan \theta_{fi}$ for front end drive, and if $\tan \theta_{ri}$ for rear wheel drive, satisfy Equations A1.30(b) and A1.30(a) respectively. The percentage correction is generally $100(\tan \theta)/(\tan \theta_i)$.

Moulton and Best[6] have preferred to relate the percentage correction, with front wheel drive, to the condition which produces zero deflection of the front suspension, i.e. $\tan_{fi} = H/L$, Equation A1.28. This is a matter of personal choice; we must understand and state which criterion is being used as a reference.

A1.19 ANTI-PITCH RATE OF CAR SUSPENSION: WORKED EXAMPLES

When a car has a pitching angle φ the front suspension has a deflection $a\varphi$ and the rear suspension a deflection $b\varphi$. The corresponding forces developed are $a\varphi S_{cf}$ and $b\varphi S_{cr}$, so that the anti-pitch rate is

$$a^2 S_{cf} + b^2 S_{cr} \tag{A1.33}$$

Example 1.12

Pitching movement resulting from different ratios of front and rear suspension frequencies, Fig. 3.13.
(a)   Vertical movement of front end excited by transverse ridge. The decaying vibration excited by a single impulse follows Equation 3.15, i.e. $x = e^{-nt} A \cos (\omega_c t)$.
   Assumptions: $A = 0.04 \, m$, $\omega_c = 2\pi \times$ frequency $= 2\pi$
   $n = W/2F_d = 0.8$.
   Points are taken every 30°, i.e. at intervals of 0.083 s. There seems no point in reproducing all of them. The amplitudes at

Table A1.1(a)

Number of complete vibrations	Amplitude (cm)	Time (s)
0	4.0	0
1	1.797	1.0
2	0.808	2.0
3	0.363	3.0

Table A1.1(b)

Number of complete vibrations	Amplitude (cm)	Time from start of movement (s)
0	4.0	0
1	1.659	1.1
2	0.688	2.2
3	0.285	3.3

Table A1.1(c)

Number of complete vibrations	Amplitude (cm)	Time from start of movement (s)
0	4.0	0
1	1.947	0.9
2	0.948	1.8
3	0.461	2.7

intervals of 1s, i.e. at the beginning of each complete cycle, are shown in Table A1.1(a).

(b) Movement of rear end excited by transverse ridge.
Assumptions are as (a) except that frequency = 0.9091 Hz, i.e. slower than the front end in the ratio 1:1.1. Time of complete cycle therefore 1.1 s; and $\omega_c = 2\pi \times 0.9091 = 1.8182\pi$. The amplitudes at the beginning of each complete cycle are shown in Table A1.1(b).

(c) Movement of rear end excited by transverse ridge.
Assumptions are as (a) except that frequency is taken as 1.1 Hz, i.e. faster than the front end in the ratio 1/0.9 (time of complete cycle 0.9 s) $\omega_c = 2\pi \times 1.1 = 2.2\pi = 6.91$ rad/s. The

amplitudes at the beginning of each complete cycle are given in Table A1.1(c).
(d)   The rear end vibrations start later than the front.
Assumptions: Two velocities (1) 50 km/hr, (2) 100 km/hr. Wheelbase = 2.7 m.
(1) At 50 km/hr speed is 50 000 m/3600 sec = $13.\dot{8}$ m/sec.
Time interval between initiation of front and rear suspension movements = $2.7/13.\dot{8} = 0.2$ s.
(2) At 100 km/hr the time interval is obviously half of the above, i.e. 0.1s.

Example 1.13

Moment of Inertia I about centre of gravity if k^2/ab- $= 1 = Wab$ kg m^2 (Equation A1.21). Assume for sprung weight, car with driver only

$$W_{sp} = 924.25 \text{ kg}$$

$$a = 1.35 \text{ m}$$

$$b = 1.4 \text{ m}$$

$$I = 924.25 \times 1.35 \times 1.4 = 1746.83 \text{ kg m}^2$$

For $k^2/ab = 0.9$, $I = 1572.15$ kg m^2.

Example 1.14

Difference between I and k^2/ab as between a horizontal transverse axis and a vertical one, each through the car centre of gravity (Section 1.11).

Car total weights of 1413.75 kg fully laden, 1014.25 kg driver only and sprung weights of 1323.75 kg fully laden, 924.25 kg driver only, are assumed. Fully laden includes 5 passengers at 68 kg each, 100 kg of luggage and a full petrol tank containing 55 kg of fuel. Driver only has one occupant at 68 kg, no luggage and only 27.5 kg of fuel.

The car is divided up into major components with assumed weights and centres of gravity. The body is reckoned to contribute 433.25 kg, split up into seats, front and rear panels, floor, lower and upper sides, bonnet top, roof, boot lid, windscreen and rear window. Centre of gravity positions are assumed for these too. From this information the centre of gravity positions are calculated in terms of the distance behind front wheels:

For sprung weight (1323.75 kg) fully laden,	1.6 m
For sprung weight (924.25 kg) driver only,	1.23 m
Complete car (1413.75 kg) fully laden,	1.58 m
Complete car (1014.25 kg) driver only,	1.24 m

The moments of inertia about the transvrse horizontal and vertical axes, through the appropriate centres of gravity, are then calculated:

(1) By using the centre of gravity positions of the components. Where W_1 is the weight of a component and x_1 the distance of its C.G. from the vehicle or sprung weight C.G., as appropriate,

$$I_1 = W_1 x_1^2 \quad \text{and} \quad I_{\text{total}} = W_1 x_1^2 + W_2 x_2^2 + \ldots + W_n x_n^2$$

(2) By adding to this the calculated moments of inertia of the major body panels, assumed flat, about their own centres of gravity. The resulting totals are then compared with the appropriate values of Wab to get values of the ratio k^2/ab. The results are as follows:

(a) Transverse axis, sprung weight, fully laden.
$$I = 1910.2 + 282.9 = 2193.1 \text{ kg m}^2$$
$$Wab = 1323.75 \times 1.6 \times 1.15 = 2435.7 \text{ kg m}^2$$
$$k^2/ab = 2193.1 \quad 2435.7 = 0.90$$

(b) Transverse axis, sprung weight, driver only.
$$I = 1309.5 + 282.9 = 1592.4 \text{ kg m}^2$$
$$Wab = 924.25 \times 1.23 \times 1.52 = 1728.0 \text{ kg m}^2$$
$$k^2/ab = 1592.4 \quad 1728.00 = 0.922$$

(c) Vertical axis, total weight, fully laden.
$$I = 2254.3 + 297.2 = 2551.5 \text{ kg m}^2$$
$$Wab = 1413.75 \times 1.58 \times 1.17 = 2613.46 \text{ kg m}^2$$
$$k^2/ab = 2551.5 \quad 2613.6 = 0.976$$

(d) Vertical axis, total weight, driver only.
$$I = 1626.8 + 297.2 = 1924.00.1 \text{ kg m}^2$$
$$Wab = 1014.25 \times 1.24 \times 1.51 = 1899.1 \text{ kg m}^2$$
$$k^2/ab = 1924 \quad 1899.1 = 1.013$$

All the k^2/ab ratios seem high: the results are included because they are believed to show tendencies. They indicate that the ratio can be appreciably higher for the steering than the pitching condition. This increases the attraction of lowering the pitching frequency, and excitation, by means other than increasing k^2/ab.

Example 1.15

Anti Pitch (Sections A1.13, A1.17).
   To calculate the pitch angle of a car under deceleration with and
without front and rear suspension characteristics arranged to reduce
brake drive.
Assumptions:
Vehicle weight $W = 1055$ kg $= 10\,350$ N;   Front   end   total
$W_f = 537.1$ kg, $a = 1.35$ m, $W_{usf} = 100$ kg $= 981$ N,
$W_{spf} = 437.1$ kg $= 4288$ N; Rear end total $W_r = 517.9$ kg, $b = 1.4$ m,
$W_{usr} = 100$ kg $= 981$ N, $W_{spr} = 417.9$ kg $= 4099.6$ N.
   The assumed front suspension frequency of 1.0 Hz implies a
combined front suspension rate S_{cf} derived from

$$1 = \frac{1}{2\pi}\left\{\frac{S_{cf}}{437.1}\right\}^{1/2}, \text{ i.e. } 4\pi^2 = \frac{S_{cf}}{437.1},$$

from which $S_{cf} = 17\,256.0$ N/m. This implies a front static deflection of $4288/17256 = 0.248$ m $= 9.78$ in.
   The assumed rear suspension frequency of 1.1 Hz implies a rear
spring rate which can be similarly derived from $(2.2\pi)^2 = S_{cr}/417.9$
from which $S_{cr} = 19\,962.6$ N/m. This implies a rear static deflection
of $4099.6/19\,962.6 = 0.205$ m $= 8.09$ in. Having the spring rates in
N/m makes it convenient to give the spring weights also listed in
Newtons.
   Assume height of centre of gravity 0.64m; percentage front
braking 65› which gives $p = 0.65$. At 0.9 g braking the weight
transference is

$$\frac{855 \times 0.9 \times 0.64}{2.75} = 179.1 \text{ kg} = 1757 \text{ N}$$

   If the suspensions incorporate no anti-dive the dip angle or
attitude change is

$$\frac{57.3}{2.75}\left(\frac{1757}{17\,256} + \frac{1757}{19\,962.6}\right) = 3.96°$$

This is excessive; the headlamp dip angle is $1\frac{1}{2}°$ to $2°$.
   Now suppose we take $\theta_f = 15.11°$, $\tan \theta_f = 0.27$ and $\theta_r = 16.17°$,

$\tan \theta_r = 0.29$. The attitude change is reduced to:

$$\frac{57.3 \times 855 \times 9.81 \times 0.9}{2.75^2}\{0.64 - 0.65 \times 1.35 \times 0.27 - 0.35 \times 1.4 \times 0.29$$

$$\times \left\{\frac{1}{17\,256} + \frac{1}{19\,962.6}\right\} = 6.1797(0.64 - 0.2369 - 0.1421) = 1.61°$$

The percentage reduction in the pitch angle is

$$100\left\{\frac{3.96 - 1.61}{3.96}\right\} = 59.3\%$$

This can also be calculated from equation A1.31 to be:

$$100\left\{\frac{0.65 \times 1.35 \times 0.27 + 0.35 \times 1.4 \times 0.29}{0.64}\right\} = 59.2\%$$

The vertical movement of the centre of gravity, Equation A1.26, is given by

$$\frac{pF \tan \theta_f - (1 - p)F \tan \theta_r}{S_{cf} + S_{cr}}$$

in which

$$F = 855 \times 0.9 = 769.5 \text{ kg} = 7548.8 \text{ N}$$

$$= \frac{7548.8(0.65 \times 0.27 - 0.35 \times 0.29)}{17\,256 + 19\,962.6}$$

$$= \frac{558}{37\,218.6} = 0.015 \text{ m} = 0.59 \text{ in}$$

Example 1.16

Attitude change, rear drive, live axle (Sections A1.15, A1.16 and A1.17).
Assume driving force $F = 2300$ N and $b = 1.4$.
(1) Assume $\theta_r = 16.17°$, $\tan \theta_r = 0.29$.
     The reaction point at the vertical through the centre of gravity $= 0.29 \times 1.4 = 0.406$ above the ground and therefore $0.64 - 0.406 = 0.234$ m below the C.G.

The pitching moment = $2300 \times 0.234 = 538.2$ Nm and the attitude change

$$= \frac{(57.3 \times 538.2)}{2.75^2}\left(\frac{1}{17\,256} + \frac{1}{19\,962.6}\right) = 0.4406°$$

The vertical force under the centre of gravity = $(2300 \times 0.406/1.4 = 667$ N and the lift = $667/(17\,256 + 19\,626.6) = 0.018$ m ($= 0.71$ in).

(2) Now assume $\theta_r = \tan^{-1} 0.64/1.4 = 24.56°$, ($\tan \theta_r = 0.457$). There is by definition no pitching moment and therefore no attitude change.
The vertical force = $(2300 \times 0.64)/1.4 = 1051.4$ N and the lift = $1051.4/(17\,256 + 19\,926.6) = 0.028$ m ($= 1.11$ in).

Example 1.17

Pitch frequency (Section A1.18).
$I_p = 2193.1$ kg m^2, fully laden (Example 1.14), $S_{cf} = 17\,256$ N/m,
$I_p = 1592.4$ kg m^2, driver only, $S_{cr} = 19\,963$ N/m
Anti-pitch rate = $a^2 S_{cf} + b^2 S_{cr}$ ($a = 1.6$ m, $b = 1.15$ m) (Equation A1.33)

$$= 1.6^2 \times 17\,256 + 1.15^2 \times 19\,963$$
$$= 44\,175.4 + 26\,401.07 = 70\,576.5 \text{ Nm/rad}$$

Pitch frequency $= \dfrac{1}{2\pi}\left(\dfrac{70\,576.5}{2193.1}\right)^{1/2} = 0.903$ Hz, fully laden

For driver only, $a = 1.23$ and $b = 1.52$.
So anti-pitch rate = $1.23^2 \times 17\,256 + 1.52^2 \times 19\,963$
$$= 26\,106.6 + 46\,122.52 = 72\,229.12 \text{ Nm/rad}$$

Pitch frequency $= \dfrac{1}{2\pi}\left(\dfrac{72\,229.12}{1592.4}\right)^{1/2} = 1.07$ Hz

A1.20 ANTI-ROLL RATES

When cars with independent suspension roll, their suspension rates operate at the wheel track. If this wheel track is T and the suspension rate at each wheel is $S_c/2$, then the anti-roll rate of the suspension is

$$\frac{T^2 S_c}{4} \tag{A1.34}$$

The total anti-roll rate of a car with independent suspension all round is therefore

$$\frac{T_f^2 S_{cf}}{4} + \frac{T_r^2 S_{cr}}{4} \qquad (A1.35)$$

If the car has an axle at either or both ends, using coil springs or torsion bars, then instead of the wheel track T we have to use the spring track T_s and the corresponding anti-roll stiffness at each end is

$$\frac{T_s^2 S_s}{4} \qquad (A1.36)$$

on the suspension alone. Because of the difference between the spring and wheel tracks the effect of tyre deflections has to be calculated separately. The relationship $T^2 S/4$ is the fundamental one, with the appropriate suffix for the spring, tyre or combined rate of the appropriate end of the car, and with S the total rate at that end of the car, i.e. that for the two wheels.

When an axle relies on leaf springs the twisting and sideways bending to which these springs are subjected result in anti-roll rates in excess of 50% above those to be expected from the spring track alone. Because of the variation in spring design, in the attachment to the axle and in the materials used in the spring eye bushes, no hard and fast rule for the excess can be given.

Cars may be fitted with anti-roll rods or their equivalent. Whatever form these may take it is convenient to express their effect as a rate at each wheel, when the fundamental equation will allow the calculation of the additional anti-roll stiffness. A useful rule of thumb is that the anti-roll rate at the wheel should not exceed 50% of the suspension rate there; figures in excess of this will spoil the ride by virtue of the high accelerations of the head sideways caused by the high roll excitation which is induced when a bump or hollow is met by wheels on one side of a car only.

A1.21 ROLL ANGLES IN CORNERING

One interest in the anti-roll stiffness is in its effect on the roll angle of a car when cornering. Figure A1.13 illustrates the state of affairs. The total sideways force due to the sprung weight is $W_{sp} a$ N, where a is the centripetal acceleration, m/s^2. It is customary to refer to

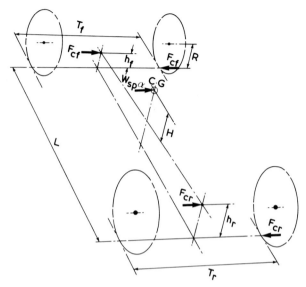

Fig. A1·13   Dimensions and forces for a cornering car

cornering severity ad 0.5 g or any other proportion of the acceleration due to gravity (0.5 g = 4.905 m/s²).

The major rolling moment of the sprung weight about its roll axis is $W_{sp}aH$ Nm. Roll angle can be reduced by reducing H; this implies either increasing the height of the roll axis or reducing the height of the centre of gravity. It can also be reduced by increasing the anti-roll stiffness of the suspensions. A secondary rolling moment is that due to the sideways overhang of the centre of gravity from the roll axis, due to its total roll angle. This total roll angle is made up of:

(1)   The roll angle on the tyres φ_{us} due to the weight trransference of the unsprung weight, usually takes as acting at the height of the wheel centre. The weight transference due to the unsprung weight is

$$\frac{W_{us}aR}{T} \text{ N} \tag{A1.37}$$

and the roll angle due to it is

$$\varphi_{us} = \frac{4W_{us}aR}{T^2 S_t} \text{ rad} \tag{A1.38}$$

The average

$$\varphi_{usa} = 2aR\left(\frac{W_{usf}}{T_f^2 S_{tf}} + \frac{W_{usr}}{T_r^2 S_{tr}}\right) \tag{A1.39}$$

(2) The roll angle on the tyres, φ_{rc}, due to the weight transference from the sprung weight acting at the roll centre height. This is $W_{sp}ah/T$ and the roll angle on the tyres due to this

$$\varphi_{rc} = \frac{4W_{sp}ah}{T^2 S_s} \tag{A1.40}$$

The average roll on the tyres due to this is

$$\varphi_{rca} = 2a\left(\frac{W_{spf}h_f}{T_f^2 S_{tf}} + \frac{W_{spr}h_r}{T_r^2 S_{tr}}\right) \tag{A1.41}$$

(3) The roll angle θ on the suspension and tyres due to the sprung weight causing weight transference.

In calculating the overhand moment we must use the total roll angle, θ_t. There can only be one total roll angle for the car. Because we are basing our initial calculations on the average tyre deflections, front and rear, from causes (1) and (2), we must work to a common roll angle of the sprung mass, θ_{sp}.

Having in this way arrived at our total roll angle, we can get the actual front and rear angles θ_{spf} and θ_{spr}, when we want to calculate the weight transferences front and rear, by subtracting from the total roll angle the actual tyre roll angles, front or rear, due to the unsprung weight and the height of the roll centre.

The roll angle of the sprung weight,

$$\theta_{sp} = \frac{4W_{sp}H(a + \theta_{sp} + \varphi_{usa} + \varphi_{rca})}{T_f^2 S_{cf} + T_r^2 S_{cr}} \tag{A1.42}$$

The total roll angle $\theta_t = \theta_{sp} + \varphi_{usa} + \varphi_{rca}$. The actual sprung weight roll angle at the front end.

$$\theta_{spf} = (\theta_t - \varphi_{usf} - \varphi_{rcf}) \tag{A1.43(a)}$$

so that the front end weight transference is:

$$W_{tf} = \frac{W_{usf}aR}{T_f} + \frac{W_{spf}ah_f}{T_f} + \frac{(\theta_t - \varphi_{usf} - \varphi_{rcf})T_f S_{cf}}{4} \tag{A1.44(a)}$$

Correspondingly the actual sprung weight roll angle at the rear,

$$\theta_{spr} = (\theta_t - \varphi_{usr} - \varphi_{rcr}) \qquad \text{(A1.43(b))}$$

and the rear end weight transference is:

$$W_{tr} = \frac{W_{usr}aR}{T_r} + \frac{W_{spr}ah_r}{T_r} + \frac{(\theta_t - \varphi_{usr} - \varphi_{rcr})T_rS_{cr}}{4} \qquad \text{(A1.44(b))}$$

For a given weight transference W_t the roll angle is

$$\frac{4W_t}{ST} \qquad \text{(A1.45)}$$

so that the total roll angle on the tyres at the front end,

$$\varphi_{tf} = \frac{4W_{tf}}{S_{tf}T_f} \qquad \text{(A1.46(a))}$$

and at the back

$$\varphi_{tr} = \frac{4W_{tr}}{S_{tr}T_r} \qquad \text{(A1.46(b))}$$

The roll angle on the front suspension,

$$\theta_{sf} = \frac{(\theta_t - \varphi_{usf} - \varphi_{rcf})T_fS_{cf}}{4} \frac{T_f4}{T_f^2} S_{sf}$$

$$= \frac{(\theta_t - \varphi_{usf} - \varphi_{rcf})S_{cf}}{S_{sf}} \qquad \text{(A1.47(a))}$$

and on the back suspension,

$$\theta_{sr} = \frac{(\theta_t - \varphi_{usr} - \varphi_{rcr})S_{cr}}{S_{sr}} \qquad \text{(A1.47(b))}$$

A1.22 MOMENT OF INERTIA IN ROLL: WORKED EXAMPLES

Example 1.14 contains calculations of the rotating moment of inertia of the car about horizontal transverse and vertical axes passing through the centre of gravity of the car. Example 1.18 gives the results of a similar calculation to obtain the rotating moment of inertia of the sprung weight of that same car about a fore and aft axis through its centre of gravity. The value of k^2/ab so calculated for this example is 0.53 (driver only) and 0.49 (fully laden).

The application of the centre of percussion theory, used in Section A1.12 for steering reactions, can be used also in relation to pitching and rolling. If we consider the case where $k^2/ab = 1$, a disturbance applied to the front wheels causes pivoting about the rear wheels and has therefore a moment arm of $(a + b)$. When $k^2/ab = x < 1$, the pivoting point is bx behind the centre of gravity and the moment arm in applying the pitching force is therefore $(a + bx)$. The result, in terms of disturbance, is that the effective moment of inertia against the disturbance originating from the front wheels is:

$$\frac{(a + b)x}{a + bx} \tag{A1.48}$$

as compared with the situation where $k^2/ab = 1$.

For the corresponding condition of a disturbance through a wheel or wheels on one side of the care exciting roll the ratio is

$$\frac{2Tx}{T + Tx} \tag{A1.49}$$

For pitching with $x = 0.9$, $a = 1.6$ and $b = 1.15$ the ratio is

$$\frac{2.75 \times 0.9}{1.6 + (1.15 \times 0.9)} = 0.939$$

For roll, with $x = 0.5$ and $T = 1.47$ m, the ratio is

$$\frac{2 \times 1.47 \times 0.5}{1.47 + (1.47 \times 0.5)} = 0.67$$

Under pitch excitation from the front the preferred oscillation point is $0.9 \times 1.15 = 1.035$ m behind the centre of gravity.

Under roll excitation the corresponding oscillation point is

$$0.5 \times 0.735 = 0.368 \text{ m}$$

from the centre of gravity. If these oscillation points applied, a given deflection y of that corner of the sprung weight due to the single front wheel of a car passing over a bump would result in a roll angle of $y/1.103 = 0.907y$ rad and a pitch angle of $y/2.635 = 0.380y$ rad.

With angular accelerations proportional to the relative angular displacements this means that the sideways acceleration of a driver's or passenger's head is 2.39 times as great as the fore and aft acceleration. This ratio applies for the quantities assumed; these are felt to be reasonably representative. Subjective observation is that the sideways accelerations are considerably higher than the fore and aft ones.

EXAMPLES

Example 1.18

Roll frequency (Section A1.20).
Front and rear tracks $T_f = T_r = 1.47$ m

$$\text{Anti-roll stiffness} = \frac{1.47^2 \times 17\,256}{4} + \frac{1.47^2 \times 19\,963}{4} \text{(from Equa-}$$

tion A1.35)

$$= 9322.1 + 10\,784.5 = 20\,106.6 \text{ Nm/rad}$$

By the methods outlined in Example 1.14, which give $k^2/ab = 0.53$ for driver only, and 0.49 fully laden:
(1) Inertia $= 265$ kg m^2, driver only

$$\text{Frequency} = \frac{1}{2\pi}\left(\frac{20\,106.6}{265}\right)^{1/2} = 1.39 \text{ Hz}$$

(2) Inertia $= 353$ kg m^2, fully laden

$$\text{Frequency} = \frac{1}{2\pi}\left(\frac{20\,106.6}{353}\right)^{1/2} = 1.20 \text{ Hz}$$

Example 1.19

Bounce frequency (Section A1.21).
Assumptions: fully laden
$S_{cf} = 17\,256$, $S_{cr} = 19\,963$, $W_{sp} = 1323.75$ kg, fully laden

$$W_{spr} = \frac{1323.75 \times 1.6}{2.75} = 770.18 \text{ kg}$$

$$W_{spf} = 1323.75 - 770.18 = 553.57 \text{ kg}$$

$$\text{Front end bounce frequency} = \frac{1}{2\pi}\left\{\frac{17\,256}{553.57}\right\}^{1/2} = 0.89 \text{ Hz}$$

Rear end bound frequency $= \dfrac{1}{2\pi}\left\{\dfrac{19\,963}{770.18}\right\}^{1/2} = 0.81$ Hz

Overall bounce frequency $= \dfrac{1}{2\pi}\left\{\dfrac{17\,256 + 19\,963}{1323.75}\right\}^{1/2} = 0.844$ Hz

Assumptions: driver only
$W_{sp} = 924.25$ kg, driver only

$W_{spr} = \dfrac{924.25 \times 1.23}{2.75} = 413.39$ kg

$W_{spf} = 924.25 - 413.39 = 510.86$ kg, S_{cf} and S_{cr} unchanged

Front end bounce frequency $= \dfrac{1}{2\pi}\left\{\dfrac{17\,256}{510.86}\right\}^{1/2} = 0.925$ Hz

Rear end bound frequency $= \dfrac{1}{2\pi}\left\{\dfrac{19\,963}{413.39}\right\}^{1/2} = 1.106$ Hz

Overall bounce frequency $= \dfrac{1}{2\pi}\left\{\dfrac{17\,256 + 19\,963}{924.25}\right\}^{1/2} = 1.01$ Hz

Example 1.20

Weight transference and roll angles (Section A1.21).
Take driver only conditions, assumptions are
$S_{sf} = 18\,500$, $S_{tf} = 256\,600$, $S_{cf} = 17\,256$
$S_{sr} = 21\,647$, $S_{tr} = 256\,600$, $S_{cr} = 19\,963$
$W_{sp} = 924.25$ kg, centre of gravity 1.23 m behind front wheels, wheelbase $L = 2.75$ m, $W_{spf} = 510.86$ kg, $W_{spr} = 413.39$ kg
$W_{usf} = 100$ kg, $W_{usr} = 100$ kg, $h_f = 0.15$ m, $h_r = 0.20$ m
$H = 0.5$ m, $T_f = T_r = 1.47$ m, $R = 0.33$ m
Take $a/g = 0.5$, $a = 4.905$ m/s².
    The average roll angle on the tyres due to the unsprung weight (Equation A1.39)

$$\varphi_{usa} = 2aR\left(\dfrac{W_{usf}}{T_f^2 S_{tf}} + \dfrac{W_{usr}}{T_r^2 S_{tr}}\right)$$

$$= 2 \times 4.905 \times 0.33\left(\dfrac{100}{1.47^2 \times 256\,600} + \dfrac{100}{1.47^2 \times 256\,600}\right)$$

$$= 0.001168 \text{ rad} = 0.06691°$$

The average roll angle on tyres due to the roll centre height

$$\varphi_{rca} = 2 \times 4.905\left(\frac{510.86 \times 0.15}{1.47^2 \times 256\,600} + \frac{413.39 \times 0.2}{1.47^2 \times 256\,600}\right)$$

$$= 0.002818 \text{ rad} = 0.1615°$$

Roll angle due to the sprung weight (Equation A1.42)

$$\theta_{sp} = \frac{4 \times 924.25 \times 0.5(4.905 + \theta_{sp} + 0.0039861)}{1.47^2 \times 17\,256 + 1.47^2 \times 19\,963}$$

$$\theta_{sp} = \frac{1848.5(\theta_{sp} + 4.90899)}{80\,426.5} = 0.02298371(\theta_{sp} + 4.90899)$$

$0.977106\ \theta_{sp} = 0.111827$ and $\theta_{sp} = 0.115481$ rad
$\theta_t = \theta_{sp} + \varphi_{usa} + \varphi_{rca} = 0.1195$ rad $= 6.845°$
$\varphi_{usf} = 0.0011677$

$$\varphi_{rcf} = \frac{4 \times 4.905 \times 510.86 \times 0.15}{1.47^2 \times 256\,600} = 0.0027114$$

$\varphi_{usr} = 0.0011677$

$$\varphi_{rcr} = \frac{4 \times 4.905 \times 413.39 \times 0.2}{1.47^2 \times 256\,600} = 0.002925 \text{ rad}$$

$\theta_{spf} = \theta_t - \varphi_{usf} - \varphi_{rcf} = 0.1156$ rad
$\theta_{spr} = \theta_t - \varphi_{usr} - \varphi_{rcr} = 0.1154$ rad
  Front end weight transference W_{tf}

$$= \frac{100 \times 4.905 \times 0.33}{1.47} + \frac{510.86 \times 4.905 \times 0.15}{1.47}$$

$$+ \frac{0.115588 \times 1.47 \times 17\,256}{4}$$

$$= 110.11 + 255.69 + 733.01 = 1098.81 \text{ N}$$

  Rear end weight transference W_{tr}

$$= 110.11 + \frac{413.39 \times 4.905 \times 0.2}{1.47} + \frac{0.11537 \times 1.47 \times 19\,963}{4}$$

$$= 110.11 + 275.87 + 846.40 = 1232.4 \text{ N}$$

Total roll angle on tyres, front end
$= 4W_{tf}/S_{tf}T_f = 0.01165$ rad $= 0.6677°$
Total roll angle on tyres, rear end $= 0.01307$ rad $= 0.7489°$
Roll angle on suspension, front end $= (0.11559 \times 17\,256)/18\,500$
$(6.178 + 0.6677 = 6.846°)$ $= 0.1078$ rad $= 6.178°$
Roll angle on suspension, rear end $= (0.11538 \times 19\,963)/21\,647$
$= 0.1064$ rad $= 6.097$ $(6.097 + 0.7489 = 6.846°)$.

Now consider the effect of increasing the front suspension spring rate in roll to the maximum suggested figure of 1.5 times normal figure by the use of an anti-roll rod.

Assumptions: $S_{sf} = 18\,500 \times 1.5 = 27\,500$ N/m,
$S_{cf} = 25\,042$ N/m. Other assumptions unchanged from previous part. φ_{us} and φ_{rc} are unchanged.

$$\theta_{sp} = \frac{1848.5(\theta_{sp} + 4.90899)}{97\,251} = 0.019008\,\theta_{sp} + 0.093308$$

$$= 0.09512 \text{ rad}$$

$\theta_t = 0.099$ rad $= 5.678°$
$\theta_{spf} = 0.09910 - 0.0011677 - 0.0027114 = 0.09522$ rad
$\theta_{spr} = 0.09910 - 0.0011677 - 0.0029255 = 0.095008$ rad
Front end weight transference W_{tf}
$= 110.11 + 255.69 + 876.34 = 1242.4$ N
Rear end weight transference W_{tr}
$= 110.11 + 275.87 + 697.02 = 1083.01$ N
Total roll angle on tyres, front end $= 0.01317$ rad $= 0.755°$
Total roll angle on tyres, rear end $= 0.01148$ rad $= 0.658°$
Roll angle on front suspension $\theta_{sf} = (0.09522 \times 25\,042)/27\,750$
$(4.924 + 0.755 = 5.679°)$ $= 0.08593$ rad $= 4.924°$
Roll angle on rear suspension $\theta_{sr} = (0.09501 \times 19\,963)/21\,647$
$(5.0205 + 0.6581 = 5.679°)$ $= 0.0872$ rad $= 5.0205°$

A1.23 WEIGHT DISTRIBUTION FRONT AND REAR

The weight distribution between the front and rear of a car has to be considered in relation to:

(1) The percentage changes of sprung weight between the driver only condition and the fully laden. To avoid unacceptable attitude changes between these two conditions, with high percentage weight changes, either the springing has to be relatively hard or the spring rate has to be progressive or a means of standing height correction has to be provided, on the

rear suspension at least. Associated with this also is the difficulty of specifying damper characteristics which are a good enough compromise between the two limits of sprung weight, or which are arranged to vary with that sprung weight.

Associated with this also is the problem of maintaining a bounce frequency for the fully laden condition which is sufficiently higher than the front suspension bounce frequency to minimise pitch, without being excessively high in the driver only condition.

(2) The stability of the car in slippery conditions or in relation to wind forces at the slight yaw angles which are associated with cornering or, probably more importantly, with slight attitude changes due to road disturbances when driving along a straight road.

(3) The achievement of acceptable or desired handling behaviour, which as we shall see later is affected both by the average weight carried by front and rear tyres and by the weight transference during cornering.

REFERENCES

1. Timoshenko, S., *Vibration Problems in Engineering*, 3rd Edn, D. Van Nostrand, London (1955)
2. Wilson, W. Ker., *Vibration Engineering*, Charles Griffin (1959)
3. Olley, M., 'National Inçuence on Passenger Car Design', *Proc Inst Auto Engrs*, Vol. XXXII (1937–38)
4. Olley, M., 'Road Manners of the Modern Car', *Proc Inst Auto Engrs*, Vol. XLI (1946–47)
5. Bastow, D., 'Vehicle Attitude Changes Due to Acceleration and Braking', *J Auto Engng*, Vol. 5, No. 1 (1974)
6. Moulton, A. E. and Best, A., 'From Hydrolastic to Hydragas', *Proc Auto Div Inst mech Engrs* (1978–79)
7. Bastow, D., 'Aspects of Car Rear Suspension', *Proc Auto Div Inst mech Engrs*, Vol. 190, 53–56 (1976)

Appendix 2: Steering calculations and worked examples

A2.1 STEERING ANGLES OF INNER AND OUTER FRONT WHEELS

Ignoring tyre slip angles, Fig. A2.1, it is clear that the steering angle required for each front wheel is different from the other, and that the difference between the two increases as the turb radius diminishes – however the radius of the turn is defined. For an extreme relationship the smallest radius likely to be use in practice should be taken. Example 2.1, based on Fig. A2.1, shows the calculations necessary to arrive at the outer wheel lock angle for an inner wheel lock angle of 40 degrees. For this calculation the effective front track, T_{fk}, is the distance apart of the intersections of the kingpin axes and the ground; if e is the offset of the middle of the contact patch from the kingpin axis, then $T_{fk} = T_f - 2e$. The equations necessary to arrive at the relative angles and radii of turn can be understood by reference to Fig. A2.1.

Assume θ_i inside wheel lock angle

$$\frac{L}{R_{ri} + e + \frac{(T_r - T_f)}{2}} = \tan \theta_i$$

i.e.
$$R_{ri} + e + \left\{ \frac{T_r - T_f}{2} \right\} = \frac{L}{\tan \theta_i} \tag{A2.1}$$

$$R_{fi} = \frac{2.75}{\sin \theta_i} \tag{A2.2}$$

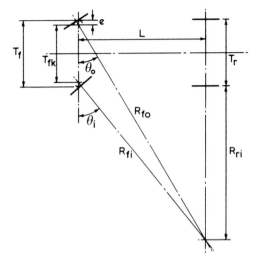

Fig. A2·1   For the exact steering angles the front datum points are where the kingpin axes meet the ground, less than the front track by twice the kingpin offset from the middle of the contact patch

$$\frac{L}{R_{ro} - e - \left\{ \dfrac{T_r - T_f}{2} \right\}} = \tan \theta_o \qquad (A2.3)$$

$$R_{fo} = \frac{L}{\sin \theta_o} \qquad (A2.4)$$

A2.2   DIFFERENT INNER AND OUTER WHEEL LOCK ANGLES

To obtain the differences in lock angles that are required, one or more four-bar chains are used. The conventional, and mostly obsolete, axle uses a single four-bar chain as shown in Fig. A2.3. If we assume that we know θ_i and θ_o, the maximum lock angles for inner and outer wheels, that T_{fk} is fixed, in this case the distance apart of the kingpin axes at track rod level, and that a dimension y has either been chosen or has been determined by clearance considerations, then the greater the angle ϕ by which the steering lever departs from parallelism with the car centre line, in the straight ahead position, the greater the angular difference between θ_i and θ_o.

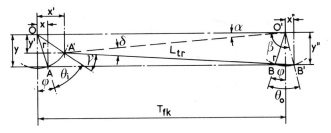

Fig. A2·2   This diagram provides the basis for the calculation of inner angles on an axle, for any desired relationship

The need therefore is to establish φ for our desired values of θ_i and θ_o obtained from Fig. A2.2.

An approximate, and possibly sufficiently accurate, value can be obtained by drawing and trial and error. It may be desirable to check this trigonometrically. Starting from the left hand end, Fig. A2.2, O is the kingpin centre at the track rod height, A the position of the left hand steering ball joint, defined by a radius r and the angle φ, from which $x = r \sin \varphi$ and $y = r \cos \varphi$. A new position A′ for the ball joint is obtained, where angle AOA′ $= \theta_i$, $x' = r \sin(\varphi + \theta_i)$ and $y' = r \cos(\varphi + \theta_i)$. The centre of the right hand kingpin at track rod level is at O′. The track rod length $L_{tr} = T_{fk} - 2x$. Join A′ to O′.

$$\text{Angle } \alpha = \tan^{-1}\left\{ \frac{y'}{T_{fk} - x'} \right\} \tag{A2.5}$$

$$A'O' = \frac{T_{fk} - x'}{\cos \alpha} \tag{A2.6}$$

For the triangle A′O′B we now know A′O′, O′B′ $= r$ and A′B′ $= L_{tr}$

$$\cos \beta = \frac{A'O'^2 + r^2 - L_{tr}^2}{2A'O'r} \tag{A2.7}$$

$$\sin \delta = \frac{A'O' \sin \beta}{L_{tr}} \tag{A2.8}$$

Lock angle

$$\theta_o = \alpha + \beta + \varphi - 90° \tag{A2.9}$$

To define the position of B', $x'' = r\sin(\theta_o - \varphi)$ and $y'' = r\cos(\theta_o - \varphi)$.

We are interested in the control angle γ. The apex angle OA'O' is

$$180° - \alpha - A'OO' = 180° - \alpha - (90 - \varphi - \theta_i)$$
$$= 90° - \alpha + \varphi + \theta_i$$

Angle O'A'B' $= 180° - \beta - \delta$, so

$$\gamma = 180° - (90° - \alpha + \varphi + \theta_i) - (180° - \beta - \delta)$$
$$= \alpha + \beta + \delta - \varphi - \theta_i - 90° \tag{A2.10}$$

The smaller the control angle the less accurate is the relationship between inner and outer steering angles and the more dependent that relationship upon play in ball joints and steering pivots and on deflections of the parts under load; and since a small control angle implies a small moment arm from the kingpin, the larger the forces in the track rod to produce a given torque about the kingpin.

Our examples have been of track rods behind the wheels. In theory track rods can be in front of the wheels; in practice there tend to be clearance problems between ball joints and wheels with such forward track rods. The choice of θ_i at 40 degrees is guided by being a probable maximum for private cars. Taxis, to meet the Metropolitan cab regulations, and commercial vehicles, buses and coaches with much longer wheelbases need angles greater than 40 degrees.

A2.3 CALCULATIONS FOR INDEPENDENT SUSPENSION SYSTEMS: WORKED EXAMPLES

Independent front suspensions of the types generally used, i.e. double wishbone or strut and link, cannot accept the errors implied by a single track rod and the general practice is to provide a single track rod to control each wheel. The length of that track rod should be fixed to match the suspension linkage characteristics; its inner end if most likely to be coupled to the rack of a rack and pinion steering gear and by implication the unequal angles θ_i and θ_o need to be obtained from equal and opposite travels of the inner ball joints. The variables to play with are the length of the steering levers, generally determined either by clearance considerations or by the available rack travel, the angle φ and the fore and aft position of the inner ball joints. Figure A2.4 gives the general picture, with the three important positions, right hand and left hand locks and the straight

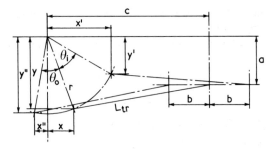

Fig. A2·3   With independent suspension and rack and pinion steering the desired inner and outer wheel angles are derived from equal rack travel in two directions

ahead, shown in Fig. A2.4(a), straight ahead, A2.4(b) left hand lock (inner wheel) and A2.4(c) right hand lock (outer wheel).

From Fig. A2.3 we see that, assuming we start with L_{tr} and a, we have first to establish c and then b from the inside lock angle. Figure A2.4(a) shows that

$$c = L_{tr} \cos \gamma + x \qquad\qquad (A2.11)$$

where $x = r \sin \varphi$ and

$$\gamma = \sin^{-1}\left\{\frac{y - a}{L_{tr}}\right\}$$

y being $r \cos \varphi$.

To arrive at b we next consider the inside lock position, since this is most likely to be fixed by clearance conditions. If however we regard both lock angles as already fixed it does not matter in which order we take the inside and outside lock positions. Let us assume therefore that we will use the inside lock angle, Fig. A2.4(b), to establish b, the rack travel from straight ahead to full lock.

$$x' = r \sin (\varphi + \theta_i) \quad \text{and} \quad y' = r \cos (\varphi + \theta_i)$$

In this case

$$b + c = x' + L_{tr} \cos \gamma' \qquad\qquad (A2.12)$$

The sign of γ' is unimportant. Having in this way arrived at b we can proceed to Fig. A2.4(c), the outside lock position. We know $c - b$, the angle $\alpha'' = \tan^{-1} a/(c - b)$ and

$$d'' = (c - b)/\cos \alpha'' \qquad\qquad (A2.13)$$

This gives us again a triangle of which all three sides are known

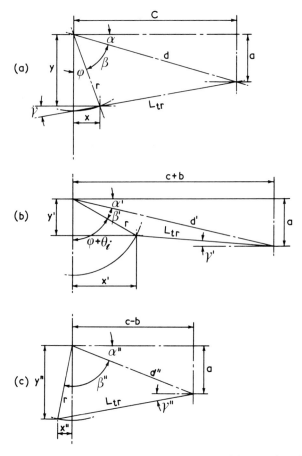

Fig. A2·4 With independent suspension and rack and pinion steering the three extreme positions are shown for the method of calculation used in the text: (a) straight ahead, (b) inner wheel on lock, (c) outer wheel on lock

and

$$\cos \beta'' = \frac{d''^2 + r^2 - L_{tr}^2}{2rd''}$$

$$\theta_o = \alpha'' + \beta'' + \varphi - 90° \qquad (A2.14)$$

The control angle for the position of Fig. A2.4(b) is

$$90° - (\varphi + \theta_i) - \gamma' \qquad (A2.15a)$$

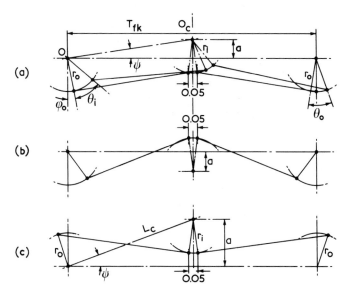

Fig. A2·5 Three of the possible arrangements when independent suspension is combined with a central steering idler are shown here: (a) steering arms behind the wheels, idler pivot in front of the wheel centre line, (b) steering arms behind the wheels, idler reversed, (c) steering arms in front of the wheels, idler pivot in front of its ball joints

if $y' < a$, or

$$90° - (\varphi + \theta_i) + \gamma' \qquad (A2.15b)$$

if $y' > a$.

An alternative possibility for an independent front suspension steering layout is the central level, Fig. A2.4(a). Symmetry suggests that the central lever shall have equal angles each side. The obvious way to tackle it is to join O to O_c, the central pivot axis, arriving at an angle ψ, and then treat the result as a variant of the axle layout. A possible alternative layout is that shown in Fig. A2.5(b) which has advantages from the ball-joint wheel clearance aspect but as drawn may have central lever pivot-engine and transmission unit clearance problems. A derivation of this is the layout of Fig. A2.6(c) which uses the forward position of the track rods and moves the central lever pivot forward out of the way of the drive unit. The angle $\psi = \tan^{-1}\{2a/T_{fk}\}$ and the length between centres of the levers $T_{fk}/2 \cos \psi$. To achieve the steering angles required, one or both of the angles OAB and ABO$_c$ must be less than a right angle. Equal

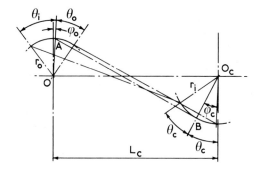

Fig. A2·6   For calculation purposes the layout of Fig. A2.5(c) is most easily dealt with by using the line joining the two pivots as a base

angles each way, θ_c, of the central lever must produce the angles θ_o and θ_i required.

It is usually desirable to make φ_c as small as possible; this means putting the two ball-joints on the centrre lever as close together as clearance requirements permit. If this minimum inner ball-joint separation is d, then the angle

$$\varphi_{c\,minimum} = \sin^{-1}\left\{\frac{d}{2r_i}\right\} + \psi \qquad (A2.16)$$

For calculation purposes it is easier to use the distance between kingpin and idler centres, L_c in Fig. A2.5(c), as the base line and this becomes line OO_c of Fig. A2.6. The resulting straight ahead position of the linkage is shown in Fig. A2.7(a); the extreme lock positions are shown in Fig. A2.7(b) and A2.7(c).

To arrive at the track rod length L_{tr}, Fig. A2.7(a), we have to choose a value of φ_o, L_{tr} is the hypotenuse of the right-angled triangle   ABC   whose   other   two   sides   are $(y_o + y_i)$ and $L_c - (x_o + x_i)$.

$$\alpha = \tan^{-1}\left\{\frac{y_o + y_i}{L_c - (x_o + x_i)}\right\} \qquad (A2.17)$$

and

$$L_{tr} = \frac{L_c - (x_o + x_i)}{\cos \alpha} \qquad (A2.18)$$

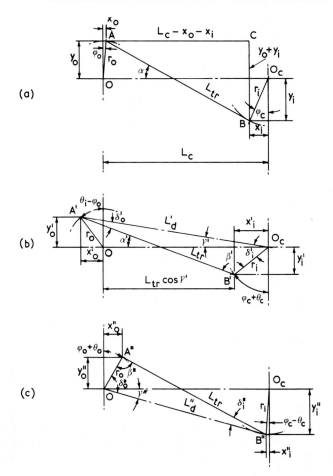

Fig. A2·7   Using the construction of Fig. 2.6, these diagrams show: (a) the straight ahead position, (b) inside wheel lock, (c) outside wheel lock

Assuming that the inside lock position of the left hand wheel is used to arrive at θ_c, the angular movement of the central lever from straight ahead to either lock, Fig. A2.7(b), the new position of the wheel ball-joint centre, A', is joined to O_c, the axis of the central lever. The length of the resulting line, L'_d is calculated by arriving at γ', its angle from the line joining the centres, which is:

$$\gamma' = \tan^{-1}\left\{\frac{y'_o}{L_c + x'_o}\right\} \tag{A2.19}$$

when

$$L'_d = \frac{L_c + x'_o}{\cos \gamma'} \qquad (A2.20)$$

For the triangle $A'O_cB'$ all three sides are known and the relationship

$$\cos\beta' = \frac{L_{tr}^2 + r_i^2 - L_d^2}{2 \times r_i \times L_{tr}} \qquad (A2.21)$$

applies. The angle

$$A'O_cB' = \sin^{-1}(L_{tr} \sin \beta')/L'_d \qquad (A2.22)$$

$$\varphi_c + \theta_c = 90° + \gamma' - A'O_cB' \qquad (A2.23)$$

$$\theta_c = (90° + \gamma' - A'O_cB') - \varphi_c \qquad (A2.24)$$

The next step, Fig. A2.7(c), is to consider the opposite lock position. The centre lever ball joint is now at B'', at an angle $(\theta_c - \varphi_c)$ to the straight ahead. Join O to B''. If B'' lies to the left of the lever pivot

$$\gamma'' = \tan^{-1}\left\{\frac{y''_i}{L_c - x''_i}\right\} \qquad (A2.25)$$

and

$$L''_d = \frac{L_c - x''_i}{\cos \gamma''} \qquad (A2.26)$$

The triangle $OA''B''$ is solved from knowledge of the three sides to find first β'' and then δ''_o.
The angle $\varphi_o + \theta_o = 90° + \gamma'' - \delta''_o$ and therefore

$$\theta_o = 90° + \gamma'' - \delta''_o - \varphi_o. \qquad (A2.27)$$

The worst control angle seems likely to be either on the central level, Fig. A2.7(b), at $180° - \beta'$ or on the wheel lever, at $90° - (\theta_i - \varphi_o) - \alpha'$, where

$$\alpha' = \sin^{-1}\left\{\frac{y'_o + y'_i}{L_{tr}}\right\} \qquad (A2.28)$$

A2.4   TORQUE STEER COMPONENTS

To calculate the couple generated when two shafts transmit torque through an articulated CV joint, the effective radius of the joint must be known as well as the operating angle. In the example, Fig. A2.8, the input shaft operates about an axis AA and the output shaft about an axis BB, transmitting a torque T. The angle between the two shaft is α and the effective radius of the joint r.

At the two points of intersection in the vertical plane XX through the two shafts, the force F transmitted from one to the other is given by the following equation:

$$F = T/2R$$

The forces F also have moments $C = 2Fe$ about the vertical axis XX acting at right angles to the output shaft, where e is the offset of the point of instantaneous interaction from the axis at right angles to the output shaft equal to $r \tan \alpha/2$. The steering torque about XX is therefore given by the equation:

$$C = 2Fr \tan \alpha/2 = T \tan \alpha/2$$

If the torque in the input shaft is clockwise when viewed from the input end, the direction of the torque steer C generated about XX will also be clockwise when viewed from below.

A2.5   INERTIA TORQUES AFFECTING STEERING

Inertia torques about the steering or king pin axis can cause reactions at the steering wheel which are felt by the driver. Although

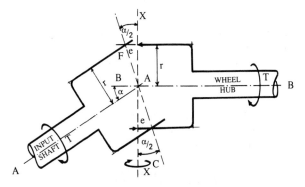

Fig. A2·8   Articulated constant velocity joint in typical driveshaft application

they also cause stresses in the steering linkage generally, it is unlikely that these stresses will be large in relation to those caused by producing steering angle on the front wheels while the car is stationary. Inertia torques are most likely to arise from three causes:

(1) errors in the steering geometry due to up and down wheel movement.
(2) gyroscopic torques due to up and down wheel movements.
(3) torques due to fore and aft accelerations of the wheel mass caused by the suspension geometry; the wheel mass has to be offset from the kingpin axis for the forces arising from these accelerations to produce torques about the kingpin axis.

(1) and (2) above should be grouped together, steering geometrry errors with up and down wheel movement produce precessional movements of the wheels which result in gyroscopic torque; wheel plane tilting with up and down wheel movement also produces precession and therefore gyroscopic torque.

The Porsche and similar type front suspensions (the parallel, fore and aft, link type) which produce the inertia torques of (3), in general, do not cause wheel plane tilting and there are no gyroscopic torques involved.

Inertia torques due to (2), and in at least one suspension design, due to (1), can also arise from rear suspensions. These torques will produce stresses in the suspension members and forces at the reaction points. In general these are not serious and can be ignored.

To arrive at torque figures for any of these causes one has to assume a form of vertical movement of the road wheels in relation to the sprung mass. There is evidence to suggest that a reasonably close approximation comes from assuming vertical simple harmonic motions of amplitude $\pm a$, where a is less than but close to the static tyre deflection, at the natural frequency of the unsprung mass.

For the unsprung mass (from Equation A1.3):

$$f_{us} = \frac{1}{2\pi} \left\{ \frac{S_s + S_t}{W_{us}} \right\}^{1/2} \text{ Hz}$$

and

$$\omega_c = \left\{ \frac{S_s + S_t}{W_{us}} \right\}^{1/2} \text{ rad/s}$$

For a simple harmonic motion of amplitude $\pm a$ and frequency $\omega_c/2\pi$ Hz, the maximum vertical velocity is $a\omega_c$ at the mid-point of its movement and the maximum acceleration is $a\omega_c^2$ at upper and lower limits of its movement.

Starting from the normal position of the wheel, the vertical displacement is $a \sin(\omega_c t)$, the vertical velocity $a\omega_c \cos(\omega_c t)$ and the vertical acceleration $a\omega_c^2 \sin(\omega_c t)$.

Amplitudes greater than $\pm$ the tyre static deflection do occur, though not often. As soon as the wheel leaves the ground, the spring rate controlling it ceases to be $(S_s + S_t)$ and becomes S_s only. The acceleration is correspondingly reduced, so that with increasing amplitude the frequency drops noticeably. Example 2.1 shows the effect of this for one particular ratio of maximum upward deflection and tyre static deflection. There is an interesting implication of this. If there is an exciting force on the unsprung mass whose frequency is proportional to the road speed and of sufficient magnitude in relation to the damping to build up to an amplitude greater than $\pm$ tyre static deflection, it is relatively easy to drive up through the vibration because increasing amplitude means decreasing frequency once the wheel leaves the ground. Slowing down however gives the wheel every chance of builing up to an amplitude limited only by the bump stop; increasing amplitude and its accompanying diminishing frequency match up with the diminishing frequency of excitation. This particular phenomenon was observed when front axles were fitted; if these were subject to wheel tramp the vibration behaved in this way.

A2.6 STEERING GEOMETRY ERRORS, BUMP AND REBOUND

The cause of steering geometry errors with up and down wheel movements is conflicting arcs from the suspension and steering linkages. There are two general causes:

(1) Incorrect relative lengths of the instantaneous radii of suspension and steering linkages.
(2) Incorrect relative heights of the ends of the two effective radii.

Figure A2.9 gives us the first part of the picture. If a link of length R is moved upward by a displacement x from the horizontal position, then in plan view it appears to shorten by a distance y. If therefore, for instance, the suspension linkage gave a straight vertical movement to the wheel at the height of the steering ball joint, but

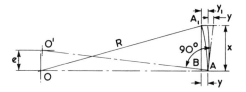

Fig. A2·9   Inward movement of link and arm end as it rises from a horizontal position. Effect of misalignment of link and tube

that steering ball joint was tied to the steering box by a link of length R, there would be a relative deflection of y which would steer the front wheel by an angle y/r where r is the effective length of the cross steering lever (y being small). If we are doing a full investigation over the range of bump and rebound movement this may be done either graphically or by calculation and can be quite lengthy. We can however make comparisons more rapidly by approximate methods.

Let us consider Fig. A2.9.

$$y = R - OB, \quad OB^2 = R^2 - \dot{x}^2, \quad OB = R - y$$

$$\therefore \quad R^2 - 2Ry + y^2 = R^2 - x^2$$

If y is small we can ignore y^2, so

$$2Ry = x^2 \quad \text{and} \quad y = x^2/2R \tag{A2.29}$$

For most cross steering layouts the effective length of the steering tube, looking along the suspension linkage axis, has a definite value. The suspension linkage, however, is most likely to be of the form shown either in Fig. A2.10 or in Fig. A2.11; there are respectively the double wishbone and the strut and link. Both are shown in their basic positions. The first has horizontal and parallel links of lengths r (upper) and R (lower), their ends d apart and the end of the lower link a above the ground. For a small lift x the inward movement of the end of the upper link is $x^2/2r$ and of the end of the lower link $x^2/2R$. Suppose our steering ball joint is located b below the lower link end. We want to find out the effective radius controlling its movement. With deflections of $x^2/2r$ and $x^2/2R$ at a distance d apart, the line joining the two lifted ends of the links will intersect the vertical through O, the original ground contact point. Let this occur at a distance c below the deflected lower link outer end. The implication of the interaction is that there has been no sideways movement of that particular point with up and down movement, i.e.

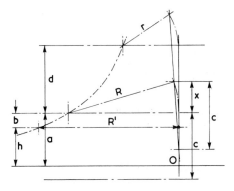

Fig. A2·10   Unequal link suspension system: point at which straight line motion occurs; locus of instantaneous centres of points on suspension upright, two link suspension system

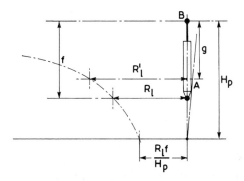

Fig. A2·11   Strut and link suspension; locus of instantaneous centres of movement of particular points

the straight line movement has been achieved; for this we know that the sideways movements of the link ends with rise and fall must be proportional to their distance from the intersection point, i.e.

$$\frac{1}{R} : c :: \frac{1}{r} : c + d$$

whence

$$\frac{c + d}{c} = \frac{R}{r} \tag{A2.30}$$

Now with our fixed location of steering ball joint b below the lower link outer end, Fig. A2.11, the effective radius of the movement at that point is R' where

$$\frac{c+d}{c-b} = \frac{R'}{r} \tag{A2.31}$$

This is another way of saying that the locus of the instantaneous centre of any point on the 'kingpost' or suspension upright is a hyperbola whose distance from that kingpost at any height h above the straight line point is

$$\frac{(c+d)r}{h} \tag{A2.32}$$

This is also the instantaneous radius and would be the correct effective length of the steering tube, looking along the suspension link axis.

The popular strut and link type shown in Fig. A2.11 is effectively an inverted version of the double linl type; the slide itself provides the straight line motion with its instantaneous centre at infinity on a line perpendicular to the sliding motion of the strut starting from its mounting/pivot point. We must therefore draw the linkage in the position in which the link of radius R_l is also perpendicular to the strut movement. It is unlikely that this will be the normal position of the linkage. The locus of the position of the instantaneous centre of any co-operating link giving the same movement of the slide with up and down movement of the wheel is again a hyperbola. The effective radius R'_l of movement of any point at a distance g below the strut pivot is

$$R'_l = \frac{R_l f}{g} \tag{A2.33}$$

and this applies whether g is less or greater than f.

The effective radius at the ground contact point H_p is below the strut pivot point is therefore $R_l f / H_p$. We note that the movement of this ground contact point lies on a radius much shorter than that of the link itself, a radical difference from the double wishbone system.

A2.7 INCORRECT RELATIVE LENGTHS OF CROSS-STEERING TUBES AND LINKAGE ARMS

We are now in a position to study the effect of condition (1) of Section A2.6, i.e. incorrect effective lengths but correct alignment

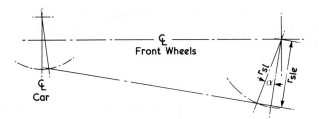

Fig. A2·12   Plan of steering linkage, showing effective length of steering lever to calculate steering angles due to errors

(initial parallelism) of the two effective radii. Suppose the effective lengths are R_l for the suspension linkage and R_{st} for the steering tube. Then for a small vertical wheel movement x the difference between the two arcs is $(x^2/2R_l - x^2/2R_{st})$. If the actual length of the steering lever is r_{sl}, Fig. A2.18, and its effective length

$$r_{sle} = r_{st} \cos \alpha \qquad (A2.34)$$

then the resulting steering angle is

$$\frac{\dfrac{x^2}{2}\left(\dfrac{1}{R_l} - \dfrac{1}{R_{st}}\right)}{r_{sle}} \text{ rad} = \frac{\dfrac{x^2}{2}\left(\dfrac{1}{R_t} - \dfrac{1}{R_{st}}\right)}{r_{sle}} \frac{360°}{2\pi} \qquad (A2.35)$$

Example 2.3 gives the calculation for a wheel deflection of 0.025 m and steering tube and linkage effective lengths of 0.7 and 0.43 m respectively. The results for the range of movement probable are shown in Fig. A2.13, Curve 1.

A2.8 INCORRECT ALIGNMENT OF STEERING TUBE AND LINKAGE

Condition (2) of Section A2.6 produces a different type of graph for the error. Consider again Fig. A2.9, equal radii R on different centres O and O' separated by e produce an error y' for a lift of x. With sufficient accuracy

$$y + y' = \frac{x^2}{2R} + \frac{xe}{R}$$

To take a simple case, where the steering tube has the same effective radius R as the link and is at the same level, the tube end and link

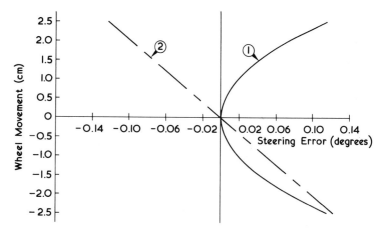

Fig. A2·13   Steering errors due to: Curve 1: diverging radii of 0.43 m and 0.7 m (incorrect lengths); Curve 2, incorrect height of ends of lever and tube (incorrect alignment); link and tube radii both 0.5 m, height error of ends 0.006 m

end both move in by the amount $y = x^2/2R$ due to their length leaving an error $y' = ex/R$ due to the offset of the link and tube centres. If e is an error due to manufacturing tolerances it is unlikely to exceed 0.1m and should be considerably less.

I have known cases of a deliberately introduced e. This may have been done to favour bump movement when there is a discrepancy in the effective lengths of the equivalent link and the steering tube. The dimension e is such a case would be determined empirically.

Example 2.4 provides a worked example of equal tube and link lengths; the results are plotted in Fig. A2.13, Curve 2.

Example 2.5 has been included to compare the effects of the different types of steering error. For this purpose a vertical wheel vibration comprising simple harmonic motion of amplitude ±0.025m at a frequency of 12 Hz, for which $\omega_c = 75.4$ rad/s, is assumed. The errors of Examples 2.3 and 2.4 combined with this vibration produce precessional angular velocities of the front wheel about its kingpin; these are shown in the graphs of Fig. A2.14; on that figure are also shown the precessional angular velocities of the front wheel, subjected to the same vertical vibration, due to a swing axle radius of 1.42 m. The gyroscope torque is the product of the rotating inertia, the velocity of rotation of that inertia about its axis and the precessional velocity

$$M_g = I\Omega\omega \qquad (A2.36)$$

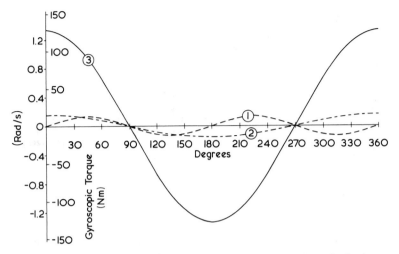

Fig. A2·14   Precession velocities and gyroscopic torques of front wheels about steering axis from various cases. Curve 1, length errors, e.g. Fig. A2.13, Curve 1; Curve 2, alignment errors, Fig. A2.13, Curve 2; Curve 3, due to swing axle, centre at other wheel

A2.9   INERTIA TORQUES DUE TO FORE AND AFT LINKS: WORKED EXAMPLES

The final source of inertia torques about the steering pivot is that due to fore and aft links forming part of a suspension. We have to assume that the part of the front unsprung weight able to turn about the steering pivot or kingpin is of mass W'_{us} kg and its centre of gravity has an offset or moment arm about the steering pivot of e m. The suspension links are assumed parrallel and of length R m (Fig. A2.15).

There are two sources of inertia torque with this layout:

(1)   If the unsprung weight has a vertical velocity of v m/s at the position with the links horizontal then the horizontal centripetal acceleration of the unsprung mass is v^2/R. The inertia torque is then

$$\frac{W'_{us}v^2e}{R} \text{ Nm} \qquad\qquad (\text{A2.37})$$

At positions above and below the links' horizontal position, when they are at an angle φ to the horizontal and the vertical

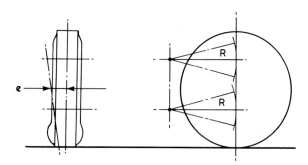

Fig. A2·15   Trailing link suspension as cause of inertia torques; relevant dimensions

velocity is v', then the inertia torque moment becomes:

$$\left(\frac{W'_{us}v^2}{R}\right)e \cos \varphi \; \text{Nm} \tag{A2.38}$$

For small deflections we can safely ignore $\cos \varphi$. On the assumption of vertical simple harmonic motion at the natural frequency of the unsprung mass and amplitude $\pm x'$ we can derive the inertia torque values over a complete cycle of vertical movement. The torque will be in one direction only.

(2)   If the unsprung weight has (substantially) vertical accelerations due to its vertical movements these accelerations, as the wheel departs from the horizontal position of the suspension links by an angle φ, will have a component fore and aft which will then produce a torque about the kingpin. For an acceleration a this torque will be, with sufficient accuracy,

$$a \sin \varphi W'_{us}e \; \text{Nm} \tag{A2.39}$$

Example 2.1

Effect of wheel leaving ground in vertical wheel vibration (Section A2.5).
Assumptions:
$W_{us} = 50$ kg, $S_s = 20\,000$ N/m, $S_t = 266\,700$ N/m

$$f_{us} = \frac{1}{2\pi}\left(\frac{286\,700}{50}\right)^{1/2} = 12.05 \; \text{Hz}$$

$$\omega_c = \left(\frac{286\,700}{50}\right)^{1/2} = 75.72 \text{ rad/s}$$

$$f'_{us} = \frac{1}{2\pi}\left(\frac{20\,000}{50}\right)^{1/2} = 3.18 \text{ Hz}$$

$$\omega'_c = \left(\frac{20\,000}{50}\right)^{1/2} = 20 \text{ rad/s}$$

Take tyre static deflection $\Delta_t = 0.033$ m and $a = 0.05$ m.

Displacement while wheel is on the ground is $a\sin(\omega_c t) = 0.05\sin\varphi$, say and when this is equal to 0.033 m we have $\sin\varphi = 0.033/0.05$, from which $\varphi = 41.3°$.

While the wheel is off the ground the displacement is $R\sin(\omega'_c t) = R\sin\theta$. At the change over point

$$\tan\theta/\tan\varphi = \left(\frac{S_s}{S_s + S_t}\right)^{1/2}$$

$$\tan\theta = \tan 43.1\left(\frac{20\,000}{286\,700}\right)^{1/2} = 0.2320$$

$$\theta = 13.06°$$

The velocity at the change point is obviously common, i.e. $0.05\cos 41.3° = R\cos 13.06°$, $R = 0.0386$ m.

Time of cycle when wheel does not leave ground = $1/12.05 = 0.083$ s.

Time of complete cycle with wheel leaving ground is

$$(2\pi - 2\varphi)\left(\frac{50}{286\,700}\right)^{1/2} + 2\theta\left(\frac{50}{20\,000}\right)^{1/2}$$

(with φ and θ now in radians)

$$t' = 4.842\left(\frac{50}{286\,700}\right)^{1/2} + 0.456\left(\frac{50}{20\,000}\right)^{1/2}$$

$$= 0.0639 + 0.0228 = 0.087 \text{ s}.$$

The frequency ratio, for this particular maximum deflection, is 0.956.

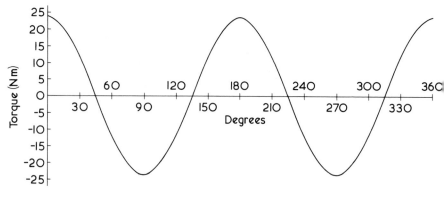

Fig. A2·16

Example 2.2

Steering geometry errors, link lengths (Section A2.6).

(1) Effective link length of the double wishbone suspension at any position where a link does not exist (see Fig. A2.16).

Take $r = 0.3$ m, $R = 0.5$ m, $d = 0.25$ m. From Equation A2.30,

$$\frac{c + d}{c} = \frac{R}{r}$$

$$\frac{c + 0.25}{c} = \frac{0.5}{0.3}, \quad c = 0.375 \text{ m}$$

With $b = 0.1$

$$\frac{c + d}{c - b} = \frac{R'}{r}$$

so that $R' = 0.682$ m.

(2) Effective link length of the strut and link suspension at any position other than at the link.

Take $f = 0.35$, $H_p = 0.7$, $R_l = 0.4$ m and $g = 0.3$. From Equation A2.33

$$R'_l = \frac{R_l f}{g} = \frac{0.4 \times 0.35}{0.3} = 0.467 \text{ m}$$

$$R'_l \text{ at gound level} = \frac{0.4 \times 0.35}{0.7} = 0.2 \text{ m}$$

Example 2.3

Steering geometry errors (Section A2.6); different effective lengths of suspension link and steering tube.
   Assume $R_l = 0.43$ m, $R_{st} = 0.7$ m and $r_{sle} = 0.14$ m.
   For a wheel lift of x, (Fig. A2.17) the inward movement of the end of the link is, from Equation A2.29

$$y_e = \frac{x^2}{2R_l}$$

and that of the end of the steering tube

$$y_{st} = \frac{x^2}{2R_{st}}$$

$$\text{So, steerring error} = \frac{(x^2\,2R_l - x^2\,2R_{st})}{r_{sle}}\text{rad}$$

$$= \frac{x^2}{2\times0.14}\left(\frac{1}{0.43} - \frac{1}{0.7}\right) = 3.204x^2\text{rad}$$

When $x = 0.025$ the steering error is 0.002rad or 0.1147°.

Example 2.4

Steering geometry errorrs (Section A2.8); equal effective lengths of steering tube and suspension link, incorrect alignment (wrong vertical position of inner or outer end of steering tube in relation to link). Assume $R_l = R_{st} = 0.5$ m, $e = 0.006$ m, wheel lift 0.025 m. The steering error will be:

$$\frac{e \times \text{wheel lift}}{R_l r_{sle}} = \frac{0.006 \times 0.025}{0.5 \times 0.14} = 0.002143 \text{ rad} = 0.1228°$$

Example 2.5

Gyroscopic torques.
   The movement assumed is that of the unsprung weight at an amplitude of ±0.025 m and at a frequency of 12 Hz, $\omega_c = 75.4$ rad/s,

i.e.

$$\text{Deflection} = 0.025 \sin \theta \text{ m}$$

$$\text{Velocity} = 0.025\omega_c \cos \theta = 1.885 \cos \theta \text{ m/s}$$

$$\text{Acceleration} = 0.025\omega_c^2 \sin \theta = 142.13 \sin \theta \text{ m/s}^2$$

$$\text{Maximum acceleration} = 142.13 \text{ m/s}^2 = 14.48 \text{ g}$$

$\theta = (\omega_c t)$ and we take readings every 30° or 0.524 rad. The time interval between points at 30° intervals is $0.524/75.4 = 6.95 \times 10^{-3}$ s.

There are three cases to be considered: precession due to:

(1) incorrect lengths of link and steering tube
(2) incorrect alignment of link and steering tube, and
(3) swing axle effect.

For (1) with link and steering tube lengths of 0.43 m and 0.7 m respectively, the steering error is $3.204x^2$ rad (Example 2.3).

For (2) with link and tube lengths each 0.5 m and incorrect height of 0.006 m for one end of steering tube (Example 2.4), steering error $= 0.0857x$ rad.

For (3) assume a swing axle radius of 1.42 m. The angular or precessional velocity of the wheel is then

$$\frac{\text{linear vertical velocity (m/s)}}{1.42} \text{ rad/s}$$

(1) Angular change from $\theta = 0$ to $\theta = 60°$ is 3.204 $(0.025 \times 0.866)^2 = 1.502 \times 10^{-3}$ rad.
     Time interval $= 13.88 \times 10^{-3}$ s

$$\text{Angular velocity} = \frac{1.502 \times 10^{-3}}{13.88 \times 10^{-3}} = 0.108 \text{ rad/s}$$

(2) Angular velocity of precession is (Example 2.4) 0.0857 time the linear velocity and at 30° this velocity is 1.885 cos 30°
     $= 1.632$ m/s.
     The angular velocity of precession is 1.632×0.0857
     $= 0.14$ rad/s.
(3) The angular velocity of precession is $1.885/1.42 = 1.33$ rad/s at the mid-position. The angular velocities of precession have to be multiplied by $I_p \omega$. If we are considering wheel out-of-balance as a possible source of the unsprung mass vertical vibration we should assume $\omega = \omega_c = 75.4$ rad/s.

On the basis of the tyre and wheel being represented by a mass of 18 kg concentrated between rradii of 0.33 m and 0.18 m,

$$I_p = 18 \frac{(0.33^2 + 0.18^2)}{2} = 1.27 \text{ kg m}^2$$

So the maximum gyroscopic torques are:

(1) from incorrect lever and steering tube lengths as assumed,

$$0.108 \times 1.27 \times 75.4 = 10.34 \text{ Nm}$$

(2) from incorrect alignment of lever and steering tube, as assumed,

$$0.14 \times 1.27 \times 75.4 = 13.41 \text{ Nm}$$

(3) from swing axle effect, pivot at other wheel, as assumed,

$$1.33 \times 1.27 \times 75.4 = 127.4 \text{ Nm}$$

It is fair to point out that such a swing axle effective radius is small in relation to general practice.

Figure A2.14 shows the precessional velocities through a complete cycle of θ from 0 to 360° ($\theta = \omega_c t$) from (1) to (3) above. To a different scale, noted in the graph, Fig. A2.14 also shows the gyroscopic torque generated by these precessional velocities for the wheel inertia and angular velocity listed.

Example 2.6

Inertia torques from fore and aft links (Section A2.9).

Assume $R = 0.3$ m, $x' = 0.025$, $f_{us} = 12$ Hz, $\omega_c = 75.4$ rad/s, $W'_{us} = 40$ kg, $e = 0.05$ m

(1) At links horizontal (assumed mid-stroke or normal position) velocity $v = 1.885$ m/s

$$\text{Inertia torque} = \frac{40 \times 1.885^2 \times 0.05}{0.3} = 23.69 \text{ Nm}$$

(2) At extreme deflection 0.025 m,

$$\varphi = \sin^{-1} \frac{0.025}{0.3} = 4.78° \ (\sin \varphi = 0.08\dot{3})$$

Acceleration = 142.13 m/s²
Torque = 142.13 × sin 4.78 × 40 × 0.05 = 23.69 Nm
The resulting torque curve is plotted in Fig. A2.16.

A2.10 EFFECT OF WEIGHT TRANSFERENCE IN CORNERING

Because of the differences in loads carried by inner and outer wheels when cornering, the relationship between sideways force and drift angle is not that obtained by taking a cross section of the curves of Fig. 7.32 on any given vertical, which would produce curve 1 of Fig. 7.33 for the chosen static wheel load of 4500 N, but the mean of the curves 2 and 3 which represent the corresponding sections of the curves of Fig. 7.32, taking account of the weight transfer in cornering represented by the lines joining the 4500 N load point on the base to the ends of the cross line showing the inner and outer wheel loads at a chosen sideways acceleration (0.5 g in the case illustrated). The inverted triangle of Fig. 7.32 shows how one can get a drift angle for the 0.5 g sideways acceleration by drawing verticals from the ends of the cross line and finding a line passing through the top end of the static load line which cuts these two verticals at the same drift angle. On the assumption of linearity one can divide the vertical into say four equal parts and get also the drift angles at 0.125 g, 0.25 g and 0.375 g sideways accelerations. In early studies, this procedure carried out for the two ends of the vehicle gave drift angles at front and rear for the four sideways accelerations and would then, by difference, give the under- or over-steer as shown for a particular case in Fig. A2.23.

In obtaining these results it is easy to obtain by inspection for each sideways acceleration the limiting drift angles between which the result will lie. If a is the lower, b the higher of these two angles; if for the inner wheel F_{c1} and F_{c2} respectively be the cornering forces at b and a drift angles; and correspondingly F_{c3} and F_{c4} for the outer wheel; then the drift angle required to produce the total cornering force F_{cf} is:

$$a + (b-a)\left\{\frac{F_{cf} - (F_{c2} + F_{c4})}{(F_{c1} + F_{c3}) - (F_{c2} + F_{c4})}\right\} \qquad (A2.40)$$

Most corners are taken at comparatively small steering angles. At 65 km/hr, for instance, 0.3 g sideways acceleration implies a radius of curvature of 110.8 m, which on a wheelbase of 2.75 m implies a steering angle of 1.42°. Even at 30 km/hr this same sideways acceleration only implies a steering angle of 6.7°. The average driver seldom exceeds 0.3 g sideways. We can therefore assume, see Chapter 4, that the steering angle on both front wheels will be the same, without any likelihood of serious error.

The curves of Fig. 7.32 relate cornering force and drift angle. It is more general practice to plot sideways acceleration and drift angle. The relationship between sideways acceleration, car roll angle and weight transference is dealt with in Section A1.21 and Example 1.20. The roll angle line is derived as a part of the calculations to get the cornering weight transfers; it is required for reasons given in Section A2.11, item 3.

A2.11   SIDEWAYS FORCES: EFFECT OF INFLUENCES OTHER THAN LATERAL G

Although the main component of the sideways force at each end of the car is the load carried there multiplied by the sideways acceleration, there are three other factors involved: (1) drag distribution, (2) self-aligning torque, and (3) camber thrust.

(1) Because of the weight tranference the sideways forces provided by inner and outer wheels are different (Fig. 7.32 and 7.33). Because of the drift angles there is an extra 'rolling' resistance at each wheel of $F_c \tan \theta$, F_c being the cornering force and θ the drift angle, normally the same for inner and outer wheels. Each end of the car therefore provides an extra outward force on the front wheels

$$\frac{T(F_{co} - F_{ci}) \tan \theta}{L} \qquad (A2.41)$$

The outward force on the rear wheels is reduced by the same amount.

(2) Section 7.9 explained why a tyre running at a drift angle and so generating sideways force also provides a self-aligning torque. The sum of the self-aligning torques for all four wheels divided by the wheelbase also provides an extra sideways force to be generated by the front wheels, and diminishes by the same amount the sideways force to be produced by the rear wheels. Self-aligning torque varies with the load carried, the inflation pressure and the wheel diameter, which determine the length of the contact patch, and the tread width. In Fig. A2.18, curves A and B show the effect of rim size on self-alignment torque, for a given load. Curve C has been added to be appropriate to the particulars used in Example 2.9. Figures 7.21 and 7.22 show how self-aligning torque varies with drift or slip angle, load carried and inflation pressure, and also by inference with tread width. Although for strict accuracy the self-aligning torque for

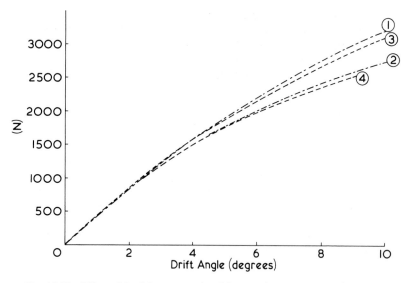

Fig. A2·17   Effect of load increase and weight transference on cornering power: Curve 1, 5000 N normal load; Curve 2, 5000 N normal load, allowance for weight transfer; Curve 3, 4500 N normal load; Curve 4, 4500 N normal load, allowance for weight transfer

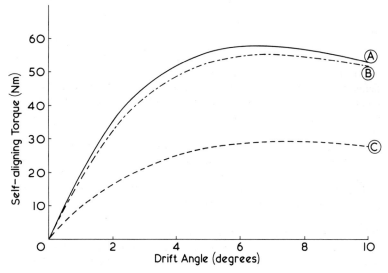

Fig. A2·18   Self-aligning torque: Curve A, 6–16 tyre, 4-ply; Curve B, 6–15 tyre, 4-ply; Curve C, values used for calculated example

each wheel should be that approprriate to its load, cornering force and drift angle, in practice one can with sufficient accuracy use at each end of the car the mean load per tyre and the drift angle there to arrive at the totals.

(3) Camber thrust; for cross-ply tyres a reasonable approximation for this is given by:

$$\frac{\text{Load carried} \times \text{Camber angle (deg)}}{57.3} \qquad \text{(A2.42)}$$

Figure 7.24 gives figures for a specific tyre and inflation pressure for such tyres. For radial ply tyres camber thrust tends to be less than this. Section A1.21 shows how to arrive at the total roll angle of the car. The final camber angle of each wheel takes account of tyre roll angle, suspension roll angle and the effect of the latter on the wheel attitude. The total camber thrusts at each end of the car are added to the outward forces there.

A2.12 CORNERING BEHAVIOUR: WORKED EXAMPLES

One way of arriving at the steady state cornering behaviour of a car has been described. The results in a particular case have been shown in Fig. A2.23.

Between straight ahead running and steady state cornering there lies a trransient stage, during which the car is taking up its appropriate roll angle and the tyre treads are assuming their deflection patterns. Straight ahead driving includes a series of reactions to disturbances such as gusts and road camber changes or irregularities. These reactions are very short duration transient stages. In pursuing the question of how transient stage behaviour may differ from steady state cornering it is useful to know how long a transient stage may last. From some observed figures the author[7] suggests that an 80 km/hr (50 mile/hr) side wind could produce a roll moment equivalent to a sideways acceleration of 0.05 g. An approximate calculation suggests that this moment would require 0.125 s to produce the car's resultant roll angle. At 100 km/hr (62 mile/hr) this would imply travelling a distance of 3.5 m. A 3° road camber would need a time of 0.105 s and at the same speed of 100 km/hr a distance of about 3.0 m to achieve a smaller roll angle, equivalent to a sideways acceleration of 0.035 g. Such transient effects, even for the fairly extreme conditions of side gusts and road camber assumed, are of such short duration that the driver can only react to their residual effects.

The two aspects of car suspension likely to affect transient handling behaviour are:

(1) In the initial unrolled state, when subjected to a sideways force due to either wind or road camber, the weight transference at each end is that due to the height of the roll centre there; the influence of roll stiffness is lacking. At such low sideways forces the influence of weight transfer may not be very important, but it will be initially different from that in the steady rolled state.

(2) As the car begins to roll, the weight transfer is affected by the roll rate on the suspension and also by the damper forces at the roll velocity concerned. These will be initially zero, increase as roll velocity increases and then diminish again as the roll angle approaches its final value. Damper settings are an acknowledged way to vary the transient stage weights transfer as between the two ends of a car, within the limits set by other suspension requirements, and so to vary handling behaviour. Assuming that $k^2/ab \leqslant 1$ for the car about a vertical axis through its centre of gravity, the first stage in starting to turn is to produce a sideways force at the front of the car only and so initiate a yaw acceleration; this builds up a yaw velocity which increases to v/R_{cf} rad/s, v being the car velocity and R_{cf} the final radius of the curve being traversed. From starting the curve to attaining a desired steady state R_c will diminish from infinity to R_{cf}. When the corner is started the back end of the car is running inside the front end. In the final state the back end of the car is hanging out by the drift angle of the rear tyres: Fig. A2.19 shows the initial and final states with the tyre tracks. Figure A2.20 shows that the effect of drift angle on the rear tyres is to move forward the centre about which the car turns on a corner.

It can be seen from these diagrams that in the transient stage, while the rear drift angle is developing, there are associated yaw acceleration and yaw velocity. These are likely to give an impression of oversteer.

Inspection of Fig. 7.32 suggests that at the sideways forces which are likely to occur in road camber and wind initiated transients the weight transference is unlikely to be important; it does become so when we are considering the transient stage leading up to steady state cornering. The behaviour of a car subjected to wind or road

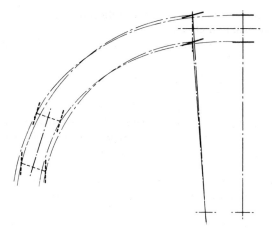

Fig. A2·19   Rear end of car swinging out as car takes up attitude angle; the transient stage. The final rear drift (attitude) angle is large enough to put the rear wheel tracks outside the front. This is still neutral steer, i.e. front and rear drift angles are equal

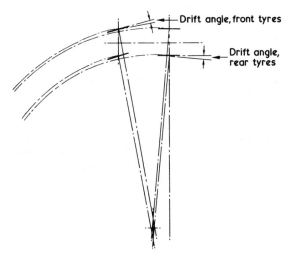

Fig. A2·20   Effect of drift angle on centre about which car turns. The parallel lines from front and rear wheel centres, for equal drift angles on inner and outer tyres, show that the actual drift angles are marginally different

camber excited transverse forces is determined principally by the relation of the sideways forces front and rear to the drift angles which these sideways forces develop, i.e. by the relationship of the tyre 'capacity' to the sideways forces. Road camber induced sideways forces are shared out between front and rear ends in the proportion of the load carried at each end. To get acceptable understeer reactions to road camber changes therefore tyre inflation at the two ends of the car is the easiest and perhaps (with equal tyre sizes all round) the only way. With side wind gusts the sharing out of side forces between front and rear depends on the centre of pressure of the car shape to various wind yaw angles; and we have to differentiate between the influence of wind yaw angles as a secondary effect and as a prime cause of a disturbance.

Suppose for example a car, not subject to a side wind, runs onto a road with a sideways slope (road camber). It will drift down the slope. If the front and rear drift angles are unequal a yaw velocity results. The curved path due to a greater front drift angle provides an outward force at the centre of gravity which opposes that due to road camber. The resulting disturbance is therefore less, and requires less driver reaction, than that caused by a greater rear drift angle, where the path curvture produces a sideways force at the centre of gravity which adds to that due to road camber and so provides a progressively increasing effect.

Now consider the result of a car shape whose centre of lateral pressure is well forward (a condition which has often occurred). The first result of a road camber thrust to the left, forr instance, deflects the front of the car to the left and at the very small wind yaw angles, due to the car continuing on its way, produces a sideways wind force urging the front of the car still further to the left, i.e. accentuating the disturbance already created, an oversteer effect. The exsitence of this effect and the need to counteract it has been responsible in the past for the provision of high understeer characteristics to give straight line stability against road camber or other similar disturbances.

When considering side gusts however a centre of pressure at or near the centre of gravity produces the same result as a road camber thrust; if that result is an understeer effect then the car is stable both to camber and side wind disturbances. The centre of pressure usually does vary with the angle of the wind to the car.

The transient effect when going into a more or less steady state corner of higher sideways acceleration than road camber or side winds are likely to provide will continue into the tyre behaviour area where weight transfer is important. It is here therefore that damper characteristics have more effect and where we are more concerned with the transition from the initial, unrolled, weight transference where the height of the roll centre determines it to the final condition where roll centre heights, front and rear anti-roll stiffness, roll angle, camber thrusts and so on are all important factors. The rate at which these various influences build up and the difference between the initial and final weight transferences are therefore important.

Example 2.7

Drift angles related to cornering force and weight transference (Section A2.10 and Figs. 7.32, 7.33 and A2.17).

(1) Assumptions: Tyre characteristics of Fig. 7.32, load carried per wheel 4500 N, average cornering force per wheel 2500 N (assumed front wheels), weight transference 2250 N.

In Fig. 7.32 a vertical is drawn on the normal, 4500 N, load line to a height of 2500 N. A transverse line is drawn at this height 2250 N each way, i.e. from 2250 N to 6750 N. The ends of this line are joined to the 4500 N point on the base line. We want first to find the drift angle required to provide the cornering force at this mean load and weight transference. The ends of the transverse line are, on the left, well above the 10° line and, on the right, between the 6° and 8° lines.

From the right hand end of the line draw a vertical upwards. From the left hand end of the line draw a vertical downwards. The left hand vertical cuts the 8° line at 1880 N and the 10° line at 2120 N. The right hand vertical cuts the 8° line at 2790 N and the 10° line at 3315 N. At these tyre loads the total cornering force at 8° is 4670 N and at 10° is 5435 N. We require 5000 N. So the drift angle required is

$$8 + \frac{(330 \times 2)}{765} = 8.86° \quad (5000 - 4670 = 330,$$

$$5435 - 4670 = 765)$$

The cornering forces are: inner wheel = 1983.5 N, outer wheel = 3016.5 N. If the suspension has a linear rate and there are no bump buffers to modify the curve, within the deflection range concerned, the triangle whose base is the 4500 N line at 2500 N cornering force and apex the 4500 N point on the base line will define the weight transference at smaller cornering forces, i.e. 450 N at 500 N cornering force, etc. We can therefore arrive at drift angles at 500, 1000, 1500, and 2000 N

344 STEERING CALCULATIONS AND WORKED EXAMPLES

cornering forces. The results are:

Cornering force, N	500	1000	1500	2000	2500
Drift angle, deg.	1.17	2.45	3.99	6.07	8.86

These are plotted in Fig. A2.17.
(2) The effect of increasing load.
  Assumptions: Tyre characteristics of Fig. 7.32, load carried per wheel 5000 N, average cornering force per wheel 2750 N (assumed front wheels), weight transference 2500 N.
  These three quantities are increased approximately in proportion. The construction of (1) above is repeated with the following results (also plotted in Fig. A2.17):

Cornering force, N	550	1100	1650	2200	2750
Drift angle, deg.	1.32	2.77	4.51	6.87	10.07

Example 2.8

Effect of drag distribution, self-aligning torque and camber thrust on sideways forces at front and rear (Section 2.34).
  Assumptions: As example 2.7 (1), track 1.43 m, wheelbase 2.75 m.

(1) Drag distribution.
  From Example 2.7 we know that the cornering forces of inner and outer wheels are respectively, at their maximum, 1983.5 N and 3016.5 N and the drift angle is 8.86°. The fore and aft components of these forces are:
Inner wheel: 1983.5 × sin 8.86 = 305.5 N
Outer wheel: 3016.5 × sin 8.86 = 464.6 N
The difference is therefore 159.1 N and the resulting extra sideways force at the front wheels is:

$$\frac{159.1 \times 1.43}{2.75} = 82.73 \text{ N}$$

(2) Self-aligning torque.
  Figure A2.18 shows self-aligning torque for two tyre sizes and at a particular load. Let us assume a linear relationship

between load and self-aligning torque, use curve B and assume this is at 4500 N load; then for the inner wheel and 8.86° drift the self aligning torque will be $(53.7 \times 2250)/4500 = 26.85$ Nm and for the outer wheel will be $(53.7 \times 6750)/4500 = 80.55$ Nm. The total torque is 107.4 Nm and this produces an extra sideways force at the front wheels of $107.4/2.75 = 39.05$ N.

It is clear that with the assumptions we have made we can ignore the load differences and take the figure as that for two wheels at normal load, i.e. in the case above $53.7 \times 2 = 107.4$ Nm.

There will be a corresponding outward force on the front wheels from the same effect on the rear wheels. The outward force on the rear wheels is diminished to the same extent as the front outward force is increased.

(3) Camber thrust.

Taking the camber thrust as the load carried by the wheel multiplied by the tangent of the camber angle, Fig. 7.31(b), we have to find the camber angles concerned.

At the front it is assumed that the wishbones are unequal and initially parallel. It is also assumed that the top link is 0.3 m long, is 0.4 m above the ground and the links are disposed to give straight line motion to the ground contact point. It is further assumed that the roll angle at say 0.5 g sideways acceleration is 5°. The upward deflection of the outer front wheel and the downward deflection of the inner are each $(1.43/2) \sin 5° = 0.062$ m. The inward deflection of the end of each upper triangle level is $0.062^2/(2 \times 0.3) = 0.0064$ m. This implies an inward (in relation to the car) lean of each wheel of $0.0064/0.4$ rad $= 0.92°$.

If the wheels initially have zero camber, the outward (on the corner) lean of the front wheels is then 5.92°, inner and 4.08° outer. With wheel loads of 2250 N inner and 6750 N outer the outward forces are

$$2250 \tan 5.92 + 6750 \tan 4.08 = 233.3 + 481.5 = 714.8 \text{ N}$$

The combined outward forces on the two front wheels due to the three causes are therefore 836.6 N. The total including the drag distribution and self-aligning torque on the rear wheels is likely to be between 900 and 950 N.

Our total of 5000 N outward force on 9000 N load implies therefore a sideways acceleration of say $(5000 - 925)/9000 = 0.45$ g

Example 2.9

Steady state handling (Section A2.12).

Car particulars as in Example 1.20, driver only condition. Front anti-roll rod giving 1.5 times total front roll rate compared with that on suspension springs alone, 0.5 g sideways acceleration.

S_{sf} = 18 500 N/m (but = 27 750 N/m in roll), S_{tf} = 256 600 N/m, S_{cf} = 17 256 N/m (but = 25 042 N/m in roll), S_{sr} = 21 647 N/m, S_{tr} = 256 600 N/m, S_{cr} = 19 963 N/m, W_{sp} = 924.25 kg, centre of gravity = 1.23 m behind front wheels, Wheelbase = 2.75 m, W_{spf} = 510.86 kg = 5011.5 N.

W_{spr} = 413.39 kg = 4055 N, W_{usf} = W_{usr} = 100 kg = 981 N, h_f = 0.15 m, h_r = 0.20 m. H = 0.5 m, T_f = T_r = 1.47 m, R = 0.33 m, a = 0.5, g = 4.905 m/s².

Average roll angle on tyres due to unsprung weight

$$\varphi_{usa} = 2 \times 4.905 \times 0.33 \left(\frac{100}{1.47^2 \times 256\,600} + \frac{100}{1.47^2 \times 256\,600} \right)$$

$$= 0.0011677 \text{ rad} = 0.06691°$$

Average roll angle on tyres due to roll centre height

$$\varphi_{rca} = 2 \times 4.95 \left(\frac{510.86 \times 0.15}{1.47^2 \times 256\,600} + \frac{413.39 \times 0.2}{1.47^2 \times 256\,600} \right)$$

$$= 0.002818 \text{ rad} = 0.1615$$

Roll angle due to the sprung weight

$$\theta_{sp} = \frac{1848.5(\theta_{sp} + 4.909)}{97\,251} = 0.09511 \text{ rad}$$

$\theta_t = \theta_{sp} + \varphi_{usa} + \varphi_{rca} = 0.09511 + 0.001168 + 0.002819 = 0.0991$ rad
$\varphi_{usf} = \varphi_{usr} = 0.001168$ rad

$$\varphi_{rcf} = \frac{4 \times 4.905 \times 510.86 \times 0.15}{1.47^2 \times 256\,600} = 0.0027114 \text{ rad}$$

$$\varphi_{rcr} = \frac{4 \times 4.905 \times 413.39 \times 0.2}{1.47^2 \times 256\,600} = 0.0029255 \text{ rad}$$

$\theta_{spf} = 0.0991 - 0.0011677 - 0.0027114 = 0.095217$ rad
$\theta_{spr} = 0.0991 - 0.0011677 - 0.0029255 = 0.095003$ rad

Front end weight transference
$W_{tf} = 110.11 + 255.69 + 876.28 = 1242.08$ N
$W_{tr} = 110.11 + 275.87 + 697.02 = 1083.0$ N
Total roll angle on tyres, front end $= \varphi_{tf} = 4W_{tf}/S_{tf}T_f$

$$= \frac{4 \times 1242.08}{256\,600 \times 1.47} = 0.0131715 \text{ rad} = 0.755°$$

$$\varphi_{tr} = \frac{4 \times 1083}{256600 \times 1.47} = 0.0114842 \text{ rad} = 0.658°$$

Roll angle on front suspension

$$\theta_{sf} = \frac{0.09522 \times 25\,042}{27\,750} = 0.08593 \text{ rad} = 4.924°$$

(Note: $4.924° + 0.755° = 5.679°$)
Roll angle on rear suspension

$$\theta_{sr} = \frac{0.09501 \times 19\,963}{21\,647} = 0.08762 \text{rad} = 5.0206°$$

(Note: $5.0206° + 0.658° = 5.6786°$)
Total front weight $W_f = 610.86$ kg $= 5592.54$ N
Front weight per wheel $= 305.43$ kg $= 2996.27$ N
Total rear weight $W_r = 513.39$ kg $= 5036.36$ N
Rear weight per wheel $= 256.695$ kg $= 2518.18$ N
Inner front wheel weight $= 2996.27 - 1242.08 = 1754.19$ N
Outer front wheel weight $= 2996.27 + 1242.08 = 4238.35$ N
Inner rear wheel weight $= 2518.18 - 1082.97 = 1435.21$ N
Outer rear wheel weight $= 2518.18 + 1082.97 = 3601.15$ N
Cornering forces at 0.5 g sideways acceleration.
Front:

(1)   Due to sideways acceleration: 0.5 g $= 1498.14$ N per wheel
(2)   Due to drag distribution:
from front wheels, assume 9.7° drift angle

$$= \frac{2484.16 \times 9.7}{57.3} \times \frac{1.43}{2.75} = 218.68 \text{ N or } 109.34 \text{ N per wheel}$$

from rear wheels, assume 5.2° drift angle

$$= \frac{2165.94 \times 5.2}{57.3} \times \frac{1.43}{2.73} = 102.96 \text{ N or } 51.48 \text{ per wheel}$$

(3) Due to self-aligning torque: (use graph Fig. A2.18, Curve C, for 3000 N load) from front wheels = (28.9 × 2)/2.75 = 21.02 N or 10.51 N per wheel from rear wheels = (2.91 × 2)/2.75 × 2500/3000 = 17.63 N or 8.82 N per wheel

(4) Camber thrust.
Front: both wheels leaning inwards at 0.5° in relation to car (+0.5° initial chamber, −1° change with deflection due to roll; car total roll angle 5.68°)

$$\text{thrust} = \frac{1754.19 \times 6.18}{57.3} + \frac{4238.35 \times 5.18}{57.3} = 572.35 \text{ N}$$

or 286.18 N/wheel

Rear: both rear wheels leaning out at 5.68/2 = 2.84° (instantaneous centre 1.43 m away from wheel) so

$$\text{camber thrust} = \frac{5036.36 \times 2.84}{57.3} = 249.62 \text{ N or } 124.81 \text{ N per}$$

wheel

Mean outward force per front wheel at 0.5 g sideways acceleration = 1498.14 + 109.34 + 51.11 + 10.51 + 8.82 + 286.18 =

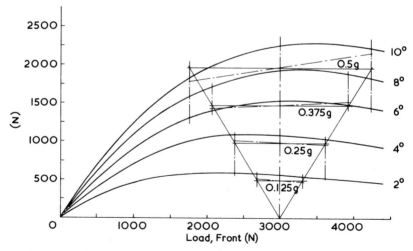

Fig. A2·21 Load, cornering force weight transference and drift angles: worked example, front wheels

1964.1 N. Using Equation A2.40

$$\text{Drift angle} = \left\{ \frac{3928.2 - 3420}{4040 - 3420} \right\} x2 + 8 = 9.64°$$

Mean outward force per rear wheel at 0.5 g sideways acceleration (Fig. A2.22) = 1259.09 − 109.34 − 51.11 − 10.51 − 8.82 + 124.81 = 1204.12 N

The results are shown in Table A2.1 and plotted in Fig. A2.21.

The understeer angle of 4.39° at 0.5 g sideways acceleration would be considered excessive. The easiest way to correct this would be to reduce the inflation pressure of the rear tyres. A possible alternative

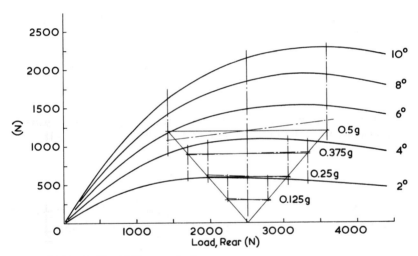

Fig. A2·22   As Fig. A2.21; rear wheels

Table A2.1

Sideways acceleration		0.125 g	0.25 g	0.375 g	0.5 g
Front drift angle, deg		1.74	3.68	6.15	9.64
Rear drift angle, deg		1.03	2.11	3.39	5.25
Understeer angle, deg		0.71	1.57	2.76	4.39
Cornering	Inner Front	505	1010	1424	1780
Force	Outer Front	474	960	1515	2152
	Inner rear	304	615	901	1071
	Outer rear	294	589	904	1335

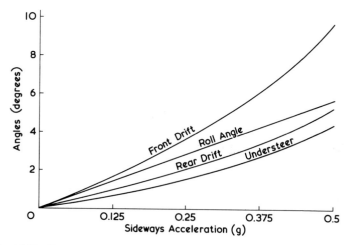

Fig. A2·23 Front and rear drift angles, roll angle, understeer angles of worked example

would be to transfer more of the weight transference to the rear wheels, by fitting an anti-roll rod to the rear suspension. If this were wholly additional to the existing front anti-roll rod the roll angle would be reduced and some would favour this.

It is a matter of interest that at 0.125 g and 0.25 g sideways accelerations the inner tyre provides more cornering force than the outer. The drag distribution effect for these two cases will be in the reverse direction from that at higher sideways accelerrations and for greater accuracy we should take account of this, rather than rely on a scaling down of the figure of 0.5 g sideways acceleration. The effect is however small.

Appendix 3: Discomfort factors analysed

A3.1 FREQUENCY/AMPLITUDE/ACCELERATION RELATIONSHIPS

Experiments at Purdue University[1] led to a criterion of unpleasantness or discomfort K; for accelerations A in m/s^2 and frequency f in Hz, $K = Ae^{0.6f}$. Table A3.1 shows values of K arrived at for two levels of sensation: uncomfortable and disturbing; and for the three directions of vibrations, vertical, longitudinal and transverse. Tables A3.2 and A3.3 list various implications of this criterion and the relationships between the different directions and the two discomfort levels.

Later experiments for which Jacklin was responsible[2] used a dummy containing a three-directional accelerometer placed on a board on the car seat. As a result of these tests the earlier criteria were modified to the following:

(1) In the vertical direction $K_v = Ae^{0.13f}$; for A in m/s^2, $K_v = 2.59$ for disturbing and 3.05 for uncomfortable conditions.

(2) In the horizontal longitudinal direction $K_l = Ae^{0.087f}$; $K_l = 1.22$ for disturbing and 1.68 for uncomfortable conditions.

(3) In the horizontal transverse direction $K_t = At$; $K_t = 0.84$ for disturbing, 0.99 for uncomfortable conditions.

The implementations of these three expressions in terms of amplitude and corresponding accelerations at various frequencies are given in Table A3.4.

Various means of combining the three K factors recorded for a given vehicle to obtain one representative of the complete vehicle were proposed. Curves representing the two Jacklin proposals are shown in Fig. A3.1. The later proposals indicate very much reduced

Table A3.1 DISCOMFORT FACTORS FOR DIFFERENT DISCOMFORT LEVELS AND THREE DIFFERENT DIRECTIONS

Direction of acceleration	Criterion	Maximum K	Ratio K uncomfortable/ K disturbing
Vertical	Uncomfortable	18.75	2.05
	Disturbing	9.14	
Longitudinal horizontal	Uncomfortable	3.35	2.62
	Disturbing	1.28	
Transverse horizontal	Uncomfortable	2.47	3.48
	Disturbing	0.71	

Discomfort factor $K = Ae^{0.6f}$, where A = acceleration, m/s, e = exponential function, f = frequency, Hz

Table A3.2 VERTICAL ACCELERATIONS, DISCOMFORT FACTOR $K = Ae^{0.6f} = 18.75$

Frequency Hz	1	2	4	6	10
Acceleration, m/s²	10.29	5.65	1.70	0.51	0.046
r, m	0.261	0.036	0.0027	0.00036	0.000012

For SHM maximum acceleration = $r\omega^2$

Table A3.3 RATIOS BETWEEN DISCOMFORT FACTORS K

Direction	Vertical Longitudinal horizontal	Vertical Transverse horizontal	Vertical Longitudinal horizontal	Vertical Transverse horizontal
Condition	Uncomfortable	Uncomfortable	Disturbing	Disturbing
Ratio	5.60	7.59	7.14	12.87

$\pm a$ = amplitude, m
f = frequency, Hz
$\omega = 2\pi f$ rad/sec
$\Delta = a \sin \omega t$, for SHM giving $A = a\omega^2 \sin \omega t$
A = acceleration, m/s²
For vertical accelerations $K_v = Ae^{0.13f}$
For longitudinal horizontal accelerations $K_l = Ae^{0.087f}$
For transverse horizontal accelerations $K_t = A_t$

Table A3.4   ACCELERATIONS AND AMPLITUDES AT DISTURBING AND UNCOMFORTABLE LEVELS OF VIBRATIONS AT DIFFERENT FREQUENCIES

Frequency	Hz		1	2	4	6	10
Vertical	Disturbing	A	2.27	2.00	1.54	1.19	0.71
	$K_v = 2.59$	a	0.057	0.013	0.0024	0.00084	0.00018
	Uncomfortable	A	2.68	2.35	1.81	1.40	0.83
	$K_v = 2.59$	a	0.068	0.015	0.0029	0.00099	0.00021
Longitudinal	Disturbing	A	1.12	1.03	0.86	0.72	0.51
horizontal	$K_l = 1.22$	a	0.028	0.0065	0.0014	0.00051	0.00013
	Uncomfortable	A	1.54	1.41	1.19	1.00	0.70
	$K_l = 1.68$	a	0.0039	0.0089	0.0019	0.00070	0.00018
Transverse	Disturbing	A	0.83	0.83	0.83	0.83	0.83
horizontal	$K_t = 0.83$	a	0.021	0.0053	0.0013	0.00059	0.00021
	Uncomfortable	A	0.99	0.99	0.99	0.99	0.99
	$K_t = 0.99$	a	0.025	0.0063	0.0016	0.00070	0.00025

sensitivity at the higher frequencies. It seems probable that this is due to the change from a hard seat to a cushion. The principal point we notice from all these curves is that they ignore the sensitive frequencies listed in Section 3.9. ISO 2631 is obviously based upon later work by various experiments. Figure A3.1 shows sample curves for different endurance times for vertical and horizontal accelerations. In ISO 2631 these accelerations are given as RMS values; they are shown here in peak (assumed sinusoidal) values for easier comparison with the other curves of Fig. A3.1. The vertical acceleration figures recognise an undue sensitivity between 4 and 8 Hz; the horizontal accelerations a sensitivity below 2 Hz.

Figure A3.1 also includes the Janeway's 'extremely uncomfortable' curve, from Reference 3. One must assume that all known results were considered in deriving ISO 2631.

Some MIRA experiments[4] showed best correlations with the subjective judgements of a varied sample by measuring the average vertical acceleration in the 0.75 to 71 Hz frequency range. Longitudinal and transverse accelerations measured at floor level appeared to be irrelevant. Later tests on their Mark II accelerometer used a freqency range of 0.2 to 50 Hz. Floor level horizontal accelerations still seemed irrelevant and also roll and pitch displacements measured by a positional gyroscope.

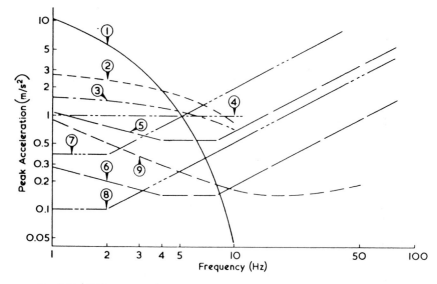

Fig. A3·1 Different experimenters have arrived at different conclusions as to the tolerance of the human body to vibration at different frequencies and in different directions. These curves show the wide variations expressed as peak accelerations

Curve 1: $K = 18.75 = Ae^{0.6f}$ (Ref. 1)
Curve 2: $K_v = 3.05 = Ae^{0.13f}$ (Ref. 2)
Curve 3: $K_t = 1.68 = Ae^{0.087f}$ (Ref. 2)
Curve 4: $K_t = A_t = 0.99$ (Ref. 2)
Curve 5: Vertical accelerations, 1 hr endurance level (ISO 2631)
Curve 6: Vertical accelerations, 8 hr endurance level (ISO 2631)
Curve 7: Horizontal accelerations, 1 hr endurance level (ISO 2631)
Curve 8: Horizontal accelerations, 8 hr endurance level (ISO 2631)
Curve 9: Extremely uncomfortable (Janeway, from Ref. 3)

REFERENCES

1. Jacklin, H. M. and Liddell, G. J., 'Riding Comfort Analysis', *Engng Bulletin*, Purdue University, Vol. 17, No. 3, Research Series No. 44 (1933)
2. Jacklin, H. M., 'Human Reactions to Vibration', *J. Soc. Auto. Engrs*, Vol. 39, No. 4 (1936)
3. Stayner, R. M., 'Vibrations in Road Vehicles', Transport Papers at 3rd Symposium of Society of Environmental Engineers, April 15–18 (1969)
4. Oliver, R. J. and Whitehead, J. P., 'A Survey of the Ride Characteristics of Contemporary Motor Cars', MIRA, Report No. 1966/11

Index